ALL ABOUT BATTERSEA

LECTOR HOUSE PUBLIC DOMAIN WORKS

ALL ABOUT BATTERSEA

HENRY S. SIMMONDS

ISBN: 978-93-89539-61-5

Published: 1882

LECTOR HOUSE LLP
E-MAIL: lectorpublishing@gmail.com

S. MARY'S, BUILT ACCORDING TO ACT OF PARLIAMENT, 14. GEO. III. OPENED NOV. 17, 1777. ABOUT 1823 AN ENTRANCE POR-TICO OF THE DORIC ORDER WAS ADDED.

ALL ABOUT BATTERSEA,

BY

HENRY S. SIMMONDS.

1882.

CONTENTS

- Introduction. 1

- Nine Elms Lane.—The King's Champion. 5

- Thorne's Brewery.—What Battersea has been called. 6

- London and South Western Railway Company's Goods Station and Locomotive Works.. 6

- Mill-Pond Bridge.—New Road.. 9

- A Royal Sturgeon caught in the wheel of the Mill at Mill-Pond Bridge. . . . 11

- Wallace's Vitriol Works.. 12

- Sleaford Street.—Coal.. 13

- Street Lighting.. 14

- London Gas-Light Company's Works and Vauxhall Gardens. 16

- On a recently-exposed Section at Battersea.. 25

- Phillips' Fire Annihilating Machine Factory Destroyed.—Brayne's Pottery.—The Old Lime Kilns.—Laver's Cement & Whiting Works.. 27

- The Southwark and Vauxhall Water Works.. 28

- Water Carriers and Water Companies.. 29

- The Village of Battersea.—Growth of the Parish.. 31

- Boundaries.—A Legal Contest between Battersea and Clapham Parishes. Clapham Common.. 33

- Lavender Hill.—The Seat of William Wilberforce.—Eminent Supporters of the Anti-Slavery Movement.—Frances Elizabeth Leveson Gower. Mr. Thornton.—Philip Cazenove.—Charles Curling, Lady George Pollock, and others. 35

- Battersea Market Gardens and Gardeners. 38

- Stages set out for Battersea from the City.—Annual Fair.—Inhabitants supplied with Water from Springs.—The Manor of Battersea before the Conquest. 40

- Battersea and its association with the St. Johns.. 41

- Henry St. John Lord Viscount Bolingbroke.. 42

- A Horizontal Air Mill.. 45

- St. Mary's Church.. 47

- The Indenture. 49

- Epitaphs and Sepulchral Monuments.. .51

- Rectory and Vicarage.. 54

- A Petition or Curious Document.. 55

- Dr. Thomas Temple.—Dr. Thomas Church.. 56

- Cases of Longevity.—The Plague.—The Three Plague Years.—Deaths in Battersea.. 57

- Vicars of Battersea from Olden Times.. .58

- Thomas Lord Stanley.—Lawrence Booth.. 60

- York House.. 60

- Battersea Enamel Works.—Porcelain.—Jens Wolfe, Esq.—Sherwood Lodge.—Price's Patent Candle Factory.. 61

- Candlemas. 67

- The Saw.—Mark Isambard Brunel's Premises at Battersea.—Establishment for the preservation of timber from the dry rot burnt down.. 68

- History of the Ferry.—The Old Wooden Bridge.. 70

- Albert Suspension Bridge.. 72

- Chelsea Suspension Bridge.. 74

- The Prince of Wales.—Freeing the Bridges "For Ever." 75

- The Stupendous Railway Bridge across the Thames.. 78

- The spot where Cæsar and his legions are stated by some antiquarians to have crossed the river. 78

- A haunted house.—Battersea Fields.—Duel between the Duke of Wellington and Lord Winchelsea.. 80

CONTENTS

- The Red House.. 81

- "Gyp" the Raven.—Billy the Nutman.—Sports. 81

- "The Old House at Home."—Sabbath Desecration. 82

- Her Majesty's Commissioners empowered by Act of Parliament to form a Royal Park in Battersea Fields.—Wild Flowers.—Battersea Park.. . . 83

- London, Brighton and South-Coast Railway Company's two Circular Engine Sheds and West-End Goods Traffic Department. 89

- Long-Hedge Farm.—London, Chatham and Dover Railway Locomotive Works. 91

- A Canvas Cathedral.. 96

- H.P. Horse Nail Company's Factory.. 98

- St. George's Church, its clergy, its graveyard, epitaphs and inscriptions (St. Andrew's Temporary Iron Church).. 100

- Christ Church, its clergy. 104

- St. John's Church.. 106

- St. Paul's Church.. 107

- St. Philip's Church.. 107

- St. Mark's Church.. 109

- St. Luke's Chapel-of-Ease.. 110

- St. Saviour's Church.. 111

- St. Peter's Church. 112

- Temporary Church of the Ascension.—St. Michael's Church.. 113

- All Saints' Temporary Iron Church.—Rochester Diocesan Mission, St. James', Nine Elms. 116

- St. Aldwin's Mission Chapel.—The Church of our Lady of Mount Carmel and St. Joseph.. 117

- Church of the Sacred Heart.—The Old Baptist Meeting House, Revs. Mr. Browne, Joseph Hughes, M.A., (John Foster), Edmund Clark, Enoch Crook, I. M. Soule, Charles Kirtland. 118

- Baptist Temporary Chapel, Surrey Lane. 122

- Battersea Park Temporary Baptist Chapel.. 123

- Baptist (Providence) Chapel. 124

- Baptist Chapel, Chatham Road.—Wesleyan Methodist Mission Room and Sunday School.—United Methodist Free Church, Church Road, Battersea.—The United Methodist Free Church, Battersea Park Road. . . . 126

- Primitive Methodist Chapel, New Road. 127

- Primitive Methodist Chapel, Grayshott Road.—Primitive Methodist Chapel, Plough Lane. 128

- St. George's Mission Hall.—Battersea Congregational Church, (Independent), Bridge Road. 129

- Stormont Road Congregational Church, Lavender Hill. 131

- Wesleyan Methodism in Battersea. 132

- Methodistic Chronology. 135

- Wesleyan Chapel, Queen's Road. 136

- Free Christian Church, Queen's Road. 137

- Trinity Mission Hall, Stewart's Lane.—Plymouth Brethren. 138

- "The Little Tabernacle."—Thomas Blood. 139

- Battersea Priory.—Alien Priories. 140

- Ursulines. 141

- Battersea Grammar School, St. John's Hill. 142

- The Southlands Practising Model Schools.—St. Peter's Schools.—St. Saviour's Infant. 143

- Christ Church National Schools.—St. George's National Schools.— Voluntary Schools. 144

- London Board Schools. 145

- London School Board, Lambeth Division. 146

- The Elementary Education Acts.—Regulations affecting Parent and Child.148

- A Coffee Palace.—Latchmere Grove.—Plague Spots.—The Shaftesbury Park Estate. 151

- The Metropolitan Artizans' and Labourers' Dwellings Association. 153

- Latchmere Allotments.—Dove Dale Place.—An Old Boiler.—Lammas Hall.—The Union Workhouse. 154

- Old Battersea Workhouse.—The "Cage."—The "Stocks." 156

- The Falcon Tavern.—A Cantata. 157

- Origin of Bottled Ale in England.—"Ye Plough Inn."—"The Old House."—Stump of an Old Oak Tree. 158

- "Lawn House," Lombard Road.—The Prizes for the Kean's Sovereigns and the Funny Boat Race.—The Old Swan Tavern.—Royal Victoria Patriotic Schools. 159

- St. James' Industrial Schools.—Royal Masonic Institution for Girls. 160

- Clapham Junction.—Battersea Provident Dispensary. 161

- Wandsworth Common Provident Dispensary.—Charity Organization Society.—The Penny Bank.—No. 54 Metropolitan Fire Brigade Station.—Origin of Fire Brigades. 162

- The Metropolitan Police.—Police Stations, Battersea.—St. John's College of the National Society.. 163

- The Vicarage House School.—Various Wharves and Factories.. 164

- Mr. George Chadwin.—T. Gaines.—Tow's Private Mad House.—The Patent Plumbago Crucible Company's Works. 165

- Silicated Carbon Filter Company's Works. 167

- Condy's Manufactory.—Citizen Steamboat Company's Works. 167

- Orlando Jones & Co.'s Starch Works. 168

- Battersea Laundries.—Spiers and Pond's.—Propert's Factory.—The London and Provincial Steam Laundry.. 170

- St. Mary's (Battersea) Cemetery.—Numerous Epitaphs and Inscriptions. Scale of Fees, etc. 172

- The Battersea Charities. 189

- Parish Officers.—Vestrymen. 190

- Battersea Tradesmen's Club.—Temporary Home for Lost and Starving Dogs. 194

- London, Chatham and Dover Railway—Battersea Park Station—York Road Station (Brighton Line).—West London Commercial Bank. London and South Western Bank.—Temperance and Band of Hope Meetings.—South London Tramways in Battersea—Fares. 195

ALL ABOUT BATTERSEA

INTRODUCTION.

London, after the lapse of centuries, has been compared to an old ship that has been repaired and rebuilt till not one of its original timbers can be found; so marvellous are the changes and transmutations which have come over the "*town upon the lake*" or, *harbour for ships* as London was anciently called, that if a Celt, or a Roman, or a Saxon, or a Dane, or a Norman, or a Citizen of Queen Elizabeth's time were to awake from his long slumber of death, he would no more know where he was, and would be as strangely puzzled as an Englishman of the present generation would be, who had never stirred further than the radius of the Metropolis, supposing him to be conveyed by some supernatural agency one night to China, who, on rising the next morning finds himself surrounded by the street-scenery of the city of Pekin. Costumes, manners, language, inhabitants have all changed! Viewed from a geological stand-point, even the soil on which New London stands is not the same as that on which Old London stood. The level of the site of the ancient city was much lower than at present, for there are found indications of Roman highways, and floors of houses, twenty feet below the existing pathways. There are probable grounds for supposing the Surrey side to have been some nineteen hundred years ago a great expanse of water. London so called for several ages past, is a manifest corruption from Tacitus's *Londinium* which was not however its primitive name this famous place existed before the arrival of Cæsar in the Island, and was the capital of the *Trinobantes* or *Trinouantes*, and the seat of their kings. The name of the nation as appears from Baxter's British Glossary, was derived from the three following British words, tri, nou, bant, which signify the 'inhabitants of the new city.' This name it is supposed might have been given them by their neighbours on account of their having newly come from the Continent (Belgium) into Britain and having there founded a city called *tri-now* or the (new city) the most ancient name of the renowned metropolis of Britain.[1] Some have asserted that a city existed on

---

[1] The inhabitants of ancient Britain derived their origin partly from an original colony of Celtæ, partly from a mixed body of Gauls and Germans. None of them cultivated the ground; they all lived by raising cattle and hunting. Their dress consisted of skins, their habitations were huts of wicker-work covered with rushes. Their Priests the Druids together with the sacred women, exercised a kind of authority over them.

Britain according to Aristotle, was the name which the Romans gave to Modern England and Scotland. This appellation is, perhaps derived from the old word *brit*, partly coloured, it having been customary with the inhabitants to paint their bodies.

According to the testimony of Pliny and Aristotle, the Island in remotest times bore the name of Albion.

The Sea by which Britain is surrounded, was generally called, the *Western*, the *Atlantic*,

the spot 1107 years before the birth of Christ, and 354 years before the foundation of Rome. The fables of Geoffrey of Monmouth state that London was founded by Brute (or Brutus) a descendant of the Trojan Æneas the son of Venus and called New Troy, or *Troy Novant* until the time of Lud, who surrounded it with walls, and gave it the name Caer Lud, or Lud's town etc. *Leigh.* A certain Lord Mayor when pleading before Henry VI. assumed from this mythological story with a view to establish a claim to London's priority of existence over the city of Rome. The Celts the ancestors of the Britons and modern Welsh were the first inhabitants of Britain. The earliest records of the history of this island are the manuscripts and the poetry of the Cambrians. Britain was called by the Romans *Britannia* from its Celtic name Prydhain. *Camden.* We need not tarry to discuss whether Londinium originally was in *Cantium* or Kent the place fixed by Ptolemy and some other ancient writers of good authority, or whether its original place were Middlesex, or whether situated both north and south of the *Tamesis* Thames. The *Trinobantes* occupied Middlesex and Essex, they joined in opposing the invasion of Julius Cæsar 54 B.C.; but were among the first of the British States who submitted to the Romans their new City at that time being too inconsiderable a place for Cæsar to mention. Having revolted from the Roman yoke they joined their beautiful Queen Boadicea and were defeated by Suetonius Paulinus near London A.D. 61. But before reducing the Trinobantes who had the Thames for their southern boundary, it is the opinion of some antiquarians that the Romans probably had a station to secure their conquests on the Surrey side, and the spot fixed upon for the station is St. George's in the Fields a large plot of ground situated between Lambeth and Southwark, where many Roman coins, bricks, chequered pavements and other fragments of antiquity have been found. Three Roman ways from Kent, Surrey and Middlesex intersected each other in this place. It is thought that after the Normans reduced the Trinobantes the place became neglected and that they afterwards settled on the other side of the Thames and the name was transferred to the New City. The author of a work entitled "London in Ancient and Modern times." p.p. 12 and 13 writes. — Let the reader picture to himself the aspect of the place now occupied by the great Metropolis, as the Romans saw it on their first visit. He should imagine the Counties of Kent and Essex, now divided by the Thames, partially overflowed in the vicinity of the river by an arm of the sea, so that a broad estuary comes up as far as Greenwich, and the waters spread on both sides washing the foot of the Kentish uplands to the south, and finding a boundary to the north in the gently rising ground of Essex. The mouth of the river, properly speaking was situated three or four miles from where London Bridge now stands. Instead of being confined between banks as at present, the river overflowed extensive marshes, which lay both right and left beyond London. Sailing up the broad stream, the voyager

---

or *Hesperian* Ocean. Herodotus informs us that the Phœnicians, Greeks, and Carthaginians, especially the first were acquainted with it from the earliest period and obtained tin there and designated it *Tin Island.* The name Great Britain was applied to England and Scotland after James I. ascended the English throne in 1603. England and Scotland however had separate Parliaments till 1st of May 1707, when during the reign of Queen Anne the Island was designated by the name of the United Kingdom of Great Britain. The terms at first excited the utmost dissatisfaction; but the progress of time has shown it to be the greatest blessing that either nation could have experienced.

would find the waters spreading far on either side of him, as he reached the spots now known as Chelsea and Battersea—a fact of which the record is preserved in their very names. A tract of land rises on the north side of the river. It is bounded to the west by a range of country, subject to inundations, consisting of beds of rushes and osiers and boggy grounds and impenetrable thickets, intersected by streams. It is bounded to the north by a large dense forest, rising on the edge of a waste fen or lake, covering the whole district now called Finsbury and stretching away for miles beyond. This tract of land, rising in a broad knoll, formed the site of London.

An old writer says "it is now certain that the spot, (viz. St. George's in the Fields) on which the city was described to have stood, was an extensive marsh or lake, reaching as far as Camberwell hills, until by drains and embankments, the Romans recovered all the lowlands about the parts now called St. George's Fields, Lambeth etc. London never stood on any other spot than the Peninsular, on the northern banks, formed by the Thames in front; by the river Fleet on the west; and by the stream afterwards named Walbrook on the East. An immense forest originally extended to the river side, and, even as late as the reign of Henry II. covered the northern neighbourhood of the city, and was filled with various species of beasts of chase. It was defended naturally by fosses, one formed by the creek which ran along the Fleet ditch, the other by that of Walbrook. The south side was protected by the river Thames, and the north by the adjacent forest."

In the reign of Nero the first notice of Londinium or, Londinum occurs in Tacitus (Ann xiv. 33.) where it is spoken of, not then as honoured with the name *Colonia* but for the great conflux of Merchants, its extensive commerce, and as a depôt for merchandise. At a later date London appears to have been *Colonia* under the name Augusta (Amm. Marcell.; xxvii. 8.) how long it possessed this honourable appellation we do not know but after the establishment of the Saxons we find no mention of Augusta. It has received at various times thirteen different names, but most of them having some similarity to the present one. However as it is not a history of England's Metropolis but *All about Battersea*[2] we write, we will at once

[2] The Manor is thus described in Doomsday-book among the lands belonging to the Abbot of Westminster:—"St. Peter of Westminster holds Patricesy, Earl Harold held it; and it was then assessed at 72 hides: now at 18 hides. The arable land is—Three carucates are in demesne; and there are forty-five villians, and sixteen bordars with fourteen carucates, there are eight bond men: and seven mills at £42 9s. 8d. and a corn rent of the same amount, and eighty-two acres of meadow and a wood yielding fifty swine for pannage. There is in Southwark one bordar belonging to the Manor paying twelve pence. From the roll of Wendelesorde (Wandsworth) is received the sum of £6. A villian having ten swine pays to the Lord one; but if he has a smaller number, nothing. One knight holds four hides of this land and the money he pays is included in the preceding estimate. The entire Manor in the time of King Edward was valued at £80, afterwards at £30; and now at £75 9s. 8d.

"King William gave the Manor to St. Peter in exchange for Windsor. The Earl of Moreton holds one and a half hides of land, which in King Edward's time and afterwards belonged to this Manor. Gilbert the Priest holds three hides under the same circumstances. The Bishop of Lisieux had two hides of which the Church of Westminster was seized in the time of William and disseised by the Bishop of Bayeaux. The Abbot of Chertsey holds one hide which the Bailiff of this will, out of ill-will (to the Abbot of Westminster) detached from this Manor, and appropriated it to Chertsey."

commence at Nine Elms.

Hide of land in the ancient laws of England was such a quantity of land as might be ploughed with one plough within the compass of a year, or as much as would maintain a family; some call it sixty, some eighty, and others one hundred acres. Villian, or Villein, in our ancient customs, denotes a man of Servile or base condition, viz, a bond-man or servant. (Fr. Vilain. L. Villanus, from Villa, a farm, a feudal tenant of the lowest class.)

ALL ABOUT BATTERSEA

Nine Elms Lane.—The King's Champion.

NINE ELMS LANE it is said derived its name from nine Elm Trees which stood in a row facing a small mansion known as "Manor House"—on the site there has recently been erected, partly out of some of the old materials, the offices and premises belonging to Haward Bros. Forty years ago, Londoners wending their way to Battersea fields regarded themselves in the country away from the smoke of town where they could rusticate at pleasure as soon as they entered Nine Elms Lane on their pedestrian excursions. Here were hedgerows, and green lanes, and market gardens, and orchards, meadows, and fields of waving corn, where reapers might have been seen in harvest-time reaping and binding sheaves of golden grain. Dikes and ditches had to be crossed.[3] In the event of high tide, which was of no uncommon occurrence, the district would be partially inundated with water, in some places people might ply in small rowing boats as easily as on the River Thames. On the site where now stands the wharf of John Bryan and Co., the celebrated Contractors for Welsh, Steam, Gas, and household Coals in general, were situated the pleasure grounds and tea gardens belonging to Nine Elms Tavern—the old tavern is still remaining. By the side of the Coal Wharf is the Causeway where watermen used to ply for hire in order to ferry people across the river. Steel has given us a lively description of a boat trip from Richmond on an early summer morning when he fell in "with a fleet of gardeners.... Nothing remarkable happened in our voyage, but I landed with ten sail of Apricot boats at Strand bridge after having put up at Nine Elms to take in melons." Within the immediate vicinity is Thorne's Brewery with its clock turret at its summit which at night is illuminated with gas so that the passers-by looking at the clock might know the hour. On the spot where Southampton Streets are, stood in olden time a large mansion surrounded by extensive grounds, said to have been inhabited by the King's Champion. The Champion *of the King, (campio regis)* is an ancient officer, whose office is, at the coronation of our Kings, when the King is at dinner to ride armed *cap a pie*, into Westminster Hall, and by the proclamation of an herald make a challenge "that if any man shall deny the King's title to the crown, he is there ready to defend it in single combat, etc., which being done," the King drinks to him, and sends him a gilt cup with a cover full of wine, which the Champion

---

[3] About ten years ago a brick sewer was constructed under the supervision of the Metropolitan Board of Works where the filthy black ditch which partly formed a boundary line between Battersea, Clapham, and Lambeth Parishes was filled up. T. Pearson constructed the sewer, and Mr. Benjamin Butcher was Clerk of the Works.

drinks, and hath the cup for his fee.

On the north side of Nine Elms Lane, nearly opposite the place where the "Southampton Arms" Tavern is situated was a windmill.

Thorne's Brewery.—What Battersea has been called.

On the site now occupied by Thorne's Brewery there used to be a Tan Yard and Fellmonger's Establishment. When the ground was opened for the purpose of drainage some old tanks were discovered in which the hides were soaked containing remains of lime and hair. In the rear of the Brewery there was a Hop Garden where that bitter plant much used for brewing was cultivated. The only regular vehicle that passed through Nine Elms Lane was the carrier's cart—the few inhabitants of the place used to "turn out" to see it pass—a marked contrast to the present hurried and incessant traffic! Facing the Railway Terminus were two Steamboat Piers for landing and taking up passengers. At race times the excitement between the rival steamboat companies was intense—"touters," men hired expressly by each of these companies to induce passengers to go down their respective piers, became at times so exasperated with each other that they fell to blows, a sight which the baser sort of the crowds assembled on such occasions enjoyed to their hearts' content.

Many things have been said by way of disparagement of Battersea and not at all reflecting credit on certain localities within the parish. Battersea has been called "the Sink Hole of Surrey." Europa Place, Bridge Road, has been designated "Little Hell," and the spot where Trinity Hall has been erected at the end of Stewart's Lane, received the epithet of "Hell Corner." Persons in the habit of receiving stolen property were said to reside in the neighbourhood; moreover, there was a gang called "Battersea Forty Theives!" "Sharpers" are said to have abounded in every direction, so that strangers going to Battersea would be "cut for the simples." But we who know something of London life know that other Metropolitan parishes have their "dens of infamy" and localities of "Blue Skin," "Jack Sheppard," and "Jonathan Wild" notoriety, that beneath the shadow of St. Paul's Cathedral and Westminster Abbey, our Houses of Parliament and Mansions of the Nobility and Aristocracy, squalor and crime, vice and grandeur walk side by side, and oftentimes hand in hand.

London and South Western Railway Company's Goods Station and Locomotive Works.

Adjoining Thorne's premises and Swonnell's Malt houses, is the London and South Western Railway Company's Goods Station, which, before the extension of that Company's line in 1848 to Waterloo Road, was originally the Metropolitan Terminus. Though this part of the line crosses the most grimy portion of Lambeth, a distance of two miles and fifty yards, yet it cost the Railway Company £800,000. The London and Southampton Railway (as it was first called) was opened on the 11th of May, 1840, which, in connexion with the opposite wharf and warehouses on the banks of the river, at that time occupied an extent of between seven and eight acres. The entrance front of the (then) Metropolitan Terminus at Nine Elms, erected from designs by William Tite, Esq., Architect to the Company, was not unhandsome though at present it has rather a dingy appearance for want of renovation, and has a central arcade which originally led to the booking office and waiting rooms now used for the manager's and clerks' offices for the goods traffic department. The railroad was commenced under the authority of an Act of Parliament which received the Royal assent on the 5th of July, 1834 (it was opened as far as Woking Common on the 21st of May, 1838). By this Act the Company were empowered to raise £1,000,000 in £50 shares, and a further sum of £330,000 by loan. Since that time several additional Acts have been passed authorizing the Company to extend their line and increase their capital. The Company's capital for the present year (1879) is £17,000,000. Mr. Wood was the Company's first Locomotive Superintendent. When the London and Southampton line was first opened all the workmen in the Company's service had a half holiday and one shilling each given to them. The Richmond Railway—this though an offshoot of the South Western, and worked by that Company, was executed by a private one. It was however sold to the South Western Company in October, 1846. It had been opened on the 27th of July previous. Number of miles open 648. The gross receipts for the year ending December 31, 1873, were £2,195,170. The railroad intersects Battersea parish to the extent of two miles and a half. The Goods Department comprises the hydraulic shed, down goods shed, carriers' shed, egg shed, the old warehouse and granary by the riverside; down office, Wandsworth Road Gate; cartage office, Nine Elms Lane. Officers of the Company.—General Manager, Archibald Scott, Esq.; Locomotive Superintendent, W. Adams, Esq.; Resident Engineer, William Jacomb, Esq.; Treasurer, Alfred Morgan, Esq.; Goods Manager, J. T. Haddow, Esq., Nine Elms; Assistant Goods Manager, Mr. W. B. Mills, Waterloo; Superintendent, R. H. Ming, Esq., Nine Elms; Chief Inspector, Mr. Robert Lingley, Nine Elms; Law Clerk, M. H. Hall, Esq.; Mr. H. B. Terrill, Cashier; Mr. J. E. Hawkins, Chief Clerk; Superintendents of the Line, E. W. Verrinder, Chief Superintendent, Waterloo Station; John Tyler, Western Division, Exeter Station; William Gardiner, Assistant Superintendent, Waterloo Station; W. H. Stratton, Storekeeper, Nine Elms Works.

Soon after the opening of the London and Southampton Railway a collision between two passenger trains occurred at the Nine Elms Terminus resulting in the death of a young woman, a domestic servant, who, with a fellow servant, had been spending the day at Hampton Court. The Coroner's Jury returned a verdict of accidental death *a deodand* of £300 was levied on the "Eclipse" locomotive engine, the moving cause of death. The Railway Company paid the £300 to Earl Spencer as Lord of the Manor, who most generously divided it amongst the deceased's relatives.

> *Omnia qua movent ad mortem sunt deodanda:*
> What moves to death, or kills him dead,
> Is deodand, and forfeited.

On the South Western Railway Stone Wharf are the agents' offices of the several depôts for the sale of Portland stone, Bath freestone, etc. Huge blocks of stone direct from the quarries are here deposited and piled block upon block. A single block in some instances weighing ten tons elevated and removed by means of a steam traveller moving on a gantry.

When the workmen were engaged in "digging out" the ground for the foundation of the goods sheds a human skeleton was discovered, on which Mr. Carter (coroner) held an inquest. Dr. Statham, who made the *post mortem* examination, stated that the skeleton was that of a male person, that there were three severe cuts upon the head either of which was sufficient to cause death. As no further evidence was procurable a verdict was given in accordance.

About forty years ago, when Mr. Gooch was Locomotive Superintendent, a fire broke out at the London and South Western Railway Works, Nine Elms Lane, which caused great destruction of property, including a very handsome clock tower. Various metals were fused and mingled into shapes fantastic, portions of which were substituted for chimney-piece ornaments in the homes of the workman and kept as mementos of this conflagration! A man of the name of Dover who it is said accidentally set the stores on fire was so frightened that it turned the hair of his head grey in one night!

At Nine Elms Locomotive, Carriage and Stores Departments are fire precautions which the Railway Company insist upon being strictly observed. A fire engine with hose and all necessary appliances is kept in a building set apart for it adjoining Heman's Street Entrance gate. A properly qualified fireman is appointed to look after the whole of the buildings by night, as a precaution against fire. The fireman's name is Thomas Lewin, and his residence is 51, Thorne Street, Wandsworth Road. His hours of duty are from 5.30 p.m. to 6.30 a.m. It is the fireman's duty to perambulate the whole of the works during the night, and to make a daily report of the circumstances in the book provided for that purpose. He is responsible that the fire engine, hose, hydrants, etc., are kept in working order and tried once a week. A statement of the trial is to be made in the fireman's report book with any suggestions or remarks. Positions of Hydrants at Nine Elms Works—There are 120 hydrants (always charged) distributed as follows:—15 in the offices, paint loft and shops beneath; 4 in the general stores; 4 in wheelwrights' and signal shops; 2 in bonnet shop; 5 in waggon shop; 4 in new waggon shop and saw mill; 5 in smiths' and carriage fitting shops; 9 in erecting shops; 2 in turning shop; 3 in tender shop; 4 in new erecting shop; 1 in permanent way shop; 4 in arches under the Viaduct; 52 in running shed; 4 at outlets of water tanks, and 2 on the coal stage. Positions of Tell-tale Clocks:—1 in the office; 1 in general stores; 1 in wheelwrights' shop; 1 in paint shop; 1 in saw mill. It is the fireman's duty to commence to "peg" each of these blocks four times every night at the following hours, viz., 8 p.m., 10.30 p.m., 1 a.m. and 3.30 a.m.

Facing the Goods Station are the Company's Wharves with an extensive river frontage. Here also formerly stood Francis' Cement Works, adjoining is Nine Elms Steamboat Pier. The South Western Railway Locomotive Works and Goods Department occupy a vast area. It is computed that about 2,000 persons are employed in the various departments. Here were formerly orchard-grounds—many a goodly tree bearing fruit and pleasant to the eye has been felled. "Woodman spare that tree!" though spoken by feminine lips would have no force of appeal in this fast age of iron railways and steam locomotives, when Railway Companies scruple not by virtue of Acts of Parliament to pull down by hundreds the dwellings of the poor, it is not to be supposed for an instant that a few fruit trees however delicious their produce or delightful their shadow should prove a peculiar obstacle in the way of this March of Civilization! On payment of sixpence, children at half-price, persons might enter these orchards with full liberty to eat as much fruit as they liked on condition that they brought none away. The old Spring Well near Nine Elms Lane, Wandsworth Road, is within the recollection of many, who by descending some six or eight steps reached with their hands the iron ladle out of which they often drank cooling draughts of nature's sparkling aquatic refreshment. Ah, everything has a history and its lesson if we did but know. We all exert unconscious influence either for good or evil,—some secret action performed; some deed of kindness done; some public boon conferred with the benefactor's name concealed shall by-and-by be proclaimed upon the house-top. A cup of cold water given in the name of a disciple of Jesus of Nazareth shall not lose its reward. Some persons wish to be remembered by posterity, even wicked parents would not like after death to be obliterated from the memories of their children. The best of all human monuments is a good character,—Solomon says, "a good name is rather to be chosen than riches."

Our forefathers never dreamed of erecting such drinking fountains[4] as we have in these days with troughs for cattle and smaller ones for mongrel barking curs to slake their thirst; the pond by the way, the wooden horse trough outside the road-side Inn, the long-handled iron pump, in some instances resembling the head and tail of the British Lion having the body of a greyhound, pleased them and suited their purpose. The site now environed by the London Gas Works was formerly a large market ground, here too grew apple, pear, and cherry trees, gooseberry bushes and currants, roses were cultivated and rendered the air fragrant with their sweet perfume. In the ditches and trenches or small channels and streams occasioned by the tidal overflow from the river, juveniles of both sexes might have been seen catching with hand and cap sticklebacks and utilizing a medicine phial or gin bottle for an aquarium. Senior boys and hobbledehoys with jovial facial aspect who had not studied ichthyology or that part of zoology which treats of fishes, attempted to catch larger fry by adopting the Izaak Walton method of angling with rod and line, and thought themselves amply rewarded if after much patient endurance the motion of their floats indicated that their baits had taken, their eyes would glisten at the sight of a few roaches and perches. Youngsters would amuse themselves by watching the newts and tadpoles, the leaping and swimming of that amphibious reptile of the *batrachian* tribe, wondering perhaps, supposing their biblical knowledge to have extended thus far, whether those were the kind of creatures that crawled out of the river Nile and crept into the houses of the Egyptians.

Mill-Pond Bridge.—New Road.

---

[4] His Grace the Duke of Westminster is the President of the Metropolitan Drinking Fountain and Cattle Trough Association.

Many a dainty dish of stewed eels have the miller's men had at Mill-pond Bridge, who not unfrequently caught alive this precious kind of anguilla as it lay concealed between the stones and mud, without the aid of eel-pot or basket. Mill-Pond Bridge derives its name from the old tidal water flour mill, the only vestige of the mill remaining is the outward carcase, which is in a ruinous condition; beneath its cover are the lock gates, the entrance of the creek where thousands of tons of coal are conveyed in barges to the London Gas Works.

NEW ROAD, as it is designated, leading from Battersea fields to the Wandsworth Road was a lane with a mud bank on both sides. In a line with the centre of the South Western Railway "Running Shed" was formerly Mill-Pond which answered the purpose of a large reservoir of water raised for driving the mill wheel.

Water mills used for grinding corn are said to have been invented by Belisarius, the General of Justinian while besieged in Rome by the Goths, 555. The ancients parched their corn and ground it in mortars. Afterwards mills were invented which were turned by men and beasts with great labour, yet Pliny mentioned wheels turned by water. *See Telo-dynamic Transmitter.*

The simplest mill for bruising grain was nothing more than two stones between which it was broken. Such was often seen in the country of the Niger by Richard and John Lander on their expedition to Africa. The manna which God gave to the children of Israel in the desert "the people went about and gathered it, and ground it in mills or beat it in a mortar," *Numbers xi.* 8.

From mills and mortars thus rudely constructed there must have been obtained at first only a kind of peeled grain which Dr. Eadie says may be compared to the German *graupe,* the English *groats,* and the American *grits* or *hominy.* Fine flour was laboriously obtained from household mills like our coffee mills. The oldest mention of flour is in Gen. xviii. 6; but bread which is made of flour or meal is named in Gen. iii. 19. In order to reduce the flour to a proper degree of fineness it was necessary sometimes to have it ground over again and cleared by a sieve.

Samson when a prisoner to the Philistines was condemned to the mill-stone to grind with his hand in the prison-house, Judges xvi. 21. In England prisoners are sent to the treadmill as a punishment.

The Talmudists have a story that the Chaldeans made the young men of the captivity carry mill-stones with them to Babylon where there seems to have been a scarcity at that time. They have also a proverbial expression of a man with a mill-stone about his neck which they use to express a man under the severest weight of affliction.

Windmills are of great antiquity and stated to be of Roman or Saracen invention, they are said to have been originally introduced into Europe by the Knights of St. John, who took the hint from what they had seen in the crusades (*Baker*). Windmills were first known in Spain, France and Germany in 1299 (*Anderson*). Wind saw-mills were invented by a Dutchman in 1633, when one was erected near the Strand in London.

A Royal Sturgeon caught in the wheel of the Mill at Mill-Pond Bridge.

Acorns was the coarse fare of the old inhabitants of Britain, when wild Britons painted their skin to make themselves appear more fierce, and native tribes in a still more barbarous condition, half naked or clad in the skins of beasts, not cultivators of the soil, subsisted on the flesh of their cattle or on the precarious produce of the chase. Packs of hungry, growling, cruel wolves[5] prowled in the woods and forests, and Druidical Priests exercised an entire control over the unlettered people they governed, and human captives seized on Britannia's shores were offered as victims in sacrifice, a holocaust to the divinities and false gods which ancient Britons worshipped!

The Accipenser, in ichthyology, a genus of fishes belonging to the Amphibia Nantes of Linnæus. The Accipenser has a single linear nostril; the cirri are below the snout, and before the mouth. There are three species of this genus. The ruthenus has four cirri, and fifteen squamous protuberances; it is a native of Russia. The huso has four cirri; the body is naked, has no prickles or protuberances. The ichthyocollo, or *isinglass* of the shops, famous as an agglutinant, and used also for the fining of wines, is made from its sound or scales. The Sturio, or Sturgeon with four cirri and eleven squamous protuberances on the back. This fish annually ascends our rivers (it has occasionally been seen in years gone by as high up the river Thames as Wandsworth) but in no great numbers, and is taken by accident in the salmon nets. It seems a spiritless fish making no manner of resistance when entangled, but is drawn out of the water like a lifeless lump. This cartilaginous fish is highly prized for food, not unlike in taste to veal. About thirty-six years ago a Royal Sturgeon was caught in the wheel of the mill at Mill-Pond Bridge then in the occupation of Mr. Hutton the Miller (who was noted as a breeder of game fowls), now the property of the London Gas-Light Company. It appears that a local tradesman named Henry Appleton was going to town and saw a great crowd, some with guns shooting at a great fish, but the Sturgeon's natural armour resisted the force of their small shot such as they were then using. Mr. Appleton upon seeing the state of affairs hastened to procure a bullet or two as a more effectual

[5] Wolves were very numerous in England, King Edgar unsuccessfully attempted to effect their total destruction by commuting the punishment of certain crimes into the acceptance of a certain number of wolves' tongues from each criminal; their heads were demanded by him as a tribute particularly 300 annually from Wales, A.D. 961.

In 1289 Edward I. issued his Royal Mandate to Peter Corbet for the extermination of wolves in the several counties of Gloucester, Worcester, Hereford, Salop, and Stafford; and in the adjacent county of Derby.

Camden at page 900 informs us certain persons at Wormhill held their lands by the duty of hunting and taking the wolves that infested the country, whence they were styled *Wolf Hunt.*

In Saxon times and during Athelstan's reign wolves abounded so in Yorkshire that a retreat was built at Flixton in that county "to defend passengers from the wolves that they should not be devoured by them." On account of the desperate ravages these animals made during winter the Saxons distinguished January by the name of the Wolf month. An *outlaw* was called a *wolf's head* as being out of the protection of law and liable to be killed as that destructive beast.

means of capturing the prize and the first shot or bullet fired was fatal to the poor sturgeon which was then landed and conveyed into the garden of Mr. Hutton's private house upon the exact spot of which at the present time stands the house (since erected) on the banks of the Creek in the occupation of Mr. Methven. It then became after the usual ceremony of asking the Lord Mayor, the property of Mr. Appleton, and was exhibited by him in York Street (now Savona Street), on premises now in the occupation of Mr. Dulley, Butcher. After being exhibited several weeks great crowds coming from all parts of London to see it, the Sturgeon was sold to a Fishmonger residing in Bond Street, who publicly exhibited it in his shop for some years with a description stating particulars, where it was captured and by whom and its length, being upwards of 9-ft. It is said to have been equal in weight to a sack of flour viz., 280 lbs.

The Sturgeon is more abundant in the Northern Coasts of Europe. It is also found in the more Southern parts. It was esteemed by the ancients as a very great luxury and it was held in high repute for the table by the Greeks and Romans and at their banquets it was introduced with particular ceremonies.

In England when caught in the Thames within the jurisdiction of the Lord Mayor of London it is a *Royal Fish* reserved for the Sovereign. The flesh is white, delicate, firm and nutritious. It is used both fresh, generally stewed. The largest species of Sturgeon is the Bielaga, or Huso. Huso (*A. Huso*) of the Black and Caspian seas and their rivers. It attains the length of 20 or 25 feet and has been known to weigh nearly 3000 lbs.

Near the site where now stands the Park Tavern at the corner of the New Road, opposite Mr. Featherstonhaugh's Brewery and not far from "The Plough & Harrow," were the flower gardens and beautiful residence of John Patient, Esq., afterwards occupied by Mr. Carne the Barge Builder. The house where Mr. Bennett, Lath-render, resides, and the house adjoining were used as a Private Asylum for the insane and was called "Sleaford House."

The picturesque and retired Country Parsonage, the residence of the Rev. J. G. Weddell, stood a considerable distance from the main road—"The Prince Alfred" tavern situate in Haine Street occupies the site. In this locality was a tenter-ground the entrance to which from the road was through a white gate.

Wallace's Vitriol Works.

A gateway at the commencement of "Hugman's Lane" which had "no thoroughfare" led to the works belonging to Peter Pariss and Son, Oil of Vitriol Manufacturers and Manufacturing Chemists. Mr. Wallace, who subsequently held these premises had them considerably enlarged to facilitate his project in working up gas liquor for making Sulphate of Ammonia, which is extensively used for agricultural purposes. The sewers in the neighbourhood became impregnated with a deleterious gas and the stench from the drains was intolerable. After considerable litigation with the Board of Works Mr. Wallace became a bankrupt.

By order of the Mortgagees on Wednesday and Thursday, March 3rd and 4th, 1880, Mr. Douglas Young sold by auction the plant and machinery of the above extensive works, including 5 large Cornish steam boilers, tubular boiler, 3 egg boilers, a bottle boiler, a 4000 gallon wrought iron tank, 12 smaller ditto, 4 large circular tanks, 5 steam barrel of various sizes, flange pipes, 3 large iron coils, about 70 tons old metal, several copper and iron boilers of various sizes, furnace fittings, weighing bridge by Hodgson and Stead, self-feeding boiler and engine, about 150,000 sound bricks, a large quantity of sound timber including balk timber, yellow deals, planks, battens, die-square, floor and lining boards, and 50 tons of breeze, several stacks of firewood, pantiles, drain pipes and other plant materials.

Sleaford Street.—Coal.

SLEAFORD STREET appears to have obtained an amount of respectability that it had not of yore. Once upon a time one side was nicknamed "Ginbottle Row," and the opposite side was called "Soapsuds Bay!" Mill-Pond Bridge was very narrow, about half its present width, with a low parapet on both sides.

If the following statement could be relied on, it would perhaps allay the fears created by certain alarmists respecting the physical limits to deep coal mining and duration of the coal supply. "There are coal deposits in various parts of Great Britain at all depths down to 10,000 or 12,000 feet. Mining is possible to a depth of 4,000 feet, but beyond this the high temperature is likely to prove a barrier. The temperature of a coal mine at a depth of 4,000 feet will probably be found as high as 120º Fahr.; but there is reason to believe that by the agency of an efficient system of ventilation the temperature may be reduced, at least during the cooler months of the year, as to allow mining operations without unusual danger to health. Adopting a depth of 4,000 feet as the limit to deep mining there is still a quantity of coal in store in Great Britain sufficient to afford the annual supply of twenty-two millions of tons for a thousand years." —Hull.[6]

"Early to bed and early to rise makes a man healthy, wealthy and wise," was a motto adopted by our forefathers when the inducements to promenade London streets by night were not so inviting as now.

"Ranelagh and Vauxhall were places of frivolous amusement resorted to even by the higher classes. From those and other haunts of folly, lumbering coaches or

[6] More than a quarter of a century ago, Professor Buckland when examined before the House of Commons, limits the supply to 400 years. Mr. Bailey in his Survey of Durham limits the supply to 200 years only. But some proprietors when examined in 1830 extended the period of total exhaustion of the mines to 1,727 years; they assumed that there are 837 square miles of coal strata in this field and that only 105 miles had been worked out.

"There were 2936 collieries in Britain in 1860; from these were raised 83,923,273 tons of coal. The greatly increasing consumption of coal has originated fears as to the possibility of the exhaustion of our mineral fuel. It appears that, while in 1820, only 15,000,000 tons were raised, in 1840, the amount had reached 30,000,000, and in 1860, it was nearly 84,000,000. At the same rate of increase the known coal, within a workable distance from the surface, would last at least 100 years. But the consumption, during the last twenty years of the century, would at the present increasing ratio amount to 1464 million tons a year, a quantity vastly greater than can be used. We need not, therefore, now begin to fear lest our coalfields should be speedily used up." —Chambers's Encyclopedia.

sedan chairs conveyed home the ladies through the dimly lighted or pitch dark streets, and the gentlemen picked their way over the ruggedly-paved thorough-fares, glad of the proffered aid of the link boys who crowded round the gates of such places of public entertainment or resort as were open at night, and who, arrived at the door to which they had escorted some fashionable foot-passenger, quenched the blazing torch in the trumpet-looking ornament which one now and then still sees lingering over the entrance to some house in an antiquated square or court, a characteristic relic of London in the olden time."

Street Lighting.

Street lighting was not known to the Greeks and Romans, it was therefore necessary for them whenever they went abroad after dark to carry flambeaux. Street lighting was first introduced at Paris about the beginning of the 16th century. An Edict was issued ordering the inhabitants to keep lights burning in their windows after nine at night. In 1558, lamps were exchanged for lanterns, and in 1671 these lanterns were ordered to be lighted from the 20th of October to the beginning of April. This however did not prove a satisfactory arrangement. At length a premium was offered by the Government for a dissertation on the best mode of lighting the streets. The successful competitors were a journeyman glazier, M. M. Bailly, Le Roy and Bourgeois Le Cheteaublanc. To the glazier was awarded a prize of 200 livres, and to the other three jointly 2,000 livres. The result of their suggestions was a general lighting of the streets by oil lamps set upon posts.

In London, lanterns were first used in 1688, and those inhabitants whose houses fronted the streets were ordered to hang out their lanterns and keep them burning from 6 to 11 o'clock at night; the number of lanterns thus used within the boundaries of the City of London was 5,000. Without the City, inclusive of the suburbs, the probability is that the number was 15,000.

In 1874, another act was passed for regulating the lighting of the City still further. Since the lighting of the streets, alleys, courts, etc., of our Metropolis with gas have come many other sanitary and social improvements, and it is not unlikely that under a wise Providence we owe to this invention as much security from the nightly depredations of burglars as much so as from the vigilance of the police.

The existence and inflammability of coal-gas has been known in England for two centuries. In the year 1659, Thomas Shirley correctly attributed the exhalations from the "burning well" at Wigan, in Lancashire, to the coal-beds which lie under that part of the country; and soon after, Dr. Clayton, influenced by Shirley, actually made coal-gas, and detailed the results of his labours in a letter to the Hon. Robert Boyle, who died in 1691. About a century later, 1753, Sir James Lowther communicated to the Royal Society a notice of a spontaneous evolution of gas at a colliery belonging to him at Whitehaven. Bishop Watson made many experiments on coal-gas, which he details in his Chemical Essays. Mr. R. Taylor, on the Coal-fields of China, says, "The Chinese artificially produce illuminating gas from bitumen coal we are certain. But it is a fact that spontaneous jets of gas derived from boring into coal-beds have for centuries been burning, and turned to that and other economical purposes. If the Chinese are not gas manufacturers, they are nevertheless gas consumers and employers on a large scale, and have evidently been so ages before the knowledge of its application was acquired by Europeans." In 1792, Mr. Murdoch, an engineer at Redruth in Cornwall, erected a little gasometer with apparatus which produced gas sufficient to supply his own house and offices, and in 1797, he erected a similar apparatus in Ayrshire. In the following year, he was engaged to put up a gas works at the Manufactory of Bolton and Watts, at Soho, Birmingham,—this was the first application of gas in a large way. Except among a few scientific men, the manufacture of gas excited but little curiosity until the year 1802, when the front of the great Soho Manufactory was brilliantly illuminated with gas on the occasion of the public rejoicings at the Peace. In 1801, M. Le Bon, at Paris, succeeded in lighting up his own house and gardens with gas from wood and coal, and had it in contemplation to light up the City of Paris.

Only within the present century has gas superseded in London the dim oil lamps. About forty years ago, oil lamps and lighted candles were used in our churches and chapels; in some places of worship evening services were dispensed with altogether. A humorous anecdote is related of Dr. Johnson: it is said, one evening, from the window of his house in Bolt Court, he observed the parish lamp-lighter ascend a ladder to light one of the small oil lamps. He had scarcely descended the ladder half-way when the flame expired. Quickly returning he lifted the cover of the lamp partially and thrusting the end of his torch beneath it, the flame instantly communicated to the wick by the thick vapour which issued from it. "Ah!" exclaimed the Doctor, "one of these days the streets of London will be lighted by smoke."—*Notes and Queries*, No. 127. Certain scientific men were incredulous as to the practicability of lighting up the whole of London with gas, and Sir Humphrey Davey asked if it were intended to take the dome of St. Paul's for a gasometer! In 1820 gas meters were patented by John Malan, in 1830 by Samuel Clegg, in 1838 by Nathan Defries and others. Mr. Daniel Pollock, father of the late Chief Baron, was governor of the first "chartered" gas company in 1812. In 1822 St. James' Park was first lighted with gas. In 1825, its safety had not then been established on the part of the Government, a committee of the most eminent scientific men immediately inspected the Gas Works, and reported that the occasional superintendence of all the Works was necessary. However, since then so rapidly has the invention of gas-lighting progressed, that now in the present year of grace, there is neither City nor town in Great Britain of any note but what is illuminated with gas and has works for its manufacture in close proximity to the houses of its inhabitants. Gas supply of London, receipts for the year 1872, £2,133,600, for 1873, £2,544,000. What is coke? Coke is the residual carbon of pit coal after the volatile matters have been expelled by heat, it has a porous texture and a lustre sometimes approaching the metallic. It is a valuable fuel, producing an intense and steady heat and leaving but little residue after combustion. The residual coke in retorts has a quantity of ash, which, besides its earthy base of silicate, usually contains sulphur and other deleterious matter. The breeze can be used in furnaces and in burning bricks. There is a considerable quantity of pure hydrogen produced by the decomposition of water in cooling coke. Attempts have been made to manufacture gas from other substances besides coal—oil, resin, peat, and even water having in their turn commanded capital for a fair trial of their merits of all

these; however, coal has alone stood the test of commercial success, those companies formed for other schemes having either been dissolved or become converts to
its superior advantages. No doubt it will be considered Utopian—Mr. Robinson
thinks that the electric light might be so modified as to be used in public dwellings!
There are exhaustless stores of latent electricity, but the difficulty is to know how
to develop and utilise it.

Street gas lit by electricity, by Mr. St. George Lane, Fox's method: trial partially
successful, Pall Mall, etc., 13th April, 1878. British Museum Reading Room illuminated by electric light, October, 1879.

London Gas-Light Company's Works and Vauxhall Gardens.

Common bituminous coal obtained from the mines of Northumberland,
Durham, York, South Wales, and a few other coal districts is the kind from which
most of the gas of this country is manufactured. The Cannel or Scotch Parrot
coals produce a gas of a much richer quality, which, though expensive, has the
advantage of superior illuminating power. Gas companies use to a very great extent coals from the following mines:—Pelaw, Leverson's Wallsend, Pelton, New
Pelton, Dean's Primrose, Garesfield, South Peareth, (The London Gas-Light Company use principally Peareth) Urpeth, Washington, Yorkshire, Silkstone, Haswell,
West Wear, Wearmouth, Brancepeth, South Brancepeth, and Ravenshaw Pelaw.
The resulting products of carbonization of these coals when an exhauster is employed will be found to give about the following average per ton:—

Gas, 9,500 cubic feet; Coke, 13 cwt., or one chaldron; Tar, 10 gallons; Ammoniacal Liquor, 13 gallons. Ammonia, a compound of Nitrogen and Hydrogen, is
converted into Sulphate of Ammonia, Sal Ammonia, Carbonate of Ammonia, etc.,
etc. Tar, which is a Hydro-carbon, after producing Naptha and light oils, becomes
useful as Asphalt, or for exterior paint work. Benzole, the base of our newly-discovered dyes, is extracted from the Naptha; which, besides, is either used as a
solvent for india-rubber and guttapercha, or yields a brilliant light when burned
in a common lamp. Gas, as it issues from the retorts, is chiefly composed of light
carburetted and bicarburetted hydrogen or olefiant gas, accompanied by condensable vapours and other gaseous impurities. The condensable vapours are principally hydro-carbon compounds which become deposited in the form of oil, and
amongst a variety of deleterious substances may be mentioned as the chief: ammonia, carbonic acid, carbonic oxide, and sulphuretted hydrogen, but the value of
coal-gas principally depends on the presence of bicarburetted hydrogen, and the
greater proportion of this the higher will be its light-giving properties.

The connection of the London Gas-Light Company's Works with Vauxhall
takes us out of the parish of Battersea for a moment into the parish of Lambeth.
Vauxhall, the early Spring Garden, was named from its site in the Manor of La
Sale Fawkes, Fawkeshall, from its possessor, an obscure Norman adventurer, in
the reign of King John.[7] The estate was laid out as a garden about 1661, in squares

[7] The true derivation is supposed to be from Falk or Faulk de Brent, a famous Norman soldier of fortune to whom King John gave in marriage Margaret de Ripariis or Red-
vers. To the lady belonged that Manor of Lambeth to which the Mansion called Faulks Hall

enclosed with hedges of gooseberries, within which were roses, beans and asparagus. Sir Samuel Morland took a lease of the place in 1665, and added fountains and a sumptuously furnished room for the reception of Charles II. and his court, and a plan dated 1681, shows the gardens planted with trees and laid out in walks and a circle of trees or shrubs. They were frequented by Evelyn and Pepys; and Addison in the *Spectator*, 1712, takes Sir Roger de Coverley there. In 1728, the gardens were leased to Jonathan Tyers, who converted the house into a tavern. The beauty of its rural scenery rendered it so much frequented that the proprietor in the year 1730, introduced vocal music, the price of admission at that time was 1s., but from the competition of others who opened public places of amusement in the neighbourhood, the proprietor introduced a great variety of amusements and raised the price of admission to 2s. During the season of 1807, the price was constantly 2s., the gardens being open only three nights in the week, and each of these nights was what was termed a gala night. Vauxhall Gardens were extensive, they contained a variety of walks illuminated with beautiful transparent paintings. Opposite the west door was a magnificent Gothic orchestra, illuminated with a profusion of lamps of various colours; and on the left was an elegant rotunda, in which the band performed in the cold or rainy weather. At ten o'clock a bell announced the opening of a cascade, with the representation of a water-mill, a mail coach, etc. Fireworks of the most brilliant description were also introduced among the attractions of the place. In numerous recesses, or pavilions, parties were accommodated with suppers and other refreshments and were charged according to a bill of fare. The ham sandwiches were of such an excellent quality and so thinly sliced that they became proverbial. The respective boxes and apartments were adorned with a vast number of paintings, many of which were executed in the best style of their respective theatres. The labours of Hogarth and Hayman were the most conspicuous. On a pedestal, under the arch of a grand portico of the Doric order, was a fine marble statue of Handel, in the character of Orpheus playing on his lyre, done by the celebrated M. Roubiliac. The number of persons who were employed in the gardens during the season is said to have amounted to 400, 96 of whom were musicians and singers, the rest were waiters and servants of various kinds. The celebrated Lowe and Beard were amongst the first singers who were engaged at Vauxhall. Upwards of 15,000 lamps were said to illuminate the gardens at one time, — the effect of the illumination was peculiarly beautiful in a moonlight night. The band of the Duke of York's regiment of Guards dressed in full uniform added to the attractions of these enchanting gardens; by military harmony, as a place of public entertainment, it became the most famous in Europe. The greatest season was in 1823, when 133,279 persons visited the gardens and the receipts were £29,590. The greatest number of persons in one night was on the 2nd of August, 1833, when 20,137 paid for admission. The carriages outside the gardens were so numerous that they extended in lines as far as Westminster Bridge in one direction and to Kennington Common in an opposite direction. The greatest number on the then supposed last night, 5th September, 1839, was 1089 persons. So fascinating did this place of amusement become that it acquired the name of the "fairy land of fancy," answering in conception to those enchanted palaces and gardens de-

---

was annexed.—*London*, by Charles Knight, Vol. I., p. 403.

scribed in the "Arabian Nights Entertainment."[8] It was in these gardens gas was manufactured by the London Gas-light Company prior to gas being made at the Company's Works in the neighbourhood of Vauxhall Row.

The London Gas-light Company was Incorporated in the year 1833.[9] The Works at Vauxhall were constructed from designs furnished by Mr. Hutchison, the Engineer. The first bed of retorts set on the Company's premises was heated by a man of the name of William Batt, June, 1834. The old man is still living, he is seventy-five years of age, and has been in the London Gas-light Company's service forty-three years. At that time the Company used a small gasometer erected in Vauxhall Gardens. It was with gas from this vessel that Mr. Green, the celebrated æronaut used to fill or inflate his great balloon. The first place lighted up with the Company's gas was Old Lambeth Market, the site now occupied by the Lambeth Baths. In December, 1858, the London Gas-light Company manufactured gas at their New Works, Nine Elms. The following month, January, 1859, an Act of Parliament came into operation to prevent gas companies from erecting other works for the manufacture of gas within ten miles of London; however, it was not until the year 1863 that the London Gas-light Company permanently removed from Vauxhall to Nine Elms.

The London Gas Works are environed with a brick wall, varying in height from ten to twenty feet, bounded on the North by Nine Elms Lane; on the South by the South-Western Railway; on the East by Everett Street; and on the West by Moat Street and Haine Street. The works within this enclosure cover an area of seventeen acres, and at the field Prince of Wales Road, about three acres more. There are five gates to the Works, but the principal entrance is in Haward Street, by the porter's lodge. At the right-hand-corner is a spacious building, on the basement is the Engineer's office, the Light office, and Messenger's lobby, which has in it a small telegraphic apparatus for communicating intelligence between this and the Chief office. The Grand Entrance is from Nine Elms Lane, opened by two pairs of massive folding doors leading into the hall, facing which is a flight of stone steps with ornamental cast-iron balusters mounted by rails on either side of polished mahogany, communicating with a similar staircase right and left which conducts to the Board room and Draughtsmen's offices. The Board room is a beautiful and commodious apartment, 33 feet by 19. It has never yet been occupied by the Board of Directors, the Board preferring to transact their business at their Chief Office, 26, Southampton Street, Strand, W.C. Secretary, A. J. Dove, Esq.; Engineer, Robert Morton, Esq.; Manager, John Methven, Esq.; Outdoor Superintendent, T. D. Tully,

[8] Vauxhall Gardens were open from 1732 to 1840, they were re-opened in 1841 and finally closed in 1859, when the theatre, orchestra, firework gallery, fountains, statues, etc., were sold, with a few mechanical models, such as Sir Samuel Morland, Master of Mechanics to Charles II. had set up here nearly two centuries previously. The site was then cleared and a church, (St. Peter's) vaulted throughout, was built upon a portion of the grounds, besides a school of arts, etc. — *John Timbs.*

[9] The London Gas-light Company Established, (Incorporated) 1833; first Works built in High Street, Vauxhall, the lease of which expired in 1865.

December 2, 1872, there was a great strike of the London Gas Stokers, 2,400 out. The inconvenience was met by great exertion, 2-6 Dec. Several were tried and imprisoned.

Esq.; Cashier, W. G. Head, Esq., with a staff of Inspectors, Collectors, Clerks, &c.

On the 31st of October, 1865,[10] a terrible gas explosion took place, when ten men were killed and many others injured. At that time the houses in Haward Street being contiguous to the works, had the window frames shattered, and similar calamities occurred elsewhere. These houses were occupied by some of the Company's employés. Lately, partly on account of the recent tidal inundations, sixteen houses belonging to the Company have been pulled down and a wall built so as to keep out the flood, in the event of extraordinary high tides. The open space between the inner and outer gates is used, as well as other open spaces about the works, for heaping up the coke mountains high, which certain youngsters in the neighbourhood would only be too delighted to have the privilege of scrambling and of bearing some of the precious fuel home to their fireless grates. Alas! much of the distress prevalent in the district is caused through the drunkenness and improvident habits of parents.

Passing through the inner gate, over which is mounted the factory bell of 2 cwt., — its size and tone would not disgrace the belfry of many a church steeple, — on the right is situated the timekeeper's office, the carbonizing foreman's lobby, the meter stores, and the stores. On the left-hand-side of the gate is the coke clerk's office, counting house, and a range of workshops, sheds, etc. for smiths, painters, fitters, and carpenters. Adjoining the coke office is the shop where all the Company's meters are tested before being sent out to the consumers. In different parts of the yard lines of iron rails are laid down, with turning tables to allow for shunting, communicating with the South-Western Railway, so as to admit trucks, which, when loaded with coke from the factory, are then conveyed to their destination. The retort houses are oblong buildings with gable wrought-iron roofs, are strongly built of brick, the walls being of immense thickness; this is necessary, not only on account of the great heat within, but on account of the large quantity of coals stowed away in the coal stores, the stock on hand being 15,000 tons.

There are seven retort houses, five of these occupy a central position in these works; they have been erected at different periods as the demand for the manufacture of gas increased. Of these retort houses No. 7 is the largest; it is 260 feet long by 80 feet wide (inside measurement), and it is 45 feet to crown of roof. Each retort

---

[10] On October 31, 1865, at the London Gas-light Company's Works, at Nine Elms, Battersea Park Road, a gas-holder exploded killing ten persons and injuring twenty-two. This was then one of the largest holders in London, its capacity being 1,039,000 cubic feet. It was 150 feet diameter, 60 feet high, with a tank depth of 30 feet, and at the instant of the explosion was nearly full, being about 50 feet to 55 feet high. The meter-house was blown to atoms, and the force of the explosion struck the side of the gas-holder, bulging it in, and at the same time driving out a portion of the top. Mr. Timbs, who records this disaster, (which happened when the late Mr. Watson was engineer) says, "As the side plates were eight to twelve gauge, the force must have been very great. With the bursting of the top there was an immediate rush of gas, which instantly caught fire, and shot up in a vast column of flame, discernible at a great distance. The concussion ripped open another gas-holder, the escaping gas caught fire, and meeting the flames from the first gas-holder, rolled away in one vast expanse of flame: an awful crash followed, and many of the neighbouring houses were shattered to pieces." — *History of Wonderful Inventions*, by John Timbs, p. 179.

house has independent shafts, but the tallest shaft faces the east end of retort house No. 2. It is a splendid piece of brick-work, the height of which is 135 feet. When the top stone was laid Mr. B. Gray, the builder, treated the men who were under him with a dinner. On this occasion sixteen persons sat on the summit and partook of this sumptuous repast. Nos. 1, 2 and 3 are ground retort houses, the other four houses are stage retort houses. With respect to the interior of these retort houses, there is plenty of room in front of the retorts for a storage of coal and good space for drawing the retorts. On the whole there is good ventilation in the roofs for allowing the smoke, etc. to escape. The floor of the stage retort houses are paved with grooved cast-iron plates. In these retort houses an open space is allowed between the furnace and the flooring in order that the coke when raked out of the retorts might fall into the coke hole below. The benches of retorts are placed in the middle of the houses. The retorts are built in settings, they are cylindrical tubes made of Stourbridge clay open through and through with mouthpieces at both ends. At the front of each bed of retorts is a furnace for heating up the retorts with the residual coke after the coals have been carbonized. The flame and hot draft of the furnaces are made to circulate thoroughly throughout the setting, traversing as great a space as possible round, under and above the retorts before egress is allowed to the main flue communicating with the chimney. The retorts are charged every six hours. Formerly, for cooling the retort lids, a pulpy mass of lime and mud of the consistence of mortar was used under the cognomen of "blue billy." This has been superseded by Morton's Patent Air-tight Lid, and Holman's Patent Lever. The two mechanical contrivances combined for this purpose are most efficient, and when financially considered must be a great saving to the Company. In the new house there are seven retorts in a bed; these, when heated sufficiently, are simultaneously charged at each end with two scoopfuls of bituminous coal; the upper retorts, on account of their retaining more heat, are charged with three scoops—each scoop contains 1 cwt. 2 qrs. of coal As soon as the lids are closed with the patent lever and cross-bar the process of gas distillation commences. In house No. 7 there are 392 mouths—total number of mouths in all the retort houses 1,793. As clay retorts when heated at first have a tendency to crack, it is necessary that the process of heating should be slow, also to get them up to their proper heat a similar caution is requisite when cooling. Apart from the manufacture of gas, in order to attend to the furnaces with the view of keeping up the heat of retorts, a certain amount of Sunday labour is involved, but it is gratifying to state that at these works labour on the Lord's day is reduced to its lowest minimum. Among several annoyances in the manufacture of gas is the choking or stoppage of ascension pipes; the person whose employment it is to look after, and if possible prevent this, is called by his fellow-workmen "the pipe jumper." Pipes connected with the mouthpieces called the ascension pipes conduct the gas to the hydraulic main, this is a large pipe at the back of the ascension pipes partly filled with water, when the works are started into which the ends of the pipes from the retorts are made to dip, and by this means forms a seal by which the gas is prevented from finding its way back either by those retorts which the workmen may be re-charging or to other parts of the bench that for the time may be out of action. The hydraulic main and its supports are very strong in order to stand the alternate and unequal heating and cooling of the benches, and the enormous strain occasioned by the large extent of pipage. Wrought iron is used in preference to cast-iron because of its lightness, strength and elasticity.

There are four lobbies for the accommodation of the stokers and seats at either end of the retort houses. The men in the carbonizing department are supplied with lockers in which to keep their provisions and clothes. Each man has a half-pint of the best Scotch oatmeal per diem allowed him to make "skilly" with. A quantity of oatmeal is put into a bucket, water is poured on and then stirred, after the meal has "settled" they dip it out with a mug to drink as often as they feel themselves thirsty. The engineer has no objection to the men having lemonade, etc., but all intoxicating drinks on the works are strictly prohibited. On Sundays, between 9 and 10 a.m., a religious service is conducted in the lobby at No. 6 retort house by the Missionary.

Scene in a retort house on week-day.—The stokers, after having been at work in the retort houses for half an hour, are "off" for nearly an hour, during which they employ their time in various ways; some play at cards, some at draughts, some at dominoes, others read the newspapers,—eight men in a group will club together and subscribe a penny each, this enables them to purchase six dailies and two weeklies, thus a group is furnished with newspaper intelligence for a week. Others of the stokers will seek to bring grist to their mill by employing the time they are off to their own pecuniary advantage either in mending their own boots and shoes or the boots and shoes of their fellow-workmen. At times some of the men may be seen mending their clothes, or washing a pair of trowsers in a bucket of water and using the wooden handle of a shovel as a substitute for a "dolly." Now and then a man will lie on his back at full length on a heap of coals, locked in the arms of Morpheus, presently he awakes out of his dreams, rubs his eyes astonished at what has transpired during the past hour. The foreman's whistle, similar to that used by a railway guard when a train is ready to start, is the signal for the men to resume their work, and to their credit be it said, they go at it manly and rush to their shovels and scoops like British sailors fly to their guns when commanded to salute a Prince or fire at an enemy! A stranger for the first time is startled when the lids or "lips" as they are called are removed from the mouths of the retorts by the bomb! bombing! a kind of percussion or shock occasioned by the gaseous vapours confined in the retorts being liberated by coming into direct contact with the atmosphere, then commences the belching forth of flame, the issuing of smoke, the raking out of carbonized coal blazing with tar in order to clear the retorts which are again quickly charged with that peculiar fossil of vegetable origin found among the carboniferous strata of the earth. It is interesting to mark the agility with which the stokers perform their duty. Five men constitute a gang,—there are three men to a scoop. Scoops are made of iron. A scoop is 10 feet long, 7½ inches wide, and 5½ inches deep with a T piece for a handle. It is placed on the ground, filled as soon as possible, then raised by two men who put underneath it a wrought iron bar called a "horse" so bent or curved in the middle on which to rest the scoop. These two men, with the aid of the man who holds the T piece, thrust the coals into the retorts as quickly as artillerymen ram cannon, and so work at each bed of retorts stripped to the waist, while the perspiration is oozing from the pores of their skin like melted tallow! Now and again a hissing noise with steam accompanied with clouds of vapour caused by buckets of water thrown on the carbonized coal taken from the retorts. No sooner is the coke thus cooled than it is (in keeping with all the movements preceding) wheeled in iron barrows to a place in the yard, where pyramidically it is piled stage upon stage until purchased by the coal contractor and coke merchants who require it for their customers. Respecting the employés at these important works—beneath the rough exterior of their sooty skin, incidental to their occupation, these sons of toil who forsooth earn their livelihood by the sweat of their brow in common with their brother man, have hearts akin to the finest specimens of humanity, and stand related to our Father in heaven, for we are all His offspring, brothers for whom the Saviour died. Whatever a man's status in social life, whatever part he may take, however humble in the divisions of industrial, honest labour, these men know that as Robert Burns says; "A man's a man for a' that."

From the hydraulic main the gas passes on to a set of condensers or coolers at the south side of the works, through which it is made to circulate until it is reduced to a temperature bearing some approximation to the surrounding atmosphere, also to separate condensable vapours before allowing the gas to pass to the purifiers. The tar well or tank is a receptacle for the overflow of the hydraulic, etc. A branch pipe from the main is inserted and sealed in a stationary lute at the bottom. The tar thus deposited as well as the ammoniacal liquor is valuable. There are five scrubbers, the tops of which are reached by flights of wooden steps with handrails and a stage or gallery above communicating from one scrubber to another. Each scrubber is a cylinder 19 feet in diameter and 70 feet high, they are made of cast-iron plates and contain a series of iron trays or gratings on which are spread layers of coke, furze, etc. Water is injected from the top by means of a revolving apparatus connected with vertical and horizontal shafting and driven by a small engine below, thereby keeping up a constant humid spray, the object being to separate the ammonia and acids from the gas.

In front of houses Nos. 4 and 5 (which by the way are the oldest retort houses inside these works) is situated the boiler and engine house. There are three boilers 28 feet by 6 in diameter. In the engine house four of Beal's exhausters occupy prominent positions, they are used to exhaust or suck the gas from the retorts and afterwards force it through the vessels for purification; two of these driven by engines of 20 horse power work 150,000 cubic feet per hour each. Two driven by engines of 12 horse power work 100,000 per hour each. Attached to the inlet of each exhauster is one of Wright's exhauster governors, it is made on the principle of pressure or suction elevating or depressing a light cylinder working in a water-lute of sufficient depth. When an exhaust is maintained on the water gauge, counter balance weights equal to the exhaust on the area of the cylinder are applied, and the oscillations, as the suction increases or diminishes, regulate to a nicety the exhaust. The whole of the machinery in this department is in excellent order and will bear the minutest inspection. Over the engine house, which is reached outside by a corkscrew or spiral iron staircase, is a workshop fitted up with machinery; it contains a horizontal engine of eight horse power, which drives two lathes, one bolt screwing machine, two drilling machines, and a saw bench. Against the wall of the engine house is one of Tangye's Special Pumps for raising water from the dock to supply the whole of the works with water for cooling purposes. Outside the engine house an apparatus called a jet exhauster has recently been erected composed of a series of vertical iron tubes, a steam boiler, a generator, and jet. A vacuum is created by a blast of steam, thereby compelling the gas to rapidly leave the retorts and at the same time the ammonia is supposed to be entirely removed by means of water which percolates through shavings with which the tubes or pipes are filled.

On the south side of the works, in addition to the coolers, there are thirteen purifiers and fifteen plots or courts including the foreman's lobby. Each purifier is of cast-iron, it is oblong in form, the cover is wrought iron riveted together in sheets, and the seal is made by means of a water-lute round the edge of the purifier. The purifying material, which is sometimes lime but principally oxide of iron, is carefully spread out on trays and these are disposed in tiers or sets in such a manner as to leave a clear open space between each succeeding layer to allow the gas to diffuse itself thoroughly throughout the mass. Lime when once fouled cannot profitably be renewed for gas purifying purposes, but the oxide of iron can be further utilized by spreading out the oxide in an open court when the oxygen of the atmosphere precipitates the sulphur and the oxide is again fit for use.

The gas passes from the purifiers to the station meter house fronting the stores on the north side of the yard, where the quantity of gas made is registered; adjoining which is Mr. Methven's the Sub-Manager's office, and a test room or laboratory where various experiments connected with the manufacture of gas are conducted. Against the north boundary is a small gas house with gas-holder, etc., all complete, occasionally used for experimenting purposes. From the station meters the gas passes to the gas-holders; each of these enormous circular vessels possesses great storage capacity. It is made on the principle that the circle of all geometrical figures is the one that a fixed circumference or outline is capable of enclosing the greatest amount of space. A gas-holder is made by riveting together light wrought iron sheets upon an angle framing and in shape resembles an inverted cup, the crown being either flat or the segment of a large sphere. It works in a circular water-tank, round which columns are erected that sustain guides at proper intervals by which the gasholder when working is supported, etc. Erected in different parts of the works, including those (two) in the field Prince of Wales' Road, are five immense gasholders with double lifts capable of holding in all 7,000,000 cubic feet of gas. The most imposing view of the Works is from the gate near the entrance of the Creek at Mill-Pond Bridge; in the creek there are sometimes as many as forty barges. On entering at this gate the eye is attracted by two ponderous lifts, which, by an arrangement of rope bands attached to shafting with revolving iron drums and pulleys supported by columns and girders and driven by two horizontal engines of twelve horse-power, are capable of lifting 500 tons of coals every twelve hours. The coals are raised from the barges in iron waggons which hold 1 ton 15 cwt. each, there are two waggons to each lift so that while one waggon is being filled the other on the stage above is being conveyed on iron rails to whatever part of the retort house the coals may be required. Each engine has a powerful brake and is worked with two levers. On the west side of the creek is the manager's residence, and an enormous gasholder with capacity to hold 2,000,000 cubic feet of gas; further on is a hand crane. In front of No. 7 retort house is one of Winshurst and Hollick's engine cranes, which is capable of lifting 200 tons of coals in ten hours by means of a chain and bucket lifted up to the hopper, a distance of nearly sixty feet, and emptied. The bucket holds 15 cwt. of coal. That portion of the Company's premises known as Mill-Pond Yard is used for the storage of pipes, bricks, fire-clay, etc. Here is the carcass of the Old Tidal Mill with lock gates; here too is the Workman's Institute and Band room. Mothers' Meetings are held at the Institute on Wednesdays at 3 p.m., on Sunday afternoons at 3 o'clock for Bible readings by a Missionary in the district.[11]

Upon the mains at their exit from the works valves are placed, each valve having a revolving pressure indicator attached, the paper of which is graduated into inches, and tenths, and marked with spaces corresponding to the twenty-four hours of the day. In the meter-house self-regulating governors are used for this purpose. From the gasholders the gas is driven through cast-iron mains or pipes,

[11] Since the above description was written in 1877 very extensive alterations have been made in these works. The Company have completed a large purifying house at the south side of the Creek, and have had constructed on the site of the Old Institute a dock for the purpose of admitting steam colliers of 1000 tons burden; and have erected a coal tramway from the same into the Works, crossing Nine Elms Lane with an iron bridge 22 feet from the roadway, which has been widened at least 20 feet. Moreover the carcass of the Old Flour Water-Mill has been pulled down the only vestiges remaining are the lock gates. Opposite Mr. Methven's residence a new institute and stables have been built. In the Works the old offices, workshops, stores, meter-house, and test rooms have been demolished, the high shaft pulled down and the jet exhauster removed. A new meter-house has been erected opposite the engine house and there has also been added new machinery. The Creek has been narrowed and the portion of ground recovered has considerably increased the size of the coke yard. A parapet has been built on both sides of the Creek to prevent the water from overflowing in the event of extraordinary high tides. Also a new stage retort house is being erected parallel with retort house No. 6. (Messrs. Kirk and Randall, Contractors). In addition, three blocks of new buildings have been erected on the west side of the road within the principal gate, is B (1) containing coke office, cashier's office and strong room; timekeeper's office, weigh office, coke foreman's office, superintendent's office and test room. On the east side of the road is B (2) containing gate-keeper's lobby and stores. At the south-east corner of the Works is B (3) consisting of workshops, lobby, etc. The whole of the three blocks were completed in about four months. (B. E. Nightingale, Builder and Contractor). The factory bell has been mounted against one of the columns belonging to the gasholder near the timekeeper's office, and a gasholder of colossal dimensions is being erected in the Company's field, Prince of Wales Road. The alterations, improvements, etc., at these Works within the last ten years have involved an outlay of about £200,000. *Yard Foreman*, Mr. A. Wilson; *Carbonizing Foremen*, Messrs. H. Walker, M. Walker, R. Johnston, W. Taylor, T. Reynolds, G. Feeney; *Purifying Foremen*, Messrs. D. Brown and H. Aylett; *Foreman of Enginemen*, Mr. G. Wilson; *Coke Foremen*, Messrs. G. Smith and C. Meredith; *Coal Gang Foreman*, Mr. W. Clowes; *Timekeeper*, Mr. R. Whitmore. Mr. R. Harvey was foreman over the men in the carbonizing department and had been upwards of forty years in the Company's employment, in consideration of his valuable services the Company have granted him, as they have also several other of their old and faithful servants, an annuity.

and from them by wrought iron service pipes to the lamps and burners which help to illuminate our Metropolis. The Company's mains extend about 170 miles, and at any point they supply gas with the same abundance and precision as at Nine Elms. At one time, the Works of the London Gas-Light Company at Vauxhall were considered the most powerful and complete in the world, and even now, in this age of rivalry and sharp competition, under the judicious management of their Board of Directors and their skilled Engineer, Robert Morton, Esq., the London Gas-Light Company maintain an honourable position among other gas-light companies, and are worthy the name they bear. The number of men employed at these works in the Winter season is about 500. There is a Sick Provident Club belonging to the works.[12]

On a recently-exposed Section at Battersea.

Extracts from a Paper read before the Geologists' Association, March 1st, 1872, by John A. Coombs, Esq.

"This section was exposed on a piece of ground recently acquired by the London Gas-light Company for a Gas-holder Station. It is situated to the north of the Prince of Wales' Road, Battersea, between the high-level lines of the London, Brighton, and South-Coast, and the London, Chatham, and Dover Railways, near the point of their separation after crossing the Thames near the Chelsea Suspension Bridge. The excavations were commenced at the latter end of last year, for the purpose of constructing two gas-holder tanks, each 185 feet inside diameter. The total length of the excavation, therefore, was about 400 feet, by about 200 feet in width, and 30 feet in depth, the direction of the longest distance being very nearly from N.W. to S.E.

The average surface of the ground was 12-ft. 9-in. above the Ordnance Datum Level, or 8 inches above Trinity High Water Mark. The general Section was as follows:—

Alluvial Soil and Vegetable Mould	2 feet
Thames Valley Gravel	22 feet
Altered London Clay (brown)	1 feet
London Clay (excavated)	5 feet

An interesting series of mammalian remains were obtained from the Valley Gravel, which, considering the limited extent of the excavation, and the number of specimens destroyed in the removal of the material, shews this section to be fully as prolific in these remains as the long-worked pits of Erith or Crayford. The specimens have been examined and identified by William Davies, Esq, of the Brit-

[12] All workmen employed by the London Gas-light Company (unless hired on other terms) are engaged on weekly hirings, and are required to give, and entitled to receive, a week's notice before leaving or being discharged from the Company's service, except in case of misconduct, for which a workman will be discharged without notice.

By order of the Board, A.J. Dove, Sec.

13th March, 1876.

ish Museum, who kindly undertook to compare them with those in the national collection. The following is a list of these remains:—

> *Elphas primigenius*, Blum. Portion of lower jaw and tooth, and the shaft of a humerus of a young individual.

> *Rhinoceros tichorhinus*, Cuv. Part of a cranium, a lumbar vertebra, a right metatarsus, and a left metacarpus.

> *Equus caballus fossilis*, Linn. A right metacarpus, a right radius, and an upper molar.

> *Bos.* sp. Cervical vertebra.

> *Cervus elaphus*, Linn. Portion of left ramus of lower jaw, and portion of a right radius.

> *Cervus tarandus*, Linn. The base of a shed antler. (This had suffered considerable attrition).

There were also found a rib and a portion of an ilium of a *Cervus* (species indeterminable), besides many other fragments too small or too much mutilated for recognition. But the most unusual fossil found in such deposits was that of *Pliosaurus*, a portion of the paddle bone of which was found associated with the remains above mentioned. This fossil, which was probably derived from the Kimmeridge Clay, shewed evident signs of attrition, but not so much as to efface the marks of muscular attachment; it was, moreover, charged with peroxide of iron. Search was made in the anticipation of shells of *Cyrena (Corbicula) fluminalis* being associated with these remains, but without success.

Immediately beneath the Thames Valley Gravel was the London Clay, possessing all the typical features of that formation, without any of the loamy gradations found in higher parts of the metropolis. The top of the clay, however, to a depth varying from 9 to 12 inches, was of a brown colour, resembling the brown (altered) London Clay found at Hampstead and elsewhere.

The clay was excavated only to a depth of a few feet, thus preventing a great number of fossils being obtained. Those found, however, are sufficient for comparison with the zones of fossils found in larger sections, and thus may afford evidence of the amount of denudation to which the clay had been subjected at this spot before the deposition of the gravel. By far the most abundant fossil found in the London Clay was the *Pentacrinus sub-basaltiformis*, which was obtained in the rounded angular, as well as the perfectly cylindrical form. The following Mollusca were also obtained:—*Nautilus regalis, Pyrula Smithii, Fusus bifasciatus, Voluta Wetherellii, Pleurotoma teretrium, Natica labellata, Dentalium*, sp., *Leda amygdaloides, Nucula Bowerbankii, Cryptodon angulatus, C. Goodallis*, and *Syndosyma splendens*. *Teredo* borings, *Serpula*, and teeth of *Lamma* complete the list of organic remains.

Septaria were abundant in the clay, many of which contained drift-wood, bored by the *Teredo*, one contained a *Nautilus regalis* as a nucleus, and several exhibited the usual crystallizations of calcite, heavy spar, and iron pyrites. Selenite, however, was very scarce in the clay, being found only in small crystals, and these by no means numerous."

In Nine Elms Lane resided Mr. Sellar, a respectable tradesman who kept a tea and cheesemonger's establishment, and who for five years discharged his parochial duties as an overseer. Greatly deploring the irreligious condition of the spiritually-benighted poor of the neighbourhood, he had erected at his own expense, a hall at the back of his premises in Everet Street, to be used for religious and secular educational purposes. Subsequently the hall was rented by the Wesleyan Methodists, and was used by them as a preaching station, Mr. Farmer acting as steward and superintendent of the Sunday school which he commenced there. When the Sunday school was opened in 1871, not more than 20 per cent. of the children who presented themselves for admission could read, and their knowledge of the sacred contents of the Holy Scriptures was *nil*. However, though the task was difficult, for seven years Mr. John Farmer, assisted by his small staff of Christian teachers:—

Plodded hard, and labour'd well
As many in Nine Elms can tell.

The hall is now engaged by the Metropolitan Tabernacle Evangelization Society. A Sunday school is still held in the place and evangelistic services conducted there every Lord's day evening.

Phillips' Fire Annihilating Machine Factory Destroyed.—Brayne's Pottery.—The Old Lime Kilns.—Laver's Cement & Whiting Works.

In this neighbourhood stood Phillips's Fire Annihilating Machine Factory. The public were frequently invited to come and see the working of the machines. At the time appointed an improvised cottage was set on fire; when fairly alight, the machines were brought to bear upon the flames and with marked success. A man and his wife had charge of the factory. One Sunday morning the man went out into the fields with his gun, leaving his wife to prepare dinner. Soon after the composition in the factory exploded, and immediately the building was enveloped in flames—the man hastened back to save his wife, but failed in his attempt to rescue her—the poor woman perished.

BRAYNE'S POTTERY for Stone-ware manufacture has been pulled down, on the site adjoining is Laver's Portland Cement Works. The Lime Kilns which had stood nearly two centuries have long since disappeared. The Whiting Works which mark the site remain among the oldest structures in this vicinity were established in the year 1666. At the entrance to the Works stood the rib bones of a Whale which the proprietor fancifully had placed there. One of the Whiting sheds formerly stood higher up the river. Mr. Laver is the owner of these works. Where Lloyd and Co's Manufacturing Joinery Works are situated were the house, timber yard and premises, owned by Mr. Robbins, father of Mrs. Cooper, Dairy, New Road. Near the spot where now stands the Royal Rifleman tavern, was a timber dock. Moored close to the river's bank was a barge house or cabin called "Noah's Ark." In the dock adjoining Noah's Ark was an old steamboat said to have been one of the first that "ran" on the Thames. The river about this part offered great attraction to swimmers and became a famous place for bathing. Hayle Foundry Wharf, Nine Elms, is now occupied by H. Young & Co., Engineers and Contractors, Founders,

Smiths, etc. Their Art Works are at Eccleston, Pimlico, and are noted for casting the statues of Lord Derby, opposite the House of Lords; John Bunyan, erected at Bedford; Wellington Memorial in St. Paul's Cathedral, and (part finished) Sir John Burgoyne.

The Southwark and Vauxhall Water Works.

THE SOUTHWARK AND VAUXHALL WATER WORKS.--The Borough Works at St. Mary Overies, in 1820, became the property of one J. Edwards, who in 1822, also purchased from the New River Company the Works on the South side of London Bridge, and combined both concerns under the designation of the "Southwark Water Works." The whole being thus possessed by one opulent individual. In 1805, several persons united to give effect to a scheme for organising the South London Water Works (subsequently called the Vauxhall) and by an Act of Parliament passed in July, 1805, they were incorporated as a Company, with authority to raise capital for attaining their object amounting to £80,000 in 800 shares of £100 each. In June, 1813, another Act was obtained for empowering the Company to raise a further sum of £80,000. The operations of this Company commenced inauspiciously for their interests by reason of their having originally adopted wooden pipes, and having then been compelled to substitute iron in their place. The principal works were on the south side of Kennington Lane, formerly Kennington Common, near to Vauxhall. These companies experienced various vicissitudes in their progress, until in 1845, when an amalgamation took place under an Act of Parliament, to which we owe the creation of the Southwark and Vauxhall Water Company as it now exists. The area of the district supplied extends for about 13 miles E. and W., and 3 miles N. and S., the home district stretching from Rotherhithe to Clapham and the suburban and rural districts from Wandsworth to Richmond. Thus an area of 39 miles south of the Thames receives a supply of water distributed to about 80,000 houses, having a population of 550,000. The Company's property at Battersea consists of one Pumping Station, standing on freehold land of some 50 acres, and six Cornish Engines, erected by Messrs. Harvey and Co., with a total of 1,200 horse power; two Reservoirs of about 10 acres, containing about 46,000,000 gallons of water, and six filter beds, having an area 10¾ acres, with a filtering capacity for 1,300,750 gallons of water per hour. The Filters are to a certain depth filled with sand, through which the water percolates, leaving the impurities on the surface to be removed at pleasure. There are 18 fires or furnaces in the boiler house, the daily consumption of coal is about 22 tons. The water at this station is pumped partly over a stand pipe 186 feet high,[13] and the remainder through an air vessel to a height of about 380 feet. The Company have considerable property at Hampton and Peckham. The Registrar General's return shews the Company possess about 685 miles of mains and service pipes, 100 miles of which (mains) are perpetually charged, and could be made available for constant supply should circumstances render it desirable. *Office*, Sumner Street, Southwark; *Chief Engineer*, Thos. W. Humble, Esq.; *Resident Engineer*, Mr. John Sampson. Adjacent to the Water Works are premises belonging to Harvey and Co., Machine, Hydraulic,

[13] A gentleman told the writer that this was vulgarly called by the sobriquet of "Punch's Tuning Fork!"

and Mining Engineers of Hayle, Cornwall.

Water Carriers and Water Companies.

Fitz Stephen (William) a learned Monk of Canterbury, being attached to the Service of Archbishop Becket was present at the time of his murder. In the year 1174 he wrote in Latin the life of St. Thomas, Archbishop and Martyr, in which as Becket was a native of the Metropolis, he introduces a description of the City of London with a miscellaneous detail of the manners and usages of the Citizens; this is deservedly considered a great curiosity, being the earliest professed account of London extant. He describes the springs and water courses which abound in the vicinity of Old London as "sweet, salubrious, and clear," so that all that the inhabitants and water-carriers had to do was to draw water from the wells and springs, or dip their vessels in the pellucid stream of the river which was fit for culinary and all ordinary and domestic purposes. London then though considered a "Great City" was as a small town when compared with its teeming population of nearly 5,000,000 which people its City and environs now.[14] Since that time the Majestic Thames and its tributary streams have been so polluted with sewerage and other deleterious and poisonous matter as to induce some of the most scientific men of the age to consider not only the desirability but the necessity of obtaining for London a pure water supply. It is asserted as a fact that in England and Wales alone upwards of eight hundred persons die every month from typhoid fever; a disease which is now believed to be caused almost entirely through drinking impure water, and Dr. Frankland, the official to whom is entrusted the analysing of such matters reports "The Thames Water" notwithstanding the care that is taken to filter it by certain Water Companies is so much polluted by organic matters as to be quite unfit for dietetic purposes.

The first conduit erected in the City of London (Westcheap now Cheapside) was commenced in the year 1235 but was not completed till 50 years afterwards (1285). The Citizens, who had to fetch their water from the Thames often met with opposition from those who resided in the lanes leading down to the river who monopolized the right of procuring a water supply by stopping and imposing a duty upon others who sought to obtain it. This state of things as might be expected became unbearable and in 1342 an inquisition was made and persons were sworn to inquire into the stoppages and annoyances complained of in the several Wards. In the fifteenth century the authorities of the City had erected New Conduits and had laid down leaden pipes. "In 1439 the Abbot of Westminster granted to Robert Large, the Lord Mayor, and the Citizens of London, and their successors, one head of water containing twenty-six perches in length and one in breadth, together with all the springs in the Manor of Paddington for an annual payment of two peppercorns." In the sixteenth century owing to the increased population and the drying up of the springs other means of supply were obtained in the neighbourhoods of Hampstead Heath, Hackney, and Muswell Hill. An Act of Parliament applied for by the Corporation was passed in 1544 for the purpose of obtaining

---

[14] The London Metropolitan District covers an area of 690 square miles—contains 6612 miles of streets. 528,794 inhabited houses; Population (June 1873) 4,025,559.

from these springs an increased supply for the North Western portions of the City. The scheme however was not carried out until the year 1590 when another important source of supply had been procured. In 1568 a conduit was constructed at Dowgate, for the purpose of obtaining water from the Thames. "In 1580 Peter Morice, an ingenious Dutchman brought his scheme for raising the Thames Water high enough to supply the upper parts of the City, and in order to show its feasibility he threw a jet of water over the steeple of St. Magnus Church, a lease of 500 years of the Thames Water, and the places where his mills stood, and of one of the arches of London Bridge was granted to Morice, and the Water Works founded by him remained until the beginning of the present century." About the same time that Morice propounded his scheme for utilizing the Water of the Thames, Stow informs us that a man of the name of Russel proposed to bring water into London from Isleworth. In 1591 an Italian named Frederick Genebelli said that he could cleanse the filthy ditches about the city such as the Fleet River, Hounsditch, etc., and bring a plentiful supply of pure, wholesome water to the City through them, but his offer does not appear to have been accepted.

"In 1606 nearly £20,000 was expended in scouring the River Fleet, which was kept open for the purpose of navigation as high as Holborn Bridge." An Act was passed in 1609 for bringing water by means of engines from Hackney Marsh, to supply the City of London; the profits arising from the enterprise were to go to the College of Polemical Divines, founded by Dr. Sutcliffe, at Chelsea. At the close of Queen Elizabeth's Reign an Act was passed empowering the Corporation to cut a river for the purpose of conveying water from Middlesex and Hertfordshire to the City, but nothing was done in this direction till after the accession of James I to the throne. In 1605 and 1606 Acts of Parliament were passed empowering the Corporation to bring water from the Springs of Chadwell and Amwell to the northern parts of the City. The Corporation transferred their power in 1609 to Hugh, afterwards (Sir Hugh) Middleton, Citizen, and Goldsmith, who with characteristic energy entered into the vast scheme which was effectually carried out at an immense expense. On Sept. 29th, 1613 the New River was opened, and London from this source received an abundant supply of water. The New River Company was incorporated in 1620. The City was supplied with its water by the conveyance of wooden pipes in the streets, and small leaden ones to the houses.

Among the Records known as the *Remembrancia* preserved among the Archives of the City of London. London, 1878. Some curious particulars are mentioned respecting the applications made by various noblemen to be allowed to have pipes, of the size of a goose-quill, attached to the city pipes, for the purpose of supplying their houses with water. "In 1592 Lord Cobham applied to the Lord Mayor for a quill of water from the conduit at Ludgate to his house in Blackfriars, but the consideration of the request was postponed, and in 1594 Lord Burghley wrote to the Lord Mayor and Alderman in support of Lord Cobham's application. Lady Essex and Walsingham asked for a supply of water for Essex-house in 1601, and obtained the Lord Chamberlain's (Earl of Suffolk) influence to further their suit; but on June 8th, 1608, the Lord Mayor wrote to Lord Suffolk that the water in the conduits had become so low, and the poor were so clamorous on account of the dearth, that it became necessary to cut off several of the quills. 'Moreover,' he added, 'complaints had been made of the extraordinary waste of water in Essex-house, it being taken not only for dressing meat, but for the laundry, the stable, and other offices, which might be otherwise served.' As London extended itself westward, and the City came to join Westminster, the drain must have been great upon the water supply, which was originally intended for a considerably smaller area. In 1613 Lord Fenton applied for a quill of water for his house at Charing Cross, but the Lord Mayor refused to grant the request on the ground that the conduits did not supply sufficient water for the City. Sir Francis Bacon (afterwards the great Lord Verulam) asked, in 1617, for a lead pipe to supply York-house, and Alice, Countess of Derby, requested to be allowed a quill of water in the following year. This celebrated lady, afterwards married to Lord Chancellor Ellesmere, lived in St. Martin's-lane, and we learn from the City letter-book (quoted in the index to the *Remembrancia*) the amount of water supplied to her was at the rate of three gallons an hour. In subsequent years, we notice among the applicants for quills of water the celebrated names of Sir Harry Vane, Denzell Holles, the Dukes of Albemarle and Buckingham, and the Earl of Northumberland." Cavendish and Watt demonstrated that water is composed of 8 parts of Oxygen and 1 part of Hydrogen. In freezing, water contracts till it is reduced to 42° or 40° Fahr. It then begins to expand till it becomes ice at 32°. Water was first conveyed to London by leaden pipes, 21 Henry III. 1237.—*Stow.*

So late as Queen Anne's time there were water-carriers at Aldgate Pump. The Water Works at Chelsea were completed and the Company incorporated in 1722. London Bridge ancient water works were destroyed by fire, 29th Oct., 1779.

Commissioners for Metropolitan Water Supply appointed 27th April, 1867; Report Signed 9th June, 1869; London supplied by Nine Companies. The New River (the best) East London, Chelsea, Grand Junction, Southwark, and Vauxhall, Kent, West Middlesex, Lambeth, and South Essex; who deliver about 108,000,000 gallons daily, 1867; about 116,250,000 gallons daily, 1877.

In 1880, the Nominal Capital of Eight Water Companies was £12,011,320.

The Village of Battersea.—Growth of the Parish.

THE VILLAGE OF BATTERSEA lies on the south side of the Thames opposite Chelsea, to which it has some historical relationship on account of its having been the seat of our Porcelain manufacture and of Saxon origin. It is situated about four miles South West of St. Paul's Cathedral. Battersea is a polling place for the Mid-divisions of the County in the Wandsworth Division of the West Brixton Hundred. Wandsworth Union and County Court District, Surrey Arch-Deaconry, and late Winchester, but now Rochester Diocese;[15] it is also within the jurisdiction of

[15] An alteration has been made in the Diocesan arrangement. Since 1877, Battersea together with other parishes in East and Mid-Surrey has been added to the See of Rochester, and therefore is under the jurisdiction of the Bishop of that Diocese. The See of Rochester was founded A.D. 604. St. Augustin or Austin (the first Bishop of Canterbury A.D. 598). Consecrated Justus, the first Bishop of Rochester. The See of West Saxons (afterwards Winchester, A.D. 705) was founded A.D. 635. The first (arch) Bishop of London was Theanus,

the Central Criminal Court, Metropolitan Board of Works, Metropolitan Police, and Wandsworth Police Court. The Parish is divided into four Wards. Penge[16]

A.D. 176 (?). Battersea is now considered to be of sufficient importance to be made a Rural Deanery, and Canon Clarke, the Rural Dean. Southwark Archdeaconry. "Diocese (Fr. from Gr. dioikesis, administration and dioikeo, to govern) the territory over which a bishop exercises ecclesiastical jurisdiction. At first, a diocese meant the collection of churches or congregations under the charge of an archbishop. The name came afterwards to be applied to the charge of a bishop, which had previously been called a parish. England and Wales are divided ecclesiastically into two Provinces, viz., Canterbury and York, the former being presided over by the Primate of all England, and the latter by the Primate of England, each of which is sub-divided into dioceses, and these again into Archdeaconries and Rural Deaneries and Parishes. A Diocese is synonymous with the See of a Suffragan bishop." (Chamber's Encyclopedia). In England, the Archbishop of Canterbury has the right of crowning the King, and the Archbishop of York the right of crowning the Queen.

Twelve years ago, the County of Surrey was divided for Electoral purposes into three Divisions named respectively East, West, and Mid-Surrey. At the time the Division was made in 1868 the Constituency of Mid-Surrey numbered only 10,500. Now (March 1880) we have on the Register 20,400 electors distributed in the following manner:—

Battersea Polling District	7,092
Coulsdon Polling District	152
Horley Polling District	465
Kingston Polling District	2,649
Reigate & Red Hill Polling District	1,271
Richmond Polling District	2,727
Sutton Polling District	1,975
Wandsworth Polling District	2,596
Wimbledon Polling District	1,606

[16] The Village of Penge stands adjacent to the boundary with Kent, to the London and Brighton Railway, and to the London, Chatham and Dover Railway near the Crystal Palace, four miles N.N.E. of Croydon; includes new streets on what was formerly a common with picturesque oaks; and has a post office of the name of Penge Bridge and Penge Lane. The Chapelry contains also the Crystal Palace with its Railway Station; and it ranks politically as a Hamlet of Battersea. Acres, 840; population in 1851, 1,169; in 1861, 5,015; houses, 668; population 1868, nearly 10,000. Villas are very numerous, and King William 4th Naval Asylum, the Watermen's Alms Houses, and the North Surrey Industrial Schools are here. The Naval Asylum is for decayed widows of naval officers, and was founded by Queen Adelaide. The Watermen's Alms Houses were built in 1850, at a cost of £5000, and comprises 41 residences. The Industrial Schools is for the parishes northward of the Thames, occupies a plot of seven acres, with farm and kitchen garden; and at the census of 1801 had 748 inmates. The Chapelry is threefold, consisting of Penge proper, and one formed in 1868. The livings are P. Curacies in the diocese of Winchester. Value of Penge, £750; of Upper Penge, £800. Patrons of both Trustees.—*Wilson's Gazetteer of England and Wales.*

Penge, for ecclesiastical purposes, is a separate parish, and has its own Overseers and supports its own poor. The Church of St. John the Evangelist is a modern gothic stone structure with tower and spire. The population of St. John's E. Parish in 1871 was 8,345, and the area is 500 acres. The Church of Holy Trinity, South Penge, to which a district was

lies in Croydon district detached from the main body seven miles distant. The entire parish comprehends an area of 3183 acres.[17] Acres of the main body, 2177 of land 166 of water.—*Wilson's Gazetteer of England and Wales*. In 1792, there were two places of worship, viz., the Parish Church and the Old Baptist Meeting House in York Road; the number of houses within the parish at that period was 380. The following tabular statement will give but an inadequate conception of the growth of the parish since then:—

	Date of Year.	Population.	Number of Houses.
	1831	5540[18]	
	1839	4,764	801
Main Body	1841	6,616	
Entire Parish	1841	6,887	
Main Body	1861	19,600	3,125
Of Entire Parish	1861	24,615	3,793
Ditto	1871	67,218	
Ditto	1880		15,208
Including 13,202 in Penge Hamlet.			
Main Body, not including Penge	1877	79,000	11,500

In 1840 the rateable value was about £28,000.
In 1856 the rateable value was about £79,100.
In 1876 the rateable value was about £331,846.
In 1880 the rateable value was about 416,000.

Anno Domini 1658, the Hamlet of Penge, seven miles from the Parish Church, contained twelve families. The Commissioners who were vested with power to unite or separate parishes did nothing in this case, they could not find a convenient place in the Hundred or County to unite it to. The nearest place of public worship was Beckingham in Kent, about a mile distant.

Boundaries.—A Legal Contest between Battersea and Clapham Parishes. Clapham Common.

With respect to the true etymology of the name Battersea,[19] it was anciently

---

assigned in 1873, is built of brick with stone dressings consisting of chancel, nave and side aisles. The foundation stone was laid by the Right Hon. the Earl of Shaftesbury, R.G., April 17, 1872. The Church cost £7,500, and is capable of seating 1,000. The Register dates from 1874. The living is a vicarage. There are Chapels for Independents, Baptists, and Wesleyans, and National Schools.

[17] According to the Post Office Directory of the Six Home Counties, edited by E. R. Kelly, M.A., F.R.S., 1874, Battersea comprises 2,203 acres of land and 159 water.

[18]   Of whom 3021 were females.

[19] Some of the old inhabitants of Battersea have a notion that Battersea took its name

written Battries-ey, and in Doom's-day Book Patries-ey, probably a mistake for Patrice-ey and signifying St. Peter's Isle, the termination ey, from the Saxon eze or ize, often occurring in the name of places adjacent to great rivers; as Putney, Molesey, Chertsey, etc. Battersea has a history dating from the time of Harold. At the Norman Conquest it passed into the hands of William the Conqueror, who exchanged it with the Abbey of St. Peter's, at Westminster, for lands at Windsor.

The earliest record we have of Battersea appears in Doomsday Book, where it is written Pattricesy. Some authors have supposed that because Petersham, which belonged to St. Peter's Abbey, Chertsey, is there spelt Patricesham, that the earliest form of Battersea originated its connexion with St. Peter's Abbey, the *c* they say in both these words was sibilant and therefore did not differ very much in pronunciation from that it is now, though they admit that it is a "curious anomaly that while P in *Patricesy* has been changed into B the P in *Patricesham* remains unchanged." What the final syllable represents is less clear as there are now no traces of Battersea having been an island although there may have been once. Chelsea, it is remarked, "was originally *Ceale-hythe* or Chelc-hythe, and a haven on the Thames, not an island, just as Lambeth was '*Lambe-hithe*' or haven, but there is no recorded form of Battersea that would allow us to say that *ey* or *ea* represented *hithe*. There was, however, until about thirty years ago, a Creek, up which tradition reports that Queen Elizabeth rowed. A bright little stream rising in Tooting, and passing by Wandsworth Common, flowed into the Thames at this Creek, which is now a mere sewer, and its better character is only kept in remembrance by the name of Creek Street." The Rev. Daniel Lysons, in a book entitled "The Environs of London," published in 1792, which, through the kindness of Mr. R. J. S. Kentish, Librarian of the Beaufoy Library, we have had the privilege of consulting, says, "the name has undergone several changes. In the Conqueror's Survey, it is called Patricesy, and has since been written Battrichsey, Battersey and Battersea, each variation carrying it still further from its original signification. Of the original signification of the word, I think there can be little doubt. Patricesy in the Saxon is Peter's water or river; and as the same record which calls it Patricesy mentions that it was given to St. Peter, it might then first assume that appellation, but this I own is conjecture. Petersham, which is precisely the same in Doomsday — Patriceham, belonged to St. Peter's Abbey, Chertsey, and retains its original name a little modernised. Aubrey, Vol. I. p. 135, derives the name from St. Patrick; but Aubrey was mistaken by seeing it written Patricesy, instead of Petricesy, in Doomsday; but the Normans were not very accurate spellers. Petersham was written in the same manner with an a."[20] "The Parish of Battersea is bounded on the East by

---

originally from a great battle that was fought in shallow water knee-deep when the river was fordable, hence Battersea, Battelsea or Battlesea — as the name itself appears to be somewhat shrouded in obscurity there may be some partial truth in this oral statement though we are not acquainted with any authentic records which warrant us to affirm that Battersea derived its name from this circumstance.

[20] The Manor of Peckham in the Confessor's reign belonged to this Parish, which has since been thrown into Camberwell; Penge being still continued as part of the Manor though separated from the rest by Streatham and Lambeth. — *Manning and Bray's History and Antiquities of Surrey*, Vol. I., p. 327.

Lambeth, on the South by Camberwell, Streatham and Clapham; on the West by Wandsworth, and on the North by the River Thames. The greater part of Wandsworth Common, which extends nearly two miles in length towards Streatham, and a considerable part of Clapham Common are in the Parish of Battersea." The boundaries of Clapham Parish, according to the oldest documents of that Parish and Manor, when taken, have usually commenced at the corner of Wix's Lane, formerly called Browmell's corner. The limits of Clapham Parish where it adjoins Battersea in the early part of last century was the subject of a legal contest, that part of Clapham Common extending to Battersea Rise being claimed by both parishes. In 1716 the inhabitants of Battersea inclosed with a ditch and bank the tract of land in question, and the people of Clapham levelled the bank and filled up the ditch; in consequence of which Henry Lord Viscount St. John, the Lord of the Manor of Battersea, brought an action for trespass against those who were engaged in this work, or their employers, which was tried at the Lent Assizes at Kingston, in 1718, when the plaintiff was non-suited. The men of Battersea however were not discouraged but persevered with greater determination than ever in supporting their claim by including when they beat the boundaries of their Parish the disputed ground in their perambulations; and says Mr. Brayley "it would seem to have been eventually successful, a certain portion of the Common being now held on lease of Earl Spencer as Lord of the Manor of Battersea." —*Brayley, Surrey Mantel,* Vol. III. p. 281.

Last century Clapham Common was little better than a morass; it covers 202 acres. The number and variety of trees both English and exotic with which it is ornamented give it very much the appearance of a park. The Metropolitan Board of Works have purchased the manorial rights over the Common which is now under their supervision. "In the year 1874 (says Mr Walford) the Enclosure Commissioners for England and Wales under the Metropolitan Common Act, 1866, and Metropolitan Commons' Amendment Act, 1869, certified a scheme for placing the Common under the control of the Local Board, the Common was purchased for the sum of £17,000 and it was proposed that it should be dedicated to the use and recreation of the public for ever. By the above mentioned scheme the Board were to drain, plant, and ornament the Common as necessary, no houses were to be built thereon, but eight lodges necessary for its maintenance."

Lavender Hill.—The Seat of William Wilberforce.—Eminent Supporters of the Anti-Slavery Movement.—Frances Elizabeth Leveson Gower. Mr. Thornton.—Philip Cazenove.—Charles Curling, Lady George Pollock, and others.

The writer of a work entitled "Clapham with its Common and Environs," says, "The Mount-Pond was originally a gravel pit, excavated principally to form the turnpike road from Tooting to London. The Mount was raised, and a Pagoda Summer House planted on the top, by Henton Brown, Esq., of the firm of Brown and Tritton, Bankers, Lombard Street, member of the Society of Friends. Mr. Brown lived in the house, late in the occupation of J. Thornton, Esq., and was at great expense in forming the Mount and Pond. The Mount was larger than it now is, and planted with choice shrubs as well as trees. A bridge was thrown over the east side to connect it with the Common, and a pleasure boat was kept under it, but which after the failure of Mr. Brown, went rapidly to decay. He fenced it round with posts and rails, and in 1748 the Parish gave him leave to put down a close fence, which a subsequent Vestry refused to ratify. He was also at the expense of making a conduit from the pond to supply a reservoir in his own grounds." Lavender Hill seems to have been long noted for its nursery gardens. Situated on the Hill was Lavender Villa—at the foot of Lavender Hill was a brook. Now Lavender Hill has the appearance of a busy town. Splendid shops, handsomely decorated and well stocked line both sides of the main thoroughfare, and rows of respectable houses and semi-detached villas forming roads and streets have sprung up in all directions. The same may be said of a great portion of Battersea Rise extending to Bolingbroke Grove. Stately trees have been felled and green slopes that were are now covered with houses, with here and there a place of worship, and all this transformation has taken place within the last twelve years. Clapham Common and its immediate vicinity was in the early years of the present century the seat of the knot of zealous men who, labouring together for what they believed to be the interest of pure religion, the reformation of manners and the suppression of slavery, came to be known as the Clapham sect. One of the most distinguished of them, William Wilberforce, lived at the house known as "Broomfield," (Broomwood) on the south-west side of Clapham Common, and there his no less distinguished son, the late Bishop of Winchester, was born September 7th, 1805. "Conterminous with his fair demesne was that of Henry Thornton, the author and prime mover of the conclave, whose meetings were held, for the most part, in the oval saloon which William Pitt, dismissing for a moment his budgets and his subsidies, planned to be added to Henry Thornton's newly-purchased residence.... It arose at his bidding, and yet remains, perhaps a solitary monument of the architectural skill of that imperial mind. Lofty and symmetrical, it was curiously wainscoted with books on every side except where it opened on a far-extended lawn reposing beneath the giant arms of aged elms and massive tulip trees." — *Stephen's Essays*, Vol. II. p. 290. "In this saloon, and on the far-extended lawn, after their long years of effort, assembled in joy and thanksgiving and mutual congratulation over the abolition of the slave trade, Wilberforce, Clarkson, Granville, Sharp, Stephen, Zachary Macaulay and their younger associates and disciples. But the Villa-cinctured-Common was also the birthplace or cradle of another and hardly less remarkable and far-reaching religious movement or institution. Just as it was the dwelling place, the home or haunt of every one of the most eminent supporters of the anti-slavery movement, so was it the home or haunt of the founders of the Bible Society, its earliest ministers or secretaries, and above all the first and greatest of its presidents, John Lord Teignmouth." — *Handbook to the Environs of London*, by James Thorne, F.S.A., Part I. pp. 111, 112. Broomwood was the seat of the late Sir Charles Forbes, contiguous to which and facing the tall poplar tree is situated a spacious villa once the residence of the late Frances Elizabeth Leveson Gower, an estimable Christian maiden-lady who was a subscriber to several benevolent institutions. She used to conduct bible readings not only for the female servants of the gentry of Clapham Common but also for navvies and others of the labouring classes in her own dinng room, where they partook of her generous hospitality after their daily toil in the shape of a hearty meal.

A Good Example of liberality was given by one Mr. Thornton, of Clapham, a noble-hearted Christian merchant. One morning, when he had received news of a failure that involved him in the loss of no less than a hundred thousand pounds, a minister from the country called at his counting-house to ask a subscription for an important object. Hearing that Mr. Thornton had suffered that loss, he apologized for having called. But Mr. Thornton took him kindly by the hand and said: "My dear sir, the wealth I have is not mine, but the Lord's. It may be that He is going to take it out of my hands, and give it to another; and if so, this is a good reason why I should make a good use of what is left." He then doubled the subscription he intended to give.

The recently deceased and much lamented Philip Cazenove was for thirty years a parishioner, residing on Battersea Rise, whose name was a Synonym for kindness and Christian charity concerning whom we feel that we cannot pass a better eulogium than that recorded in *St. Mary's, Battersea, Parish Magazine* for February, 1880. "He has been a benefactor such as a parish rarely numbers amongst its church folk. The magnificent Girls' School in Green Lane was added to Miss Champion's benefaction, almost at Mr. Cazenove's sole cost. To every church building scheme, to Battersea College, to new schools, to the proposed Hospital, to every good work he was a munificent contributor. And what he did in Battersea, he did in all parts of East and South London, indeed in all parts of the metropolis and in the country. And he sought no thanks for his donations, but with a rare self-forgetfulness he seemed to avoid the acknowledgments of gratitude. His liberality, great as it was, by no means represented all that he did for good works. In our parish he took a personal interest in our Schools of all grades. He always had words of kind encouragement for the teachers. He was always ready to preside at any meeting, or to act on any committee. And as his alms deeds went far beyond his own parish so did his personal service. There was no more familiar face than his in the Board-rooms of the great Church Societies, for some of the chief of which, as the Gospel Propagation Society, he acted as Treasurer. He was an active member of the governing bodies of Guy's Hospital, and other like institutions, and everywhere he freely gave his sunny sympathy and the ripe counsels of his long experience. He was indeed a notable instance of an open-handed, simple-hearted Churchman, some would add 'of the old school,' and we would say, may God of His mercy put it into the hearts of others to perpetuate such a 'school' for truly they are a blessing and a stay to all around them. Our venerated friend was stricken with illness in the beginning of last year, and it seemed as if he would then have succumbed to the physical weakness of the action of that great loving heart. But he rallied somewhat, and during the summer and autumn he was able to sit in his garden or to drive out in his carriage. He was able to be at S. Mark's on S. Michael's Day, 1879, and to receive the Holy Communion there for the last time in the Sanctuary. With the return of winter, his weakness increased, and after a year of weariness and languor and the depression incident to his illness, he entered into the Rest, for which he had yearned, in the early morning of January 20. Philip

Cazenove, born Nov. 23, 1798; died January 20, 1880, aged 81."

> Hear what the voice from heaven proclaims
> For all the pious dead,
> Sweet is the savour of their names,
> And soft their sleeping bed.
> They die in Jesus, and are bless'd;
> How kind their slumbers are!
> From sufferings and from sins released,
> And freed from every snare.
> Far from this world of toil and strife,
> They're present with the Lord:
> The labours of their mortal life
> End in a large reward.

—Isaac Watts, 1709.

Battersea Market Gardens and Gardeners.

At a semi-detached villa situated in this part of the Common, resided the late Charles Curling, Esq., whose memory many of the poor inhabitants of Old Battersea cherish with feelings of grateful respect. He relieved the temporal wants of the needy; opened day and night schools in order that the poorest might be educated; under his excellent wife's superintendence maternal meetings were conducted; at his own expense he supported an Evangelist and a Bible Woman to work in the district.

The Villa adjoining that of Mr. Curling's was occupied by the late Misses Sarah Hibbert and Mary Ann Hibbert, who erected Alms Houses in Wandsworth Road, Clapham, for eight aged women, in grateful remembrance of their father, William Hibbert, who was for many years an inhabitant of Clapham. Not least among the benefactresses of the poor might be mentioned the names of Lady George Pollock, Lady Lawrence, Mrs. Sillem, and Mrs. Robert Jones, of this part, (all deceased). The memory of the just is blessed!

When Lysons wrote, Battersea Rise being a salubrious locality was ornamented with several villas, also it was much admired for its pleasant situation and fine prospect. Referring to the Market Gardens, etc., he says, "About 300 acres of land in the Parish of Battersea are occupied by the market gardeners, of whom there are about twenty who rent from five or six to nearly sixty acres each." Fuller, who wrote in the year 1660, speaking of the gardens in Surrey, states, "Gardening was first brought into England for profit, about 70 years ago; before which we fetched most of our cherries from Holland, apples from France, and hardly a mess of rath ripe peas but from Holland; which were dainties for ladies, they come so far and cost so dear. Since gardening hath crept out of Holland to Sandwich, Kent, and thence to Surrey; where, though they have given £6 an acre and upwards, they have made their rent, lived comfortably, and set many people at work. Oh the incredible profit by digging of ground! for though it be confessed, that the plough beats the spade out of distance for speed, (almost as much as the press beats the pen), yet, what the spade wants in the quantity of the ground it manureth, it recompenseth with the plenty of the good it yieldeth, that which is multiplying an hundred fold more than that which is sown. 'Tis incredible how many poor people in London live thereon, so that in some seasons the gardens feed more people than the field." —*Fuller's Worthies*, Pt. 3, p. 77. "These gardeners," continues Lysons, "employ in the summer season a considerable number of labourers, though perhaps not so many as is generally supposed—on an average I am informed, not one to an acre. The wages of the men are from ten to twelve, of the women from five to seven shillings by the week. Most of the women travel on foot from Shropshire and North Wales in the spring, and as they live at a very cheap rate, many of them return to their own country richer than they left it. The soil of the ground occupied by the gardeners is sandy and requires a great deal of rain. The vegetables which they raise are in general very fine; their cabbages and asparagus particularly have acquired celebrity." The asparagus first grown in or near London was raised by the Battersea gardeners. Owing to its rich and alluvial soil, Battersea has always been noted for its fine asparagus—110 heads of extraordinary size and fit for the kitchen have been known to weigh 32 lbs.[21] There was no market at Battersea, its vegetable produce was sent to the London market. In *Bibliotheca Topographica Britannica Antiquities* (British Museum) Vol. II. p. 227, is a brief note on Battersea by Mr. Theobald. This old writer says, "The lands are fruitful beyond most others and this Parish is famous in the London market for its asparagus, hence called *Battersea Bundles*. It also in the time of a noted man there, one Mr. Cuff, was famous for producing the finest melons. The common field called Battersea Field, is constantly cropped with peas, beans, wheat, etc.... Lands are here let from 50s. down to 16s. an acre.... There are three windmills on the river's brink, one for corn, one grinds colours for the potters, and another serves to grind whitelead. Being in the

---

[21] "Among other branches of industry introduced by the Flemings at Sandwich, that of gardening is worthy of notice. The people of Flanders had long been famous for their horticulture, and one of the first things which the foreign settlers did on arriving in the place was to turn to account the excellent qualities of the soil in the neighbourhood, so well suited for gardening purposes. Though long before practised by the Monks, gardening had become a lost art in England. It is said that Katherine, Queen of Henry 8th, unable to obtain a salad for her dinner in England, had her table supplied from the low countries. The first Flemish gardens proved highly successful. The cabbage, carrots, and celery produced by the foreigners met with so ready a sale, and were so much in demand in London itself, that a body of gardeners shortly removed from Sandwich and settled at Wandsworth, Battersea, and Bermondsey, where many of the rich garden grounds first planted by the Flemings continue to be the most productive in the neighbourhood of the Metropolis."

"Some of the Flemish refugees settled at Wandsworth and began several branches of industry, as the manufacture of felts, the making of brass plates for culinary utensils."

"In addition to the Flemish Churches in the City, at the West-end, and in Spitalfields, there were several thriving congregations in the suburban districts of London; one of the oldest of these was at Wandsworth, where a colony of protestant Wallons settled about the year 1570. Having formed themselves as a congregation, they erected a chapel for worship, which is that standing nearly opposite the Parish Church, the building bearing this inscription on its front: Erected, 1573; Enlarged, 1685; Repaired, 1809, 1831." —*Samuel Smile's Huguenots in England and Ireland*, p.p. 85, 86, 88, 267, 4th Edition.

neighbourhood of London so commodiously within about four miles of the City and on the banks of the river Thames, where so many conveniences of carriage are constantly to be met, and the merchant can in an hour return to his country house. Several citizens and merchants have both built handsome houses here."

Stages set out for Battersea from the City.—Annual Fair.—Inhabitants supplied with Water from Springs.—The Manor of Battersea before the Conquest.

In 1816, Stages set out for Battersea from the following places:—A coach from Pewter Platter, Gracechurch Street, and Black Dog and Camel, Leadenhall Street, daily at 11 a.m., 3 and 7 p.m., Sunday morning at 11. Red Lion, Strand, daily 11 a.m., 3 and 7 p.m. A cart, Kings and Key, Fleet Street; Bell, Bell Yard, and George and Gate, and Pewter Platter, Gracechurch Street; King's Arms, Bishopgate Within; Ship and Hope, Charing Cross, and Angel and Sun, White Hart, and Spotted Dog, Strand, daily at 2 p.m. Boats, Queenhithe, and Globe, Hungerford Stairs daily. Waterman's rates from London Bridge to Chelsea (Battersea) Bridge—oars, whole fare 2/6, sculls 1/3, with company each person oars or sculls 4d. Not more than eight persons in any passage-boat between Windsor and Greenwich. Over the water directly every person 1d. and sculler's fare 2d. No waterman could be compelled to go below the Pageants, and Ratcliff Cross Stairs, or above Vauxhall and Feathers Stairs after five, from Michaelmas to Lady Day, nor after nine in the evening from Lady Day to Michaelmas.

The annual fair held here in Battersea Square, at Easter, was afterwards suppressed. The houses in Old Battersea were irregularly built; the inhabitants were supplied with water from springs. The County Magistrates held a meeting at Wandsworth, an adjoining village, where also a Court of Request for the recovery of debts under £5 was held, under an Act obtained in the 31st of George II., the power of which was extended by an Act in the 46th of George III. The Court of Requests, which is called a court of conscience, was first instituted in the reign of Henry 7th, 1493, and was remodelled by a statute of Henry 8th, in 1517.—*Stowe.* Established for the summary recovery of small debts under forty shillings, but in the City of London the jurisdiction extends to debts of £5.—*Ashe.* There were Courts of Request in the principal corporate towns throughout the kingdom, until 1847, when they were superseded (those of the City of London excepted) by the County Debts Court, whose jurisdiction, extending at first to £20, was enlarged in 1850 to £50. The Lord of the Manor held a Court Leet at Wandsworth, at which the Headborough and constables for Battersea were appointed.

"The Manor of Battersea, which, before the conquest, belonged to Earl Harold, was given by the Conqueror to Westminster Abbey in exchange for Windsor. The Manor was valued in the Confessor's time at £80, it afterwards sunk in value to £30, and at the time of the Survey was estimated at £75. In the taxation of 1291, the possessions of the Abbey of Westminster in Battersea were rated at £15. Thomas Astle, Esq., (says Lysons) has an original deed of Archbishop Theobald, confirming a charter of King Stephen by which he exempts the greater part of the Manor from all taxes and secular payments. Dart mentions several charters relating to Battersea, viz., William the Conqueror's original grant; a charter of privilege; a grant to the Abbot of Westminster of liberty to hunt in this Manor; a charter of confirmation in Henry the First, and another of King Stephen, besides that of privilege before mentioned."

"After the dissolution of monasteries, the Manor was reserved in the hands of the Crown; a lease of it was granted to Henry Roydon, Esq., by Queen Elizabeth, for twenty-one years, in the eighth year of her reign; it was afterwards granted for the same term to his daughter, then Joan Holcroft; and was assigned amongst others for the maintenance of Prince Henry, A.D. 1610. In the year 1627, it was granted in reversion to Oliver St. John Viscount Grandison. Sir Oliver St. John was the first of the family who settled at Battersea, he married *Joan*, daughter and heir of Henry Roydon, Esq., of this place, widow of Sir William Holcroft. Lord Grandison died in 1630, and was succeeded in that title and in the Battersea Estate by William Villiers, his great-nephew, who died of a wound received at the siege of Bristol, A.D. 1644. Sir John St. John, Bart., nephew of the first Lord Grandison, inherited Battersea; from him it passed in a regular descent to Sir Walter St. John, Bart., his nephew, to Sir Walter's son, Henry Viscount St. John, and to his grandson, Henry Viscount Bolingbroke, who, by an Act of Parliament passed before his father's death, was enabled to inherit his estate, notwithstanding his attainder. The estate and manor continued in the St. John family till 1763, when it was bought in trust for John Viscount Spencer, and is now property of the present Earl Spencer."[22] — *Lysons' Environs.*

Battersea and its association with the St. Johns.

Battersea has many memorials; its historic interest culminates in its association with the St. Johns. One is stated to have been "eminent for his piety and moral virtues." Henry in 1684 pleaded guilty of the murder of Sir William Estcourt, Bart., in a sudden quarrel arising at a supper party. His case, if Bishop Burnet be correct, could be regarded only as manslaughter, but he was induced to plead guilty by a promise of pardon if he followed that advice or of his being subjected to the utmost rigour of the law on his refusal. No pardon is enrolled but it is stated that the King granted him a reprieve for a long term of years; and in the Rolls Chapel is a restitution of the Estate (Pat 36 Charles II.) for which it would seem and the reprieve conjoined he had to pay £16,000, one half of which Burnet says the King converted to his own use and bestowed the remainder on two ladies then in high favour. — *Burnet's History of his own times; fol; 1724. Vol. I. p. 600.*

Bolingbroke or Bullingbroke, a town of great antiquity in Lincolnshire, gave the title of Viscount to the St. Johns of Battersea. In 1700, Sir Walter St. John founded and endowed a free school for twenty boys, and both he and his lady afterwards left further sums for apprenticing some of the number. It was re-built in 1859. Over the gateway in the High Street, are carved the Arms of St. John, and un-

---

[22] CUSTOMS OF THE MANOR.—In this Manor, lands descended to the youngest sons; but in default of sons, they do not go to the youngest daughter, but are divided among the daughters equally.—*Lysons.*

derneath them is inscribed the motto, "Rather Deathe than false of Faythe." As we gazed upon the above motto we were reminded of other lines which we have seen and read elsewhere. Sir Walter St. John died 3rd July, 1808, aged 87; his portrait is in the school. He built a gallery at the west end of the Old Church.

> "Dare to be right, dare to be true;
> Other men's failures can never save you;
> Stand by your conscience, your honour, your faith;
> Stand like a hero, and battle till death.

> Dare to be right, dare to be true;
> Keep the great judgment day always in view,
> Look at your work, as you'll look at it then,
> Scanned by Jehovah, and Angels and men.

> Dare to be right, dare to be true;
> God who created you, cares for you too,
> Wipe off the tears that His striving ones shed,
> Counts and protects every hair of your head.

> Dare to be right, dare to be true;
> Cannot Omnipotence carry you through?
> City, and Mansion, and throne all in view,
> Cannot you dare to be right and be true?

> Dare to be right, dare to be true;
> Prayerfully, lovingly, firmly pursue
> The pathway by Saints, and by Seraphim trod
> The pathway which leads to the City of God."

Henry St. John Lord Viscount Bolingbroke.

Bolingbroke (Henry St. John) Lord Viscount, descended from an ancient and noble family as we have already seen. His Mother was Mary, daughter of Robert Rich, Earl of Warwick. He received a liberal education at Eton and at Christ Church, Oxford, and when he left the University was considered to possess uncommon qualifications, but with great parts he had strong passions, which as usually happens, hurried him into many follies and indiscretions. Contrary to the inclinations of his family he cultivated Tory connections, and gained such influence in the House of Commons, that in 1704 he was appointed Secretary of War and of the Marines. He was closely united in all political measures with Mr. Harley; when therefore that gentleman was removed from the seals in 1707, Mr. St. John resigned his office; and in 1710, when Mr. Harley was made Chancellor of the Exchequer, the post of Secretary of State was given to Mr. St. John. In 1712, he was created Baron St. John of Lediard Tregose in Wiltshire, and Viscount Bolingbroke. But being overlooked in the bestowal of vacant ribands of the Order of the Garter, it is said he resented the affront and renounced the friendship of Harley, then Earl of Oxford, and made his court to the Whigs; nevertheless, on the accession of George 1st, the seals were taken from him. Having been informed that a resolution was taken to pursue him to the scaffold for his conduct regarding the treaty of Utrecht,

Signed 11th of April, 1713, he withdrew into France and joined the Pretender's[23] service and accepted the seals as his Secretary. But he was as unfortunate in his new connection as those he had renounced, for the year 1715 was scarcely expired, while being attainted of high treason at home, he was accused by the Pretender of neglect, incapacity and treachery, and had the papers and seals of Foreign Secretary's Office taken away. Such a complication of distressful events threw him into a state of reflection that produced by way of relief "a consolatio philosophica," which he wrote the same year under the title of "Reflection upon Exile." The next year he drew up a vindication of his conduct with respect to the Tories in the form of a letter to Sir William Wyndham. In 1718 his first wife died; in 1720 he married a niece of the famous Madam Maintenon and widow of the Marquis de Villette,[24] with whom he had a very large fortune. In 1723, after being in exile seven years, the King was prevailed upon to grant him a free pardon, and he returned in consequence to England. But his spirit was not satisfied within while he remained a mere titular Lord, and excluded from the House of Peers. His recall had been assented to by Sir Robert Walpole, but he cherished a secret dislike to Walpole and regarded him as the cause of his not receiving the full extent of the King's clemency. Walpole invited Bolingbroke to dine with him at Chelsea, but it appeared to Bolingbroke rather to shew his power and prosperity than for any other reason. Horace Walpole, the celebrated son of the Minister, says in his "Reminiscences" "Whether tortured at witnessing Sir Robert's serene frankness and felicity, or suffocated with indignation and confusion at being forced to be obliged to one whom he hated and envied, the first morsel he put into his mouth was near choking him, and he was reduced to rise from the table and leave the room for some minutes. I never heard of their meeting more." He distinguished himself by a multitude of political writings till the year 1735, when being thoroughly convinced that the door was shut against him, he returned once more to France. In this foreign retreat

[23] Pretenders, a name given to the son and grandsons of James II. of England. The Old Pretender, James Francis Edward Stuart, Chevalier de St. George, born 10th June, 1688, was acknowledged by Louis XIV. as James III. of England, in 1701 proclaimed and his standard set up, at Braemar and Castletown, in Scotland, landed at Peterhead in Aberdeenshire from France to encourage the rebellion that the Earl of Mar and his adherents had promoted, 25th December, 1715. This rebellion having been soon suppressed, the Pretender escaped to Montrose (from whence he proceeded to Gravelines) 4th February 1716. Died at Rome, 30th December, 1765. The Young Pretender, Charles Edward, was born in 1720, landed in Scotland and proclaimed his father King 25th July, 1745; gained the battle of Preston-Pans, 21st September, 1745, and of Falkirk, 27th January, 1746; defeated at Culloden, and sought safety by flight 16th April, 1746. He continued wandering among the wilds of Scotland for nearly six months, and as £30,000 were offered for taking him, he was constantly pursued by the British troops, often hemmed round by his enemies, but still rescued by some lucky incident, and at length escaped from the Ulst Morilaix in September. He died 31st January, 1788. His natural daughter assumed the title of Duchess of Albany; died in 1789. His brother, the Cardinal York, calling himself Henry IX. of England, born March, 1725, died at Rome in August, 1807.

[24] When he was about twenty-six years of age he was married to the daughter and co-heiress of Sir Henry Winchescomb, of Bucklebury, in Berkshire, Bart., and the same year, 1700, he entered the House of Commons, being elected for the Borough of Wotton-Basset in Wiltshire, by a family interest, his father having served several times for the same place.

he began his course of letters on the Study and Use of History for Lord Combury, to whom they are addressed. Lord Bolingbroke was born and died in the family Mansion at Battersea. The house was very large, with forty rooms on a floor; but with the exception of a wing,[25] it has long since been taken down and otherwise appropriated.[26] Dives' Flour Mills cover a portion of the site where once stood this venerable mansion. Upon the death of his father, who lived to be extremely old, Lord Bolingbroke settled at Battersea, where he passed the remaining nine years of his life in philosophical dignity. Pope and Swift, one a great poet, the other a great wit of that time, almost adored him. Arbuthnot, Thompson, Mallet, and other contemporary men of genius were his frequent visitors. Mr. Timbs says "here took place the memorable destruction of one of Bolingbroke's most celebrated works, his 'Essay on a Patriotic King,' of which the noble author had printed only six copies, which he gave to Lord Chesterfield, Sir William Wyndham, Lyttelton, Pope, Lord Marchmont, and Lord Combury, at whose instance Bolingbroke wrote the essay. Pope lent his copy to Mr. Allen, of Bath, who was so delighted with it that he had five hundred copies printed, but locked them up in a warehouse, not to see light until Lord Bolingbroke's permission could be obtained. On the discovery, Lord Marchmont (then living at Lord Bolingbroke's house at Battersea), sent Mr. Gravenkop for the whole cargo, and he had the books carried out on a waggon and burnt on a lawn in the presence of Lord Bolingbroke." Pope, when visiting his friend Lord Bolingbroke, usually selected as his study a parlour (the grate and ornaments were of the age of George 1st) wainscoted with cedar, and overlooking the Thames, in which he is said to have composed some of his celebrated works. It is well known that he received from him the materials for his famous poem the "Essay on Man."

Lord Bolingbroke was born about the year 1672, or as some think, in 1678; he was baptized October 10, 1678; died December 12, 1751, and left the care and benefit of his M.S.S. to Mr. Mallet, who published them together with his former printed works in five vols. 4to.; they are also printed in 8vo.

Lord Bolingbroke sank under a dreadful malady beneath which he had long lingered—a cancer in the face—which he bore with exemplary fortitude. "A fortitude," says Lord Brougham "drawn from the natural resources of his mind, and unhappily not aided by the consolation of any religion; for having cast off the belief in revelation, he had substituted in its stead a dark and gloomy naturalism, which even rejected those glimmerings of hope as to futurity not untasted by the wiser of the heathen." He used to ride out in his chariot every day, and had a black patch on his cheek, with a large wart over one of his eyebrows. He was thought to be essentially selfish; he spent little in the place and gave little away, so that he was not regarded much by the people of Battersea.

A popular writer states that "Bolingbroke's talents were brilliant and versatile; his style of writing was polished and eloquent; but the fatal lack of sincerity and

[25] The ceilings of three of the chambers upstairs are ornamented with stucco-work, and have in their centres oval-shaped oil paintings on allegorical subjects.
[26] Bolingbroke House was pulled down about the year 1775. The pictures were sold by auction.

ionest purpose which characterised him, and the low and unscrupulous ambition which made him scramble for power with a selfish indifference to national security hindered him from looking wisely and deeply into any question. His philosophical theories are not profound, nor his conclusions solid, while his criticism of passing history is worthless in the extreme. He was one of those clever unscrupulous men, unhappily too common, who forget that God has something to do with the government of this world as well as themselves, and who in spite of their ability, can never see that swift destruction treads like Nemesis on the heels of those who dare to trifle with the interests and destinies of a great people."

His opposition to revealed religion drew from Johnson this severe remark: "Having loaded a blunderbuss and pointed it against Christianity he had not the courage to discharge it himself, but left a half-crown to a hungry Scotchman to pull the trigger after his death."

Oliver Goldsmith in his life of Lord Bolingbroke says: "In whatever light we view his character, we shall find him an object rather more proper for our wonder than our imitation; more to be feared than esteemed, and gaining our admiration without our love. His ambition ever aimed at the summit of power, and nothing seemed capable of satisfying his immoderate desires but the liberty of governing all things without a rival."

A Horizontal Air Mill.

On the site of the demolished part of Bolingbroke House,[27] a horizontal Air Mill was erected in 1790, of a conical form, 140 feet in height, and having a mean diameter of 50 feet; it was 54 feet at the base and 45 at the top. It was originally applied to the grinding of linseed for oil, and subsequently by Messrs. Hodgson, Weller and Allaway, of malt for the Distilleries, which were at that time in extensive operation here. Mr. Thomas Fowler erected this mill, the design was taken from that of another on a smaller scale, constructed at Margate by Capt. Hooper. It consisted of a circular wheel, with large boards or vanes fixed parallel to its axis; and upon the vanes the wind acted as to blow the wheel round, one side of it being sheltered from the action of the wind by its being enclosed in frame work, with doors or shutters to open and admit the wind, or to shut and stop it. If all the shutters on one side were open, whilst all those on the opposite were closed, the wind acting with diminished force on the vanes of one side, whilst the opposite vanes were under shelter, turned the mill round; but whenever the wind changed, the disposition of the blinds had to be altered, to admit the wind to strike upon the vanes of the wheels in the direction of a tangent to the circle in which they moved.—*Dr. Paris's Philosophy in Sport.* "The Mill," says Mr. Timbs, "resembled a gigantic packing case, which gave rise to an odd story, that when the Emperor of Russia was in England in 1814, he took a fancy to Battersea Church and determined to carry it off to Russia, and had this large packing case made for it; but as the inhabitants refused to let the Church be carried away, so the case remained on the spot where it was deposited." The Mill served as a landmark for miles around, being more conspicuous an object at that time than the lofty square tower

[27] The part left standing formed a dwelling house for Mr. Hodgson.

of Watney's Distillery a little further westward is now. At length the upper par of the Mill was taken down; the lower part is still used for grinding corn. Capper referring to this Mill, says, "it had 96 shutters, which though only 9 inches broad reached to the height of 80 feet; these by means of a rope, opened and shut in the manner of Venetian blinds. In the inside, the main shaft of the Mill was the centre of a large circle formed by the sails, which consisted of 96 double planks placed perpendicularly, and the same height as the shutters; through these shutters the wind passing turned the Mill with great rapidity, which was increased or diminished by opening or shutting the apertures. In it were six pairs of stones, in which two pair more might be added. Adjacent were Bullock Houses capable of holding 650 bullocks, which were fed with the grains and meal from the Distilleries."

ST. MARY'S CHURCH.

St. Mary's Church.

ST. MARY'S CHURCH forms an interesting object from the water. It was re-built by Act of Parliament passed 14 Geo. 3. The former church, which was built of brick, was found to be in such a dilapidated state that the Vestry deemed it more than desirable to erect a new church than to enlarge and repair the old one. Their unanimous resolution in this respect met with the sanction of Earl Spencer; his lordship in compliance with a petition generously granted the petitioners in the year 1772 a piece of ground, etc. for the enlargement of the church yard. During the re-building of the church, divine service was conducted in the tabernacle at the Workhouse. The cost of its erection was about £5,000, which sum was raised by a brief by the sale of certain pews for 99 years, by the sale of some estates or docks belonging to the Parish, and by granting annuities on lives; the leases ex-pired Michaelmas, 1876. It was opened for divine service November 17, 1777. The ground given by the Earl Spencer for the enlargement of the church yard was consecrated by the Lord Bishop of Oxford, on Wednesday, the 15th of April, 1778. The Church is built of brick and has a tower with a conical copper spire at the west end, besides a clock and porch.[28] The belfry contains a set of eight bells, which, in addition to their ordinary Sunday chimes, ring out their merry peals on special occasions.

> "Ring out the old year's evil,
> The world, the flesh, the devil;
> Let them go! let them go!
> And ring in the Prince of Peace,
> Messiah's gentle reign.
> And let war and bloodshed cease,
> And righteousness obtain.
> Ring out the old year's crimes,
> And ring in the new year's birth, —
> Good words, good deeds, good times;
> Oh, were ever sweeter chimes
> Rung on this fallen earth
> Since creation's virgin anthem rang,
> And morning stars together sang?"
> "Chime on, ye bells! again begin,
> And ring the Sabbath morning in."

Six of the old bells were in the Old Church but re-cast, and two were added to them. Length of church, 88 feet; breadth, 49 feet 3 inches. — *Rev. Owen Manning, S.T.B.* In digging for the foundation of the present structure was found an ancient coffin lid of stone, on the top of which was a cross fleury. The Rev. Erskine Clarke in an article headed "S. Mary's Church in the Last Century" has furnished his pa-rishioners with some interesting details gathered from the Parish books respecting the re-building of the Parish Church. He says: "It does not appear that our ances-tors were more expeditious in carrying on business of this nature than we of the

[28] An Entrance Portico of the Doric order was added to the Church about the year 1823.

present day, as the first resolution to inquire into the state of the old Church[29] was passed by the Vestry in December, 1769, whereas the re-building was not finished till November, 1777. The first suggestion was to sell a portion of Penge Common in order to raise the money required, but it was afterwards found that the condition of the church was so bad that the money raised by this means would not be sufficient for the necessary repairs. On March 1st, 1771, it was ordered by the Vestry that an extra estimate be made of the needful repairs, allowing for enlargement of the chancel to the north wall, to elevate the roof and make galleries, and to raise the bottom of the church so high as five inches from the present coming in, and that the Vicar and Churchwardens wait upon Lord Spencer to get his sanction and assistance for this, and to enlarge the church yard. On December 14, 1771, it was resolved this Vestry is unanimously of opinion (there not being one dissenting voice) that a new Church shall be built in this Parish at an expense not exceeding £4,000: the said sum to be raised by annuities at the most advantageous rate; and the interest or annuity thereon to be paid by a rate not exceeding sixpence in the pound. That twelve gentlemen be nominated to be a Committee for carrying the above-named purposes into execution, and that the following gentlemen be the said Committee with such others as choose to attend, all having voices. Viz.:

The Revd. Mr. Fraigneau, Vicar.

Mr. Rhodes, Mr. Dixon,	} Churchwardens.	Philip Worlidge, Esqr.
Mr. Camden, Mr. Bremmer,	} Overseers.	Mark Bell, Esqr. Thos. Bond, Esqr.
Isaac Akeman, Esqr.		Thos. Misluor, Esqr.
Chrisr. Baldwin, Esqr.		Philip Milloway, Esqr.

And that any five of them be a Committee to transact the business. And that the said Committee may adjourn themselves from time to time, to such place as they shall think proper and at their own expense: and that the Vestry Clerk be ordered to attend the said Committee at all times of their meeting. In the following year we find that the petition to Lord Spencer to present an additional piece of ground was granted, for the following resolution is recorded in the Parish Books on April 21st, 1772. 'That the Rev. Mr. Fraigneau, Mr. Rhodes and Mr. Dixon do wait upon the Right Hon. Earl Spencer on behalf of the Parish of Battersea, to return his Lordship their hearty thanks for his noble and generous grant of the houses and ground north and south of the present entrance to the church yard.' In March, 1773, a plan prepared by Mr. Dixon was laid before the Vestry, and it was unanimously resolved that the said plan be carried into execution with all possible expedition, and the expenses not to exceed £3,000. On March 1, 1774, it was reported to the Vestry by the Church Committee that it would be necessary to apply to Parliament for power to sell some estates belonging to the Parish, and also forty pews in the new church in order to procure necessary funds. From this time to the reopening of the Church there is no further reference to the restoration except an

[29] There is a river view of Battersea by Boydell, which shows the old Church as it stood in 1752.

order for the payment of £18 for 'alterations to the Tabernacle at the Workhouse which was used for Divine Service during the re-building of the Church.' The entire cost of the Church was £4950 13s. 9½d. The following entry is made in April, 1778. Entered by order of the Reverend Mr. William Fraigneau (Vicar), Mark Bell and John Camden, Esquires, Churchwardens. The new Church of Battersea Parish was opened for Divine Service on Sunday, the 17th of November, 1777. The additional ground for enlarging the church yard granted by Earl Spencer, was consecrated by the Lord Bishop of Oxford, on Wednesday, the 15th of April, 1778. Towards the end of the year 1778 we find the inhabitants of Battersea developing a musical taste. A faculty was applied for to erect an organ, the petitioners making their request on the ground that an organ would be 'a decent and agreeable addition and ornament to the Church.' The faculty was granted, and an organ was erected at the west end of the gallery where the present one now stands." — *St. Mary's Battersea Parish Magazine*, Nov. 1876. The organ has been removed to a place under the gallery, adjacent to the choir, and the Church has been re-seated.

The following copy of one of these leases on which the pews in St. Mary's Church were held, will be read with interest.

The Indenture.

THIS INDENTURE made the Twenty-sixth day of December, in the Year of our Lord, One Thousand Seven Hundred and Seventy Eight, and in the Nineteenth Year of the Reign of our Sovereign Lord George the Third, by the Grace of God, of Great Britain, France and Ireland, King, Defender of the Faith, &c. Between the Reverend John Gardenor of Battersea, in the County of Surrey, Clerk, Allyn Simmons Smith, John Camden and Thomas Rhodes, all of the same place Esquires, and John Lumisden of the same, Surgeon, (being five of the Trustees appointed for carrying into execution an Act of Parliament made and passed in the fourteenth year of the Reign of his present Majesty King George the Third, Intituled an Act for Re-building the Parish Church of Battersea, in the County of Surrey, and for enlarging the Church Yard of the said Parish Church) of the one part, and William Dent of Battersea in the County of Surrey, Esquire, on the other part, Witnesseth that for and in consideration of the sum of Thirty-one Pounds Ten Shillings already paid and advanced by the said William Dent to the Treasurer appointed for the purposes of the said Act of Parliament, and also for and in consideration of the Yearly Rent and Covenants hereinafter reserved and contained, they the said John Gardenor, Allyn Simmons Smith, John Camden, Thomas Rhodes, and John Lumisden, in persuance and in Execution of the powers and Authorities vested in them in and by the said Act of Parliament, have Leased, Lett and Demised, and by these presents, do Lease, Lett and Demise unto the said William Dent, his Executors, Administrators and Assigns, All that Pew situate and being in the Gallery on the North side of the said Church of Battersea, (No. 62), with the appertenances. To have and to hold the said Pew, with the appertenances unto the said William Dent, his Executors, Administrators and Assigns, from the Feast day of Saint Michael the Archangel, which was in the Year of our Lord, One Thousand Seven Hundred and Seventy Seven, for and during, and unto the full end and Term of Ninety

Nine Years thence next ensuing and fully to be complete and ended, Yealding and paying therefore Yearly and every Year during the said Term, unto such person or persons, who for the time being shall be lawfully appointed to collect or receive the same Rent or sum of Two Shillings and Sixpence of lawful money of Great Britain, on the Feast day of Saint Michael the Archangel, in every year. And the said William Dent for himself, his Executors, Administrators, and Assigns, doth Covenant and Agree to and with the said before named Trustees, their Heirs and Assigns, That he the said William Dent his Executors, Administrators and Assigns, shall and will well and truly pay or cause to be paid the Rent hereby reserved and made payable according to the reservation aforesaid, And also at his and their own proper Costs and Charge, well and sufficiently repair the said Pew so Leased to him, during all the said Term of Ninety Nine Years, Provided always that if the said Yearly Rent hereby reserved, or any part thereof shall be behind and unpaid by the space of Three Calendar Months next over or after the said Feast day of payment, whereon the same ought to be paid as aforesaid (being Lawfully demanded) then and in such case the Demise or Lease hereby made shall cease, determine, and be utterly void to all intents and purposes whatsoever. In witness whereof the said parties to these presents have hereunder interchangeably set their hands and seals, the day and Year first above Written.

Sealed and Delivered without stamps,
according to the Act of Parliament above } Wm. HOLT,
in the presence of: ROBT. CORAM.

J. GARDNOR,
ALLYN SIMMONS SMITH,
JOHN CAMDEN,
T. RHODES,
JOHN LUMISDEN.

The window over the Communion table at the east end of the church is decorated with portraits of Henry 7th, his grandmother Margaret Beauchamp and Queen Elizabeth in stained glass which was carefully preserved from the former church, and executed at the expense of the St. Johns.[30] The following will explain

[30] Here also in two circular windows pierced for additional light are figures of the Holy Lamb and Dove of Modern Execution.

The east window consists of painted glass, over the portraits of Queen Elizabeth and Henry VII. are the Royal Arms in the central compartment, and on each side, the arms and quarterings of the St. Johns. The portraits are likewise surrounded with borders containing the arms of the families allied to them by marriage. At the top is a white rose inclosed in a red, under the Crown. *St. John* bears Arg. or a chief Gu. 2 Mullets or; and Quarters: 1 Arg. A bend Arg. Cotised between 6 Martlets or, for *Delaberes*. 2 Arg. a fesse between 6 Cinquefoils Gu. for *Unfreville*. 3 Erm. on a fesse Az 3 Crosses Moline or. 4 Gu. a fesse between 6 Martlets or for *Beauchamp*. 5 Arg. a fesse Sa between 3 Crescents Gu. for *Patishall*. 6 Paly of 6 Arg. and Az on a bend Gu. 3 Eagles displayed or for *Grandison*. 7 Az 2 bars Gemelles, and in Chief a lion passant for *Tregoze*. 8 Arg. a fesse Gu between 2 Mullets of 6 points Sali for *Ewyas*. 9 A Saltire Engrailed Sa. On a Chief of the Second 2 Mullets of the first, for *Iwarby* or *Ewarby*. 10 or, 3 lions passant in Pale Sa. for *Carew*. 11 Az 3 Battleaxes Arg. 12 Sa. 2 bars Arg. in Chief, 3 plates for *Hungerford*. 13 per Pale indented Gu. and Vert over all a Chevron or. 14 Arg. 3

why the three portraits were placed at the end of the Church. "The first, that of Margaret Beauchamp, ancestor (by her first husband, Sir Oliver St. John) of the St. Johns, and (by her second husband, John Beaufort, Duke of Somerset) grandmother to Henry VII.; the second, the portrait of that Monarch; and the third, that of Queen Elizabeth, which is placed here because her grandfather, Thomas Boleyn, Earl of Wiltshire, (father of Queen Ann Boleyn), was great-grandfather of Anne, the daughter of Sir Thomas Leighton, and wife of Sir John St. John, the first baronet of the family." —*Oulton.*

Epitaphs and Sepulchral Monuments.

The epitaph written by Lord Bolingbroke on his wife reads as follows: "In the same vault are interred the remains of Mary Clara des Champs de Marcelly, Marchioness of Villette and Viscountess Bolingbroke, born of noble family, bred in the Court of Lewes 14th. She reflected a lustre on the former by the superior accomplishment of her mind. She was an ornament to the latter by the amiable dignity and grace of her behaviour. She lived the honour of her own sex, the delight and admiration of ours. She died an object of imitation to both with all the firmness that reason, with all the resignation that religion can inspire, aged 74 the 18th of March, 1750."

The interior contains some interesting sepulchral monuments, among which is one of Roubiliac in the reliefs to the memory of Viscount Bolingbroke and his second wife, niece of Madame de Maintenon, both lie in the family vault in St. Mary's Church. The epitaphs on himself and his wife were both written by Bolingbroke. That upon himself is still extant in his own handwriting in the British Museum, and is as follows:—"Here lies Henry St. John, in the reign of Queen Anne, Secretary of War, Secretary of State and Viscount Bolingbroke; in the days of King George I. and King George II. something more and better. His attachment to Queen Anne exposed him to a long and severe persecution; he bore it with firmness of mind, he passed the latter part of his life at home, the enemy of no national party, the friend of no faction, distinguished under the cloud of proscription, which had not been entirely taken off by zeal to maintain the liberty and to restore the ancient prosperity of Great Britain." Another monument commemorates the descent and preferments of Oliver St. John, Viscount Grandison, who was the first of the family that settled at Battersea. When studying the law at one of the Inn Courts, he killed in a duel the Captain of the Guard to Queen Elizabeth and Champion of England. "In 1648, Sir John St. John was buried at Battersea with such unusual pomp that the heralds were fluttered and commenced a prosecution against the Executor for acting contrary to the usage of arms and the laws of heraldry. William Riley, one of the heralds deposed 'that the funeral of the deceased was conducted in a manner so much above his degree that the escutcheons were more than were used at the funeral of a Duke; and that he never saw so many persons but at the funeral of one of the blood royal.' This burial is omitted in the register." In the south gallery is a monument to Sir Edward Wynter, an officer in the service of the East India Com-

---

Toads Sa for *Botreux.* 15 Paly wavy or and Gu. All these are quarters on one shield with a Viscount Coronet; the 11 first are quartered by St. John, Baronet.

pany in the reign of Charles 2nd, on which is recorded an account of his having singly and unarmed killed a tiger, and on foot defeated forty Moors on horseback. He appears to have been a friendless youth but obtained his promotion by virtue of his intelligence, courage and good conduct as the epitaph states:—

"Born to be great in fortune as in mind,
Too great to be within an Isle confin'd,
Young, helpless, friendless seas unknown he tried;
But English courage all those wants supplied.
A pregnant wit, a painful diligence,
Care to provide, a bounty to dispence,
Join'd to a soul sincere, plain, open, just,
Procur'd him friends, and friends procured him trust;
These were his fortune's rise, and thus began
This hardy youth, rais'd to that happy man,
A rare example and unknown to most
Where wealth is gain'd and conscience is not lost.
Not less in martial honour was his name—
Witness his actions of immortal fame!

Alone, unarm'd a tiger[31] he oppress'd
And crush'd to death the monster of a beast;
Twice twenty mounted Moors he overthrew
Singly on foot; some wounded, some he slew,
Dispers'd the rest—what more could Samson do?
True to his friends, a terror to his foes
Here now in peace his honour'd bones repose."

Vita Peregrinatio.

He died March 2nd, 1685-6, aged 64.

Near at hand is a monument—a small statue of a mourning female leaning upon an urn—erected by the benevolent James Neild, in memory of his wife Elizabeth, who died 30th of June, 1791, in her 36th year. The epitaph states:—

Here low in beauteous form decay'd
My faithful wife, my love Eliza's laid;
Graceful with ease, of sentiment refin'd,
Her pleasing form inclos'd the purest mind!
Round her blest peace, thy constant vigils keep
And guard fair *innocence* her sacred sleep,
'Till the last trump shall wake the exulting day.
To bloom and triumph in eternal day.

Conjux Mærens Posuit.

And of her father, John Camden, Esq., whose son, John Camden Neild, lived in Cheyne Walk, Chelsea, and bequeathed to Queen Victoria the whole of his

[31] Being attacked in the woods by a tiger, he placed himself on the side of a pond, and when the tiger flew at him, he caught him in his arms, fell back with him into the water, got upon him, and kept him down till he had drowned him.

property, £500,000.

At the east end of the north gallery is a beautiful marble monument most elaborately sculptured sacred to the memory of Sir John Fleet, Knt., Alderman of the City of London. He was unanimously elected Lord Mayor of the City in 1693. He received Royal favours, and all ranks of the greatest honour and esteem from his fellow citizens, having been one of their representatives in Parliament thirteen years, and constantly interested in their highest stations, in which offices and honours he was universally applauded. He was a merchant and just magistrate, constant to church, loyal to his Prince, and true to his country. He was fortunate and honest, bountiful in charity a generous benefactor and a faithful friend. — *Obit 6 Julii* 1712. *Ætat:* 65.

Another tablet is erected to the memory of Margaret Susanna Pounsett, wife of Henry Pounsett, Esq., of Stockwell, in this County, and eldest daughter of Richard Rothwell, Esq., of this Parish; Alderman of the City of London and High Sheriff of the County of Middlesex: she died on the 22nd day of March, 1820, in the 32nd year of her age, leaving two sons and three daughters. Her numerous amiable and exemplary qualities, endeared her to her family in her life — Her Christian piety and cheerful resignation alone consoled them in her death. Also of Ellen Anne Pounsett, her second daughter, who died the 7th of December, 1834, aged 22.

In the west gallery is a marble tablet sacred to the memory of Richard Rothwell, Esq., Alderman and formerly High Sheriff of the City of London, and County of Middlesex; who departed this life most deeply regretted, July 26th, A.D. 1821, in the 60th year of his age. In the public station which he filled of Magistrate and Sheriff, his strict integrity, his splendid liberality, and his genuine philanthropy, justly merited and procured the highest esteem, and warmest approbation of his fellow citizens. In his private character he was respected for the vigor of his mind, the solidity of his judgment, and the uprightness of his principles, and beloved for the urbanity of his manners, and the benevolence of his heart. In him the perplexed found an able counsellor, and the distressed an active friend. His feelings were tenderly alive to the important truths of religion, and while punctual in the performance of the duties of this life he placed his sole reliance on the merits of his Redeemer for happiness in the life to come.

On the right-hand-side of the pathway leading towards the porch of the Church is a grave stone at the bottom of which is the following inscription: —"Mrs. Sarah Eleanor McFarlane, who fell by the hand of an assassin the 29th of April, 1844, aged 46 years." This poor widow resided in Bridge Road, and obtained a subsistence by keeping a Day and Sunday School. The name of the murderer who deprived the life of his victim by cutting her throat on Old Battersea Bridge, was Augustus Dalmas, a Frenchman. This horrid crime was committed late at night. The woman who had charge of the toll seeing the helpless condition of Mrs. McFarlane conveyed her to the "Swan and Magpie" Tavern at the foot of the Bridge, where she expired exclaiming "Dalmas did it!"

In the north gallery is an upright marble tablet for Sir [George] Wombwell, Bart., of Sherwood Lodge, who died October 28th, 1846, in his 77th year.

At the east end of the south aisle is a tablet to Thomas Astle, Esq., F.S.A., keeper of the records in the Tower, and who wrote on "The Origin and Progress of Writing." He left a valuable collection of manuscripts which were deposited at Stow, the seat of his noble patron the Marquis of Buckingham, to whom he gave by his will the option of purchasing them at a fixed sum.

Rectory and Vicarage.

In the churchyard lies Arthur Collins, author of "The Peerage and Baronetage of England." His grandson, David Collins, Lieutenant Governor of New South Wales, and author of a History of the English Settlement there. William Curtis a distinguished botanical writer, author of the "Flora Londinensis," was buried here, January 31, 1731.

> "While living herbs shall spring profusely wild,
> So long thy works shall please dear nature's child,
> Or gardens cherish all that's sweet and gay
> So long thy memory suffer no decay."

The Countess de Morella, who lived in one of the five mansions which gave its old name of Five House Lane to Bolingbroke Grove, has placed a coped stone with a cross on it over the old grave of her aunt Miss Elizabeth Hofer, in the church yard near the mortuary, and has had the tablets of her family at the west end of the north gallery cleaned.

Mr. Poole, the Curator of the monuments in Westminster Abbey, is now engaged in cleaning some of the mural monuments in the Church which had become grimed with the dust of years.

In the centre of the plot in front of the portico is the family vault of Sir Rupert George, Bart. Mr. Chadwin, one of the oldest parishioners now living in Battersea, relates how Sir Rupert George came to select St. Mary's Church yard as his burying place. "He was on a visit to Lord Cremorne, at Cremorne House, on the opposite side of the Thames, and he came over to Battersea and was so impressed with the beauty of the view across the river that he purchased the vault as a resting place for himself and his family. Several of his sons and daughters are interred there, and Dr. Inglis, Bishop of Nova Scotia, the first Colonial Bishop, was also buried in the vault of Sir Rupert George, to whom he was fondly attached by the strongest ties of friendship and also closely allied by marriage." The Bishop's tablet is on the wall under the north gallery.

Charles Williams of London was an actor of some eminence at the Theatre Royal, Drury Lane. He died in the prime of life. His mortal remains were interred in the church yard. As a tribute of respect his funeral was attended by the whole body of Comedians; the pall was supported by Wilks, Griffin, the two Cibbers, and the two Mills. "There is" says Daniel Lysons, "no memorial of his grave."

It is thought that as the former Church was built of brick that probably it was not very ancient. A church is mentioned in Doomsday, a most ancient record, made in the time of William 1st, surnamed the *Conqueror*, and containing a survey of all

he lands in England. Lysons, from whom we take the liberty of making some liberal quotations, when writing about 85 years ago, says, "The Church of Battersea
s dedicated to St. Mary; it is in the Diocese of Winchester, and in the Deanery of
Southwark, the benefice is a Vicarage. Lawrence, Abbot of Westminster, first procured the appropriation of the great tithes for that Abbey about the year 1156. The
monks of Westminster were to receive out of it two marks, reserving sufficient to
the Vicar to support the Episcopal burdens and himself. The Rectory was held by
John Bishop of Winchester in the time of Philip and Mary. The principal profits of
the Vicarage accrued from the gardens, which rendered the living one of the most
valuable in the neighbourhood of London. The gardeners at Battersea paid 7s. 6d.
an acre for tithes to the Vicar. The living of Battersea is dated in the King's Book at
£13 15s. 2½d." The present living is estimated at about £1,000 with residence. "In
the Valor of 1291, usually termed Pope Nicholas' Taxation, the Rectory is valued
at 26 marks and a half: the Vicarage at £4 3s. 4d. In 1658 the Rectory was stated as
worth £80 a year, and the Vicarage at £100, and in the King's Book the Vicarage
stands at £13 15s. 2½d. Battersea was one of those parishes which in memory of the
Abbey dedicated to St. Peter, presented to the Abbot and Convent in early times,
the tithes of salmon taken in this portion of the river. The Incumbents however of
Chelsea, *Battersea*, and Wandsworth endeavoured to shake this custom off as long
ago as 1231, but failed: the composition entered into upon the occasion may be
seen in Dart's History of Westminster Abbey." — *Ecclesiastical Topography.*

A Petition or Curious Document.

"There are two terriers of Battersea in the register of Winchester fastened together of the dates of 1619 and 1636." — *Ducarel's Endowments of Vicarages,* (Lambeth Library). "Owen Ridley, who was instituted to the Vicarage of Battersea, A.D.
1570, appears to have been involved in a tedious litigation with his parishioners
and to have encountered no small degree of persecution from them. The circumstance would not have been worth recording but for two curious petitions which
it produced, the originals of which (date of both 1593) were in the possession of
the Rev. John Gardenor, Vicar, by whom, (says Lysons) they have been obligingly
communicated. One of these is from certain inhabitants to Dr. Swale, one of Her
Majesty's High Commissioners for crimes Ecclesiastical; in which they state many
grievances which they suffered from their Vicar during the space of eighteen years.
Amongst other crimes alleged against him is that of conversing with a Witch. The
object of their petition was, that he might be deprived. It is signed with thirteen
names and about thirty marks. The other petition, which is to Lord Burleigh, being the more curious of the two is here given at large. *To the Right Honourable
the Lord Burleigh, Lord High Treasurer of England.* Most humbly sheweth unto your
honor, your daiely orators, the inhabitants of Battersey, beschinge you to extend
your favor in all just causes to our mynister Mr. Ridley: (so it is right honorable)
that some have sought his deprivation, by many trobles many years together, and
in divers courts sometymes in the Archdeacon's, sometymes by complayninge to
the busshop, sometymes before the highe Commissioners, sometymes before the
Archbusshop of Canterbury, his grace: Yea and once he hath ben edicted at the
assizes. But God the defender of the innocent, hath so protected him that his cawse

beinge tryed and knowene he hath hadd a good issue of all theis trobles; yet the adversarie will not cease, but seeketh to deprive him of his life, for seekinge after Witches, and procuringe the death of a man by Witchcraft. He hath byn our Vicar theis twenty years: he is zealous in the gospell, honest in life, painefull to teache us and to catechise our youth; charitable and liberall to the poore and needy accordinge to his ability, he never sued any of all his parisheoners for tythes, althoughe he hath hadd cawse gyven by some so to doe. Of our conscience wee take him rather to hate wytches, than to seeke after them; for he hath spoken often very bitterly against them out of the bible, neither doe we thinke or suspect the woman to be a witche which is accused, but hath always lyved honestly, quietly and painefully here, to get a poore lyvinge truly. Therefor the man being such a one, whom for his virtues wee love, his trobles heretofore so greate, so many and so chandgable to the undoings of himself, his wife and children, and now so daingerous for the hope of his life, doth move us to become suitors unto your honour for him, beseechinge your honor to take notice, and to make due triall of him and his cawse, so that the truth being fownd owte, justice maie take place; Your honor will defend the innocent in his innocencee, putt an end to his tonge, many wearisome and daingerous trobles and be a patrone unto him in all his good and honest actions; so shall we be bound to thancke God for you, and pray for you for ever. Signed by Robert Cooke Alias Clarencieulx Roy d'Armes, Robert Claye, preacher, and fourteen others."

Dr. Thomas Temple.—Dr. Thomas Church.

"Dr. Thomas Temple, brother of Sir John Temple, the Irish Master of the Rolls, was instituted to the Vicarage of Battersea in 1634, and continued there during the civil wars; he was one of the ministers appointed by Cromwell to assist the Committee for displacing ignorant and insufficient School Masters and Ministers. He was likewise one of the Assembly of Divines and a frequent preacher before the long Parliament. Several of his sermons are in print. Mr. Temple was succeeded in the Vicarage of Battersea by the learned Bishop Patrick, who was educated at Queen's College, Cambridge, and was domestic Chaplain to Sir Walter St. John, by whom he was presented to this benefice. Several of his tracts were published while he was Vicar of Battersea and are dedicated to his patron. He resigned the Vicarage in 1675. He was a zealous champion of the protestant religion, both by his writings and in conversation, particularly at a conference which he, in conjunction with Dr. Jane, held in the presence of James the Second with two Roman Catholic Priests, in which he had so much the superiority over his opponents in argument, that the King retired in disgust, saying that he never heard a good cause so ill defended or a bad one so well. At the Revolution he was rewarded with the Bishopric of Chichester, and was afterwards translated to Ely. He died 1707, and left behind him a numerous collection of printed works; consisting of sermons, devotional and controversial tracts and paraphrases on the Scriptures, which are held in great estimation and which were continued by William South."

"Dr. Thomas Church, of Brazen Nose College, Oxford, who was instituted to the Vicarage of Battersea in the year 1740, distinguished himself much in the ield of controversy in which he engaged against Westley and Whitfield, and Middleton: for his successful attacks on the latter and his defence of the miraculous power during the early years of Christianity. The University of Oxford gave him he degree of D.D. by diploma. He was too zealously attached to his religion to let he opinions of Lord Bolingbroke pass unnoticed notwithstanding he had been his patron. His publication on this subject however was anonymous, it was called 'An Analysis of the Philosophical Works by the late Lord Bolingbroke,' and came out n 1755. He died in 1756, aged 49."

"The registers of this parish begin in the year 1559, and excepting the former part of the 18th century appear to be accurate. Dr. Church soon after he was instituted to the Vicarage began to transcribe a considerable part of the registers, which for many years preceding had been kept by a very ignorant parish clerk. He proceeded so far as to copy the whole of the baptisms, and with great industry rectified a vast number of mistakes and supplied many deficiencies; the difficulty of transcribing the burials of which indeed for some years there were no notices, discouraged him from proceeding any further in this laudable undertaking." — *Lysons.*

Cases of Longevity.—The Plague.—The Three Plague Years.—Deaths in Battersea.

Cases of longevity in the Parish Register: Goody Harleton, aged 108 years, buried 1703; William Abbot, 101, 1733; Wiat, 100, 1790; and William Douse, 100, 1803. The case of Rebecca, wife of Richard Harding, a waterman, is mentioned. She gave birth to four children, she died in labour of the fourth child, which was still-born. The mother was buried February 8, 1730; her three infant children, Mary, Sarah, and Rebecca were buried the 2nd of March following. Respecting the rate of mortality in London during the plague years, in the year 1603, 30,578 persons died of the plague. At the accession of Charles I. in 1625, another dreadful pestilence raged in London, which carried off 35,417 persons. In the year 1665, about the beginning of May, there broke out in London the most dreadful plague that ever infested this kingdom, which swept away 68,596 persons, which added to the number of those who died of other distempers, raised the bill of mortality in this year to 97,306. And the mortality raged so violently in July, that all houses were shut up, the streets, deserted, and scarce anything to be seen therein but grass growing, innumerable fires for purifying the air, coffins, pest-carts, red crosses upon doors, with the inscription, 'Lord have mercy upon us,' and continual cries of 'pray for us;' or the melancholy call of 'bring out your dead.' The cause of this terrible calamity was ascribed to the importation of infected goods from Holland where the plague had committed great ravages the preceding year. During the whole time of its continuance there was a great calm, for weeks together there was scarcely any wind so that it was with difficulty that the fires in the streets could be kept burning for want of a supply of air, and even the birds panted for breath. The plague as is generally agreed is never bred or propagated in Britain, but always imported from abroad, especially from the Levant, Lesser Asia, Egypt, etc. Sydenham, an old writer, has remarked that it rarely infects this country oftener than once in forty years—thank God we have happily been free from it for a much longer period. There have been various conjectures as to the nature of this dreadful distemper. Some think that insects are the cause of it, in the same way that they are the cause of blights. Mr. Boyle thought that it originated from the effluvia or exhalations breathed into the atmosphere from noxious minerals to which might be added stagnant waters and putrid bodies of every kind. Gibbon, in his *Roman History*, 4th Edition, Vol. IV, p. 327-332, gives a very particular account of the plague which depopulated the earth in the time of Emperor Justinian. He thinks that the plague was derived from damp, hot and stagnating air, and the putrifaction of animal substances, especially locusts. The Mahometans believe that the plague proceeds from certain spirits, or goblins, armed with bows and arrows, sent by God to punish men for their sins; and that when the wounds are given by spectres of a black colour, they certainly prove fatal, but not so when the arrows are shot by those that appear white. The learned Dr. Chandler, who travelled in Asia Minor, was of the opinion that the disease arose from animalcules which he supposed to be invisible.

The three Plague years.	In 1603 the number of deaths in Battersea was		22
	" 1625	ditto	61
	" 1665	ditto	113

Average of Births with Burials:—

1580-1589	Births	13	Burials	7
1680-1689	"	58	"	68
1780-1789	"	60	"	69

In 1876 the number of births in Battersea Parish was 3459, and the number of deaths 1751, not including the Hamlet of Penge.

Vicars of Battersea from Olden Times.

The subjoined is copied from "St. Mary's Battersea Parish Magazine" for November, 1875. "Vicars of Battersea from Olden Times. The following extract from 'A History and Antiquities of Surrey,' begun by the Rev. Owen Manning, enlarged and continued to the year 1814 by William Bray, Esq., printed for White, Cochrane & Co., at Horace's Head, Fleet Street, will be of interest.

Patron.	Vicar.	Institution.
Abbot and Convent of Westminster	Thomas de Sunbury	13 Nov. 1301
"	William Trencheuent	21 Nov. 1306
"	Gilbert de Swalelyve	26 Oct. 1320
"	Richard Condray	11 Dec. 1325
"	Thomas at Strete de Cadyngton	20 April 1328

"	Elias de Hoggenorton	10 Aug. 1330
"	Richard de Wolword	9 Dec. 1331
"	William Handley	26 Nov. 1366
"	John Gelle	Resigned, 1370
"	William Bakere	8 Feb. 1370-1
"	John Colyn	5 Oct. 1378
The King (the temporalities of the abbey being in his hands)	Henry Green	31 Oct. 1383
Abbot and Convent of Westminster	Henry Walyngford	Resigned, 1394
"	John Berewyk	22 Oct. 1394
"	Richard Gatyn	12 May 1402
"	William Comelond	Died, 1413
"	John Smyth	25 Aug. 1413
"	Henry Oxyn	Resigned, 1457
"	John Moreys	30 Sept. 1457
"	Thomas Huntyngton	5 Nov. 1485
"	John Heron	20 April 1487
"	Nicholas Townley	Resigned, 18 Feb. 1523-4
"	Christopher Wylson	9 Mar. 1523-4
"	Richard Rosse, L.L.D.	16 May 1530
"	John Edwyn	18 Nov. 1560
"	Thomas Mynthorne	5 Jan. 1561
Queen Elizabeth	William Gray	10 Mar. 1561-2
"	Owen Ridley	21 June 1571
Sir John St. John, Bart.	Thomas Temple, B.D.	21 Nov. 1634
Sir Walter St. John	Simon Patrick, D.D.[32]	1658
"	Gervase Howe, M.A.	22 Mar. 1675-6
"	Nathaniel Gower	20 Oct. 1701
Lord St. John	George Osborn	4 Oct. 1727
Henry Viscount St. John	Thomas Church, D.D	10 Mar. 1739-40
Frederick Lord Bolingbroke	Lilly Butler	18 June 1757
"	William Fraigneau	18 Mar. 1758

[32]   The famous Bishop of Ely.

"	John Gardenor[33]	Oct. 1778
The Crown[34]	Robert Eden, M.A.	1 Feb. 1835
"	John Simon Jenkinson, M.A.	20 June 1847
Earl Spencer	John Erskine Clarke, M.A.	2 Feb. 1872
The Registers of 1345, 1366, 1415, 1446, 1492, and 1500 are lost."		

Thomas Lord Stanley.—Lawrence Booth.

In the reign of Henry VI. Thomas Lord Stanley held possession of a valuable estate in Battersea, which, in order to prevent its confiscation at that troublesome period, he had conveyed to trustees for the benefit of himself and that of Thomas his son and heir. In December, 1460, the property was transferred by the Trustees to Lawrence Booth, Bishop of Durham, and his heirs, and in the year following the grant was confirmed by the two Stanleys. The futility of this transfer was obvious for before Edward IV. had reigned eleven years the estate had escheated to the Crown "in consequence of the action of John Stanley, who assigned the lands and tenements in trust to the Abbot of Westminster, in contravention of the statute of Mortmain. The Bishop therefore had to apply to the King and on payment of £700 he obtained a grant under Letters Patent dated July 10th, 1472, of the property forfeited by John Stanley."

Lawrence Booth was made Bishop of Durham in 1457, he built a Mansion Brygge Court at Battersea, and by the King's license enclosed with walls and towers imparked his land there, with the right of warren and free chase therein. In 1476 he was translated to the See of York. He died in 1480 and bequeathed this property to the Dean and Chapter of York as an occasional residence when the Archbishop visited London. The name of York Road perpetuates this ancient occupancy. One of the few prelates who resided here was Archbishop Holgate who was committed to the Tower by Queen Mary in 1553 for being a married man, and lost much property by illegal seizure. Strype, in his life of Cranmer, relates that the officers who were sent to apprehend the Archbishop rifled his house at Battersea and took away from thence £300 worth of gold coin; 1,600 ounces of plate; a mitre of fine gold set with very fine diamonds, sapphires, and balists; other good stones and pearls; some very valuable rings, and the Archbishop's seal in silver; and his signet, an antique in gold.

York House.

It is contended that Wolsey resided at York House, Battersea, where he was introduced to Anne Boleyne though the interview is more commonly believed to have taken place at York House, Whitehall; but Shakespere in his plays makes the King come by water, and York House, Battersea, was a residence of Wolsey and

[33]   He was many years a constant exhibitor at the Royal Academy. In 1788 he published a set of Views on the Rhine. In 1798 was printed a Sermon preached by him before the Armed Association of Battersea.

[34]   The Patronage lapsed to the Crown, Dr. Allen having been appointed Bishop of Ely, and Dr. Eden, better known as Lord Auckland, Bishop of Sodor and Man.

provided with a creek from the Thames for approach to the house. Sir Edward Wynter is said to have resided at York House, whose exploits surpassed even the heroic achievements of Lord Herbert Cherbury, who, alone in his shirt chased a host of midnight robbers from his house. Sir Edward Wynter's exploits have been already mentioned. The Mansion House was considerably altered by Joseph Benwell, Esq., the occupier who took down many of the old rooms. One of these called the painted chamber had a dome ceiling and is said to have been the room in which Wolsey entertained Henry VIII. with masquerades, and in which he saw Anne Boleyne. When the floor was removed there was found under it a chased gold ring on the side of which was inscribed "Thy virtue is thy honour." This superbly painted room with a dome forms the back ground of an ancient print representing the first interview of Henry VIII. with Anne Boleyne.

There was also another large building in 1818 standing parallel with York House but nearer the river divided into two houses, then in the possession of F. Alver and H. Tritton, Esqrs., and noted for having a very fine terrace in front next the Thames.

Battersea Enamel Works.—Porcelain.—Jens Wolfe, Esq.—Sherwood Lodge.—Price's Patent Candle Factory.

The art of transfer-printing produced from copper-plate impressions is said to have been made at Liverpool; but Mr. Binns, F.S.A., in his very interesting History of Worcester ware traces the claim of transfer-printing to the Battersea Enamel Works at York House, (the Archbishop's old palace) where Ravenet and other artists wrought in engraving plates from which impressions were taken on enamel plaques, etc., for snuff-boxes and other articles. The Liverpool claim to the invention dates from 1756. Whereas Horace Walpole writes from Strawberry Hill, six or seven miles from Battersea, to R. Bently, September 18th, 1755; "I shall send you a trifling snuff-box only as a sample of the new manufacture at Battersea which is done with *Copper plates*." The Battersea Porcelain[35] Works failed and Alderman Jansen's stock, furniture, etc., were sold by public auction, March 4, 1756. The Battersea and Chelsea wares being rarities are expensive, particularly the former. A writer in the "Athenæum" thinks it probable that some of the Battersea workmen found their way to Worcester and Liverpool.

The public may see some beautiful as well as curious specimens of Battersea enamel exhibited at Kensington Museum, lent by the Hon. W. F. B. Massey-Mainwaring. Also some bought at Mrs. Haliburton's sale. Battersea enamel 1750-60. Blue and gold, pink and gold candle-sticks, snuff-boxes, scent-bottles, needle-cases, handle for a cane, tray (circular) from Dulparry with floral medallions, tazza, Bulton's hunting subjects in brown transfer, thimble cases, etui with implements.

---

[35] In 1518 the Portuguese obtained their settlement at Macao, and through them Europe obtained its first specimen of china ware. "And because the cowrie shells which represented Oriental money, resembled as they thought, the backs of little pigs, they called them porcellana; and because the transparent and beautiful texture of china ware resembled that of the delicate cowrie shell, the same name was applied to it; whence we get, it is said, our English designation—porcelain." —See *Marratt's History of Pottery.*

Battersea enamel portrait on copper, a gentleman in armour wearing the garter, etc., etc.

Jens Wolfe, Esq., who was Danish Consul to this country, had a seat at Battersea called Sherwood Lodge. He built a gallery 76 feet long by 25, and 30 in height in the most correct style of Doric architecture for the reception of plaster casts purposely taken for this collection from the most celebrated antique statues. The most remarkable of these were those from the Fighting Gladiator and the Niobe, the Barberini Faun, the Dying Gladiator and the Farnese Hercules. The mansion was pleasantly situated and beautifully shaded with poplar, lime, and sycamore trees. It was the residence of Mrs. Fitz Herbert. Sir George Wombwell chose it as his seat and resided in it about fourteen years. Subsequently Sir Edward Hyde East dwelt here. The stable belonging to Sherwood Lodge still remains, also the old wooden-cased pump with leaden spout.

PRICE'S PATENT CANDLE COMPANY, BELMONT WORKS, BAT-
TERSEA, S.W. (ABOVE)

PRICE'S PATENT CANDLE COMPANY, BROMBOROUGH POOL,
NEAR LIVERPOOL. (BELOW)

On the site where stood York House, Tudor Lodge, and Sherwood House stands a great hive of industry known as Belmont Works or Price's Patent Candle Factory. Price's Patent Candle Company (as a private firm) was among the earliest to apply in commercial enterprise the discoveries of Chevreul, and has continued to hold the first place among candle manufacturers in Great Britain; and notwithstanding the manufacture of gas, the importation of American oils and the many competitors for supplying light-giving material this Company makes its way by dexterity between them. At the present time the store room of the Belmont Factory actually contains candles of about 240 different kinds. Until Chevreul had begun his scientific investigations in 1811, oils and fats had been regarded as simple organic substances. On the complete publication of his discoveries in 1823, the complex character of these bodies became extensively known. In 1829 the plan of separating cocoa-nut oil into its solid and liquid components by pressure, was in that year patented by Mr. James Soames of London; this patent was purchased by Mr. William Wilson and his partner, who, trading upon it under the title of E. Price & Co., perfected it as to manufacturing details. In 1831 the candle manufacture in England was set free from the excise supervision to which it had been previously subjected. From that date then its progress became possible. After a time, in order to carry out successfully certain enterprises which required more capital than the Company had at their command, Mr. Wilson's partner sold his share in the beginning of 1835 to three capitalists. With these gentlemen as sleeping partners and with the aid of two of his sons, Mr. Wilson continued under the name of Edward Price & Co. to carry on the concern until it passed in 1847 into the hands of Price's Patent Candle Company, with a capital of £500,000; of this Company Mr Wm. Wilson became the first Chairman, and his sons, Mr. James P. Wilson and Mr. George F. Wilson, the two Manufacturing Directors. It is interesting to notice that in the year 1840, while Mr. J. P. Wilson was endeavouring to produce a cheap self-snuffing candle for the coming illumination in honour of the marriage of Her Majesty Queen Victoria, then about to take place, succeeded in making such candles of a mixture of equal parts of stearic acid and cocoa-nut stearine, they gave a brilliant light and required no snuffing. These candles came rapidly into notice, they were named "Composite" because of the mixture in them. Africa supplies the palm-oil which was hitherto used almost entirely for soap-making. The imports of palm-oil into England, which amounted to about 9,800 tons in 1840, have for many years past exceeded 40,000 tons annually, and averaged 50,000 tons in 1871, 1872, 1873 and 1874. This increase of importation is undoubtedly due in very great part to the use of oil in the manufacture of candles; and it is this trade which presents to the African chiefs and kings along the West Coast the motive that they can best understand for the abandonment of the slave-trade, they learn in fact, that their subjects are of more value to their rulers when collecting palm-oil than by being sold into slavery. The cocoa-nut oil brought from Ceylon is largely used in the factory. The palm-oil from the Coast of Africa being converted by chemical processes into stearine, is freed from oleic acid by enormous pressure, is liquefied by steam, and then conveyed into the moulding machinery, by which 800 miles of wicks are continually being converted into candles. Among the earlier operations of the new Company was the acquirement in 1848 of the Night-Light Patent held by Mr.

G. M. Clarke, and in 1849 of the Night-Light business of Mr. Samuel Childs, and the erection of a new factory for the purpose of carrying on this new branch of manufacture on an extensive scale. In 1875 no less than 32½ millions of new lights were sold by the Candle Company. Geology informs us that in the age of the coal formation a great part of the earth's surface was covered by a dense and tangled vegetation composed mainly of flowerless plants growing with wonderful luxuriance in the warm damp atmosphere which must then have prevailed—the masses of vegetable matter—the decay of gigantic ferns sinking into the boggy soil formed peat which as ages rolled on became converted by heat and pressure into coal. The conditions of the earth now are so different to what they were at that geological period that we are unable to state with certainty how long the process must have taken to form the ancient beds of lignite (mineral coal retaining the texture of the wood from which it was formed) and brown coal, and the still more ancient beds or seams of true coal. From these paraffine is extracted by chemical processes—it is the chief material in the *Golden Medal Palmitine Candles* (the name given to the candles in consequence of the award to the Company at the Paris Exhibition, 1867, and other products—the name "Palmitine" having been given to them because of the presence of a beautifully pure white stearine obtained from palm-oil). The paraffine thus procured by a process of distillation yields at the same time a liquid product affording under the name of coal oil, or petrolium, one of the cheapest of the Company's light-giving materials. Price's Glycerine has obtained a world-wide reputation for its purity—much of it is manufactured from palm-oil. It was in the Company's factory that *pure* glycerine was first produced. The total of raw materials brought into work by the Company in 1877 amounted to nearly 16,000 tons. The produce in the same year was as follows;—-

Candles of all kinds	147,000,000
Night-lights	32,000,000
Oils for Lamps, Machinery and Wool-working gals.	990,000
Household and Toilet Soaps cwts.	38,000
Stearine and Candle-material sold in bulk cwts.	16,000
Glycerine of various qualities cwts.	3,500

The year's produce of candles named above would suffice to give the continuous light of one candle during about 84,000 years. The Night-lights would in like manner give the continuous light of one Night-light during about 25,000 years. In 1853 the Company took a step of much importance. Liverpool being then as now, the place of arrival of the largest importation of palm-oil, it was felt to be desirable that the Company should have in or near it a second factory, prepared to manufacture this material where it could be purchased without cost of land carriage. The capital of the Company was therefore increased and an estate of about 60 acres was purchased at Bromborough Pool, near Liverpool, on which was erected the second factory with cottages. The factory village numbers 97 houses with a population of 530. It has its own place of worship, schools, co-operative stores, rifle corps, and all the organization of a model village. At present this factory employs about 320 operatives. The London Works (Battersea) occupy an area of about 13½

acres, those at Bromborough occupy 7 acres. The buildings are all roofed with cor-
rugated iron so as to reduce inflammable material to a minimum. The area covered
by the roofs is a large one, as the buildings again, with a view to safety from fire
have generally no upper floor. This area amounts to nine acres for the two factories. The operatives number about 1,300, nearly 1,000 of whom are employed at
Battersea. Connected with each factory is a mess-room in which the work-people
can either purchase their food from the Co-operative Society established among
themselves, or can have their own provisions cooked for them. At each factory a
brief devotional service is conducted every morning. Each factory has its reading
room and library; each maintains a corps of rifle volunteers (the two establishments together providing about 300 efficient riflemen), and each during the winter has its evening school for boys employed in the Works. Bromborough enjoys
an excellent recreation ground and set of allotment gardens, but the growth of
buildings about London has precluded the London operatives from having these
privileges. During the winter months, lectures and science and art classes offer
amusement and instruction to those who desire one or the other. In each factory
a medical officer pays a daily visit, and attends to all who may be ailing; a weekly
payment of one penny from each man and a half-penny from each boy being required in return for this privilege. On the whole this is one of the best regulated
firms in the Metropolis.

Mr. JAMES PILLANS WILSON, *Consulting Adviser.*
Mr. JOHN CALDERWOOD, *General Manager.*
Mr. W. H. WITHALL, *Secretary.*
Mr. KINGSTON GEORGE WOODHAM, *Superintendent.*
Mr. S. J. ROBERTS, *Chief Engineer.*
Mr. G. CHILDS, *Superintendent Night-Light Department.*
Mr. J. DAY, *Superintendent Bromborough Pool Works,* near Birken-
head.[36]

Though hour-glasses were invented at Alexandria B.C. 149, and water-clocks
about the same period, yet it does not appear that hour-glasses and clepsydras or
water-clocks were known in England during the reign of Alfred the Great. Sun
dials might be, but were of no use from eve to morn and when the days were
sunless. In order to allot certain portions of time to particular objects, eight hours
to sleep, meals and exercise, eight to the affairs of government, and eight to study
and devotion, Alfred contrived the expedient of having wax candles made of equal
weight and twelve inches in length, with marks upon them at regular distances.
The combustion of one candle lasted four hours, and each intermediate part, an
inch in distance, denoted a period of twenty minutes. Six of these candles lasted
twenty-four hours. The duty of tending these candles was entrusted to one of Alfred's domestic Chaplains who had to give the Monarch notice of their working.
As currents of air rushed through the unglazed windows and chinks in the walls
of the Royal residence as to render the combustion irregular and the register inac-

[36] The writer has had the privilege of consulting a pamphlet entitled "A Brief History
of Price's Patent Candle Company (Limited)," printed by Spottiswoode & Co., New Street
Square, London, 1876. For private circulation only.

urate, the ingenious King surrounded the candles with horn and wooden frames to make them burn steadily in all weathers.

It was a custom in olden time to conduct a sale or auction by inch of candle. A small piece of candle being lighted the bystanders were allowed to bid for the merchandize that was offered for sale—the moment the candle went out the commodity was adjudged to the last bidder.

There was also excommunication by inch of candle, when the sinner was allowed to come to repentance while a candle continued to burn; but after it was consumed he remained excommunicated to all intents and purposes.

Candlemas.

CANDLEMAS, a feast of the Romish Church, celebrated on the 2nd of February, in honour of the purification of the Virgin Mary. It is borrowed from the practice of the ancient Christians, who on that day used abundance of lights both in their churches and processions, in memory as is supposed of our Saviour's being on that day declared by Simeon "to be a light to lighten the Gentiles." In imitation of this custom, the Roman Catholics on this day consecrate all the tapers and candles which they use in their churches during the whole year. At Rome, the Pope performs that ceremony himself; and distributes wax candles to the Cardinals and others, who carry them in procession through the Great Halls of the Vatican or Pope's Palace. This ceremony was prohibited in England by an Order of Council in the year 1548.

Some writers affirm that Candlemas was first instituted by Pope Gelasius I. in 492. "The Romans were in the habit of burning candles on this day to the goddess Februa, the mother of Mars; and Pope Sergius seeing it would be useless to prohibit a practice of so long standing turned it to Christian account by enjoining a similar offering of candles to the Virgin. The candles were supposed to have the effect of frightening the devil and all evil spirits away from the persons who carried them, or from the houses in which they were placed." It is evident that the numerous superstitious notions and observances connected with candles and other lights in all countries had a remote origin, and may be considered as relics of the once universally prevalent worship of the sun and of fire, for mankind had so far forgotten the One living and true God as to worship the creature instead of the Creator who is God over all blessed for evermore.

A bright spark at the candle denotes that the party directly opposite is to receive a letter. Windy weather is prophesied from the waving of the flames without (apparent) cause, and wet weather if the wick does not light readily. There is a tradition in most parts of Europe to the effect that a fine Candlemas portends a severe winter. In Scotland the prognostication is expressed in the following distich:—

"If Candlemas is fair and clear
There'll be twa winters in the year."

It is said that condemned criminals making the *amende honorable* at the church doors were constrained to bear in their hands a wax taper of six pounds weight.

That it is only thirty-two years since a woman convicted of the offence of brawling in church, stood, by sentence of the Ecclesiastical Court, in a white sheet and with a candle in her hand, *coram publico*, in a church in Devonshire. By the superstitious in olden times in England the rescued parts of Candlemas tapers were supposed to possess supernatural virtues. "Candlemas Bleeze" was until recently, a bonfire festival still observed in sequestered parts of Scotland. A "winding sheet," a "thief" in the candle, etc., were regarded as evil omens, and anxious fears excited if suddenly a hollow cinder were ejected from the fire to know whether it resembled a cradle or a coffin!

About a century ago London was so infested with gangs of highwaymen that it was dangerous to go out after dusk. In 1705 an Act of Common Council was passed for regulating the nightly watch of the City. A number of strong able-bodied men had to be provided by each Ward. Every person occupying any shop, house or warehouse had either to watch in person or pay an able-bodied man to be appointed thereto. Watchmen were provided with lanterns and candles and armed with halberts; to watch from nine in the evening till seven in the morning from Michaelmas to the first of April, and from ten till five from the first of April till Michaelmas. Thus they went their nightly rounds calling "Lantern and a candle! Hang out your Lights!" for during dark nights a certain number of householders in each street had to hang out lanterns with a whole candle, and the Watchman thundered at the door of those delinquents who neglected to do so. The total number of Watchmen appointed by this Act was 583.

Facing Price's Candle Factory was a field which was rented by the Company and used as a cricket ground for their employés. Queen's Terrace and streets adjacent now cover this portion of land.

Among the State Papers is a letter dated August 22, 1580, from Archbishop Sandys to John Wickliffe, keeper of his house at Battersey, in which he directs him to deliver up the house to the Lords of the Council so that it might be turned into a prison for obstinate papists. During the Commonwealth, York House was sold to Sir Allen Apsley and Colonel Hutchinson for the sum of £1,806 3s. 6d., but it was reclaimed by the See after the Restoration.

The Saw.—Mark Isambard Brunel's Premises at Battersea.—Establishment for the preservation of timber from the dry rot burnt down.

Brayley in his History of Surrey says, "Besides this Mansion (near York House) there are several handsome seats fronting the river and various large manufacturing establishments, Chemical works, and melting furnaces, etc. are extensive along its banks, greatly to the annoyance of the market gardeners and florists who complain grievously of the injury they sustain by the smoke and noxious vapours of the numerous steam engines now employed in this hitherto rural district. The establishment here for the preservation of timber from the dry rot, called *Kyanizing* from the name of its inventor, was destroyed by fire on the 20th of March, 1847; and the conflagration extended to other neighbouring works. The process was carried on by forcing tar through the pores of the wood, and here was a large pond of hat fluid, the blaze of which set fire to immense piles of timber which had either undergone the process, or were in a state of preparation for it." —*Brayley, Surrey Mantel, Vol. iii. P. 447.*

A very useful thing is that dentated instrument called the *Saw*. Pliny says that the saw was invented by Dædalus. According to Apollodolus Talus invented the saw. Talus it is said having found the jaw-bone of a snake employed it to cut through a piece of wood and then formed an instrument of iron like it. Saw-mills were erected in Madeira in 1420. At Bresdan in 1427. Norway had the first saw-mills in 1530. The Bishop of Ely Ambassador from Mary of England in the escort of Rome describes a saw-mill there 1555. The attempts to introduce saw-mills into England were violently opposed, and one invented by a Dutchman in 1663 was forced to be abandoned. Saw-mills were erected near London about 1770. The excellent saw machinery at Woolwich Dockyard is based upon the invention of the Elder Brunel, 1806-13. Sir Mark Isambard Brunel was the son of a Normandy farmer, and born at Hacqueville, near Rouen, on the 25th of April, 1769. He early shewed an inclination for mechanics, and at school preferred the study of the exact sciences to the classics. In 1786, he became a sailor in the French Navy. In the revolutionary period of 1793, having involved himself by his political opinions he escaped from Paris to the United States. Brunel's career as an engineer began 1794 when he was appointed to survey for the Canal which now connects Lake Champlain with the river Hudson, at Albany. He afterwards acted as an architect in New York. On his return to Europe in 1799, he married the daughter of William Kingdom, Esq., Plymouth, and settled in England. Here he soon established his reputation as a mechanician by the invention of a machine for making block pulleys for the rigging of ships. The erection of steam saw-mills in Chatham Dockyard, a machine for making seamless shoes for the army, machines for making nails and wooden boxes, for rolling paper and twisting cotton hanks, and lastly a machine for producing locomotion by means of Carbonic acid gas, which however though partially successful was afterwards abandoned. "But the great work by which his name will be transmitted to posterity is the Thames Tunnel which, though almost a complete failure as a commercial transaction is nevertheless a wondrous monument of engineering skill and enterprise. It was commenced in March, 1825, and opened to the public in 1843, after a multitude of obstacles and disasters." He held extensive premises at Battersea on the site now occupied by the Citizen Steam-boat Company, where his celebrated saw and veneer mills were burned down about the year 1814. He was elected a Fellow of the Royal Society in 1814; was appointed Vice-President in 1832. He was Knighted in 1840. Died Dec. 1849, in his eighty first year, universally respected.

Sir Richard Phillips, who had an opportunity of inspecting Brunel's machinery at Battersea, eulogizes his fame and speaks of his merits and scientific genius thus:—"A few yards from the toll-gate of the Bridge on the western side of the road stand the workshops of that eminent, modest, and persevering mechanic Mr. Brunel, a gentleman of the rarest genius who has effected as much for the mechanic arts as any man of his time. The wonderful apparatus in the Dockyard at Portsmouth with which he sets blocks for the navy, with a precision and expedition that astonish every beholder, secures him a monument of fame and eclipses all rivalry." At Battersea Works Sir Richard witnessed four circular saws, two of them 18-ft. in diameter and two of them 9-ft. in diameter, besides other circular saws much smaller used for the purpose of separating veneers. He saw planks of mahogany and rosewood sawn into veneers the 16th of an inch thick. By the power that turned those tremendous saws he beheld a large sheet of veneer 10-ft. long by 2-ft. broad separated in ten minutes "so even and so uniform that it appeared more like a perfect work of nature than one of human art." In another building Sir Richard was shown Mr. Brunel's manufactory for shoes, where the labour was sub-divided so that each shoe passed by aid of machinery through twenty-five hands complete from the hide as supplied by the currier. By this means a hundred pairs of strong and well-finished shoes were made per day. He remarks, "each man performs but one step in the process, which implies no knowledge of what is done by those who go before or follow him. The persons employed are not shoemakers, but wounded soldiers, who are able to learn their respective duties in a few hours. The contract at which these shoes are delivered to Government is 6s. 6d. per pair, being at least 2s. less than were paid previously for an unequalled and cobbled article." The shoes thus made for the Army were tried for two years but afterwards abandoned from economical views.

Sir Richard Phillips in his "Morning Walk from London to Kew" (page 42) says, "at the distance of a hundred yards from Battersea Bridge an extensive pile of massy brick work for the manufacture of soap has recently been erected, at a cost it is said of sixty thousand pounds. I was told it was inaccessible to strangers and therefore was obliged to content myself with viewing it at a distance." This soap factory stood by the water side, a little to the east of the Bridge, erected by Mr. Cleaver. There were some large turpentine works in this parish, which belonged to Mr. Flocton.

Battersea has three bridges across the Thames communicating with Chelsea.

History of the Ferry.—The Old Wooden Bridge.

The history of the Ferry prior to the erection of the OLD WOODEN BRIDGE at Battersea can be traced back some two or three centuries. It was much used as a means of transporting passengers, goods, etc., over this part of the river. At the commencement of the reign of James I. the Ferry from Battersea to Chelsea or Chelchehith Ferry was in full operation. When James I. ascended the throne "by Letters Patent for the sum of £40, the King gave his dear relations Thomas Earl of Lincoln, and John Eldred and Robert Henley, Esquires, all the ferry across the river Thames called Chelchehith Ferry, or Chelsea Ferry." In addition to which some grants of land were included and the Grantees were empowered to transfer their rights to "our very illustrious subject William Blake." In 1618 the Earl of Lincoln, who owned Sir Thomas More's house in Chelsea which Sir Thomas More had purchased from Sir Robert Cecil, sold the ferry to William Blake. In 1695 it belonged to one Bartholomew Nutt. The ferry appears to have been rated in the parish books in 1710 at £8 per annum. Between the year 1765 and 1771 the ferry produced an average rental of £42 per annum. Sir Walter St. John by virtue of his manorial rights held possession of the ferry, at his death in 1708, the ferry with the rest of the property went to his son Henry, who died in 1742 having left the family estate to his son Henry the famous Viscount Bolingbroke, at whose death in 1751, in consequence of his having no issue or progeny of his own, the estates with the title descended to his nephew Frederick (son of his half-brother, John Viscount St. John) who obtained an Act of Parliament in 1762 to sell his estate, which, as we have already observed, was purchased in 1763 by the Trustees of John, Earl Spencer. Earl Spencer being anxious to replace the ferry with a bridge, in 1766 obtained an Act of Parliament which empowered him to build the present bridge. The bridge is in Battersea and Chelsea Parishes (the marks defining the boundary line of these Parishes meet in the centre) it was not to be rated to the land tax, or any public or parochial rate; nor deemed a County bridge, so as to subject the Counties of Surrey and Middlesex to repair the same. In the event of any casualty occurring to the bridge thereby rendering it "dangerous and impracticable" the Earl had to provide a convenient ferry at the same rate of tolls as the bridge. Some old writers who have written on the Antiquities and History of Surrey, state that the bridge was built at the expense of fifteen proprietors each of whom subscribed £1,500. Mr. Walford says in 1771, "Lord Spencer associated with himself seventeen gentlemen, each of whom was to pay £100 as a consideration for the fifteenth share of the ferry and all the advantages conferred on the Earl by the Act of 1766. They were also made responsible for a future payment of £900 each towards the construction of a bridge. A contract was entered into with Messrs. Phillips and Holland to build the bridge for £10,500. The work was at once commenced, and by the end of 1771 it was opened for foot passengers and in the following year it was available for carriage traffic. Money had to be laid out for the formation of approach roads, so that at the end of 1773 the total amount expended was £15,662. For many years the proprietors realized only a small return upon their capital, repairs and improvements absorbing nearly all the receipts. In the severe winter of 1795 considerable damage was done to the bridge by reason of the accumulated ice becoming attached to the (timber) piles and drawing them on the rise of the tide, and in the last three years of the eighteenth century no dividends were distributed." The bridge is 726 feet long and 24 feet wide. It originally had 19 openings, the centre opening had a space of 31 feet, and the others decreased in width equally on each side to 16 feet at the ends, but in consequence of the serious hindrances which the structure caused to navigation on the Thames within the last few years the bridge has undergone alterations in order to widen the water-way, four of the openings have been converted into two and strong iron girders have been introduced. The centre opening is now 75 feet wide with a clear head-way of 15 feet at Trinity High Water Mark. In 1799 only one side of the bridge was lighted with oil lamps. "In 1821 the dangerous wooden railing was replaced by a hand rail of iron, and in 1824 the bridge was lighted with gas the pipes being brought over from Chelsea although Battersea remained unlighted for several years afterwards." In the year 1878, the bridge, which had hitherto remained in the hands of the descendants or friends of the original proprietors came into the possession of the Albert Bridge Company under their Act of Incorporation. Its revenues in 1792 were about £1,700. About nine years ago its yearly income was estimated at £5,000.

Battersea Bridge Tolls by Act of Parliament 6° George III. 1766.

For every description of vehicle drawn by one horse, ass, mule or other beast		4d.
"	two	6d.
"	three	9d.
"	four	1s.
For every horse, ass mule or other beast laden and not drawing		1d.
For every hackney carriage with plates returning empty per horse		1d.
For every foot-passenger whatever		½d.
For every drove of oxen or neat cattle per score and after that rate in any greater or less number.		10d.
For every drove of calves, hogs, sheep or lambs per score and after that rate in any greater or less number.		5d.

On a Notice Board dated 6th October, 1824, are the following words: "Notice is hereby given that no trucks, wheelbarrows or other carriages will be permitted to be drawn upon the foot-paths of this bridge. By order of the Proprietors."

The Bridge though convenient has an unsightly appearance and unworthy its position across a river spanned by some of the finest bridges in the world. At the foot of the Old Bridge is a toll-house with walls twenty inches in thickness, facing which is a painted board with charges for tolls headed "Old Battersea Bridge Tolls by Act of Parliament 6° George III., 1766."

Albert Suspension Bridge.

ALBERT SUSPENSION BRIDGE, conceived originally many years ago by the Prince Consort, it was not until 1864 that an Act for its construction was obtained. Although the works were commenced soon after the necessary powers were conferred upon the Company, they were retarded by the action of the Metropolitan Board of Works. That body proposed to embank the river from Pimlico to Battersea Bridge, Chelsea; the execution of that work would involve questions affecting the bridge level and approaches. Not until 1867 did the Board obtain their Act, and not until the Autumn of 1870 did their engineer determine the open question affecting the approaches and levels of the Albert Bridge. In the mean-time the powers of the Bridge Act expired, but were revived on application to Parliament on condition that the bridge should be constructed on Mr. Ordish's rigid suspension principle. This principle is now generally well known, it having been carried out in practice on several instances, notably in that of the Francis Joseph Bridge at Prague, which is 820 feet long and has a centre span of 492 feet, and two side spans of 164 feet each. The Ordish system consists in suspending the main girders which carry the road-way by straight inclined chains, which are maintained in their proper position by being suspended by vertical rods at intervals of 20 feet from a steel iron cable. The total length of the Albert Bridge is 710 feet and 41 feet in width between the parapets, which are formed of the main girders, which are of wrought iron 8 feet deep and continuous; the upper portion is perforated in order to lighten and improve the structure. The main girders are connected transversely by cross girders placed 8 feet apart, on these the planking is laid for the carriage road-way, which is formed of blocks of wood placed with the grain vertically on the planking. The roadway is 27 feet in width. On either side is a foot-way 7 feet wide, paved with diamond-shaped slabs of Ransome stone 12 inches square and 1½ inches thick, laid on the planking with a layer of tar and asphalted felt interposed. The slabs in the centre of the footpath are of a grey color with an ornamental border. The four towers carrying the main chains of the bridge are placed outside the parapet girders; they are placed in pairs, each pair being connected at a height of 60 feet from the platform level by an ornamental iron work. The towers are of cast-iron and consist each of an inner column 4 feet in external diameter, and surrounded by eight 12-inch octagonal columns placed 12 inches from the central shaft, the whole group being connected together at intervals by disc pieces of collars of cast-iron. The straight chains are composed of rolled iron bars, united end to end by riveted joints and having swelled heads only at the extreme ends. The curved cable from which the straight chains are suspended to preserve their equilibrium is of steel wire and is 6 inches in diameter. It is composed of a series of strands of straight wires, about 900 in number, bound together by a coiled wire of smaller diameter. The bridge is divided into a centre with two side openings, the former a span of 400 feet, and the latter 155 feet each. There is a clear headway of 21 feet at the centre of the bridge from the under side of the platform to Trinity high water mark, the height being reduced to 10 feet at the abutments. The piers carrying the four towers are formed of cast-iron cylinders sunk down to the London clay and filled with concrete. The foundations of the piers consist also of cast-iron cylinders, the bottom or cutting ring being 21 feet in diameter, 4 feet 6 inches high and 1 3/8 inches thick. The next ring above this is 5 feet high and tapers from 21 feet at its junction with the cutting ring to 15 feet at the top, from which point the pier is constructed with cylinders 15 feet in diameter up to the level at which the towers commence. The thickness of the metal in the coned and upper rings is 1¼ inch. The bottom or cutting rings are noticeable as being the largest cylindrical castings ever made in one piece. One of the chief peculiarities in the Albert Bridge is the method introduced by Mr. Ordish in forming the anchorage. The arrangement is perfectly independent of the great mass of masonry generally employed in anchorages the anchorages being contained within an iron structure. It consists of a cast-iron cylinder 20 feet 6 inches deep and 3 feet internal diameter enlarged at the bottom into a chamber 5 feet diameter for anchoring the chains. The cylinder is water-tight, and is provided with a manhole and steps, so that the anchorage can be examined at any time, and cleaned and painted when necessary. This cylinder is set vertically in a surrounding bed of concrete, the bottom being 26 feet below the road-way bed. From this proceeds a vertical anchorage chain, connected to the end of the main girder, to which is also connected the principal back chain and the wire cable. The horizontal strain is thus taken through the main girders and the vertical lift by the mass of concrete in which the cylinder is embedded, and which is about one-tenth the quantity required in ordinary anchorages. The bridge commands an extensive and picturesque prospect, having on the one hand Battersea Park and on the other the Thames Embankment. Messrs. Williamson and Company were the contractors for the bridge and Mr. F. W. Bryant was their engineer. The cylinders for the piers were cast by Messrs. Robinson and Cottam, of Battersea; the cast and wrought iron work for the superstructure was supplied by Messrs. A. Handyside and Company of Derby and London, and the steel wire cables by the Cardigan Iron and Steel Works, Sheffield. There are twenty upright lampposts in keeping with the character of the bridge each bearing a lamp. One rather taller than the rest stands in the middle of the road approaching the bridge, at the base of which toll-bars are swung on iron hinges to obstruct the carriages, the others are placed at certain distances apart opposite each other on either side of the pathways. There are also four small lodges at which to receive carriage and foot tolls. The bridge was opened 31st December, 1872, at 1 p.m.; re-opened the 23rd of August, 1873, at 12.30 p.m. Estimated cost of bridge with approaches, etc., etc., about £90,000. Battersea Old Bridge belongs to the Albert Bridge Company.

Off Park Road, Battersea, is an antique cottage, the birthplace and residence of Mr. Juer, who for several years discharged the duties of Overseer and other Parochial offices in a manner creditable to himself and highly satisfactory to the parishioners. From family records he has been able to trace that his ancestors have occupied this dwelling for the last three centuries. Mr. Juer died Nov. 30, and was interred Dec. 6, 1878, in the family vault in St. Mary's Church-yard, where there had been no burial for 25 years. Canon Clarke read the burial service, and many of the old parishioners were present who respected the memory of the deceased.

Chelsea Suspension Bridge.

CHELSEA SUSPENSION BRIDGE is an elegant structure on the suspension principle, (from the site of Ranelagh to Battersea Park): it measures 347 feet between the towers and 705 between the abutments. It was made at Edinburgh and erected in 1857 after designs by the late Mr. Thomas Page, the architect of the New Bridge at Westminster, at a cost of £85,319. It was opened on the 28th of March, 1858. The roadway is suspended upon chains, which hang from two massive and ornamental piers in the river, the ends being firmly secured by solid masonry on the shores. On a portion of the iron-work of the beautiful arches connecting the towers of this magnificent bridge, beneath the escutcheon representing the Royal Standard, are emblazoned the following Latin inscriptions in old German characters:—*Anno Regni Vicesimo Victoria, Anno Domini*, 1857, *Gloria Deo in Excelsis*. The large globular lamps at the top of the piers are lighted only when the Queen sleeps in London.

Tolls paid for passing over this Bridge were:—

For every foot-passenger	½d.
For every description of vehicle drawn by one horse and other beast of draught	2d.
For each and every additional horse or other beast drawing	1d.

For every horse, mule or ass not drawing	1d.
For every wheelbarrow or truck not drawn by any horse or other beast	1d.
For every score of oxen or neat cattle and so in proportion for any greater or less number	8d.
For every score calves, sheep or lambs, and so in proportion for any greater or less number	4d.

Hackney coaches and licensed cabs without passengers, waggons, carts and drays unladen with two or more horses, to pass over the bridge upon payment of half the above toll. And all post chaise returning without passengers and return post horses, to pass over the bridge free. By virtue of an Act of Parliament 9th and 10th Victoria, cap. 39. By order of the Commissioners of Her Majesty's Works and Public Buildings, 1858. Office of Works, 12, Whitehall Place, Westminster.

The Prince of Wales.—Freeing the Bridges "For Ever."

Londoners may congratulate themselves that they are at last allowed to cross the bridges which connect the opposite banks of the Thames at the western end of this great city without paying toll. The Metropolitan Board of Works have expended £538,847 19s. in freeing these five bridges — viz.: Lambeth Bridge, £36,059; Vauxhall Bridge, £255,230 16s. 8d.; Albert and Battersea Bridges, (including Parliamentary costs), £170,305; Albert Bridge Company (taxed costs of arbitration), £2,253 3s. 1d.; Chelsea Bridge, £75,000. On Saturday, the 24th of May, 1879, Her Majesty Queen Victoria's birthday was appropriately chosen for the occasion and great preparations had been made for giving *éclat* to the ceremony. The route taken by the Royal Party (which included the Prince and Princess of Wales—two of their children, Prince Albert Victor and Prince George of Wales, attired in naval costume as naval cadets; the Duke and Duchess of Edinburgh, the Crown Prince of Denmark) which was gay with Venetian masts, bannerets, streamers and flags. The Circular Engine Shed in Victoria Bridge Road and that portion of the railway bridge which spans the Thames belonging to the London, Brighton and South-Coast Railway Company were lavishly festooned and decorated with coloured flags most profusely. Shortly after 3 p.m. came three open carriages each drawn by two horses and the well-known scarlet livery of the Court Mews on the hammer-cloths. At the south side of Lambeth Bridge the Prince was received by Sir James M'Garel Hogg, M.P., Chairman of the Board of Works; the Archbishop of Canterbury, Lord Middleton, Sir Henry Peek, Sir James Lawrence, M.P., Mr. Alderman McArthur, M.P., Mr. Selway, M.P., Mr. Coope, M.P., and other notabilities. The keys having been surrendered with the customary formalities, a Royal salute having been fired from the banks of the river and the bands having played the National Anthem, Mr. J. M. Clabon handed the Prince of Wales an address, folded and tied with green tape, after a moment's parley His Royal Highness with a smile and an approving nod of the head from the Princess, who was by express wish a joint participator with the Heir Apparent in the ceremony of opening the bridge, handed back the address asking that it might be read as he wished to reply, then Sir James M'Garel Hogg untying the tape and unfolding the address read as follows:—

"To their Royal Highnesses the Prince and Princess of Wales. May it please your Royal Highness—It is with great gratification that we, the Chairman and Members of the Metropolitan Board of Works, receive your Royal Highnesses on the occasion of your opening free to the public the five bridges over the Thames, from Lambeth Bridge on the east to Battersea Bridge on the west, which serve to connect important districts on the two sides of the river. London, which in many respects stands at the head of the great cities of the world, has too long, we fear, in the matter of free passage across the river, been behind the capitals of other countries. Until to-day there has been no free bridge in the metropolis westward of Westminster by which the population north and south of the Thames could pass from one side of the river to the other. We are glad that this reproach will now be removed. The bridges which your Royal Highnesses are about to declare free have been acquired by the board under the powers of an Act of Parliament passed in the year 1877, which had for its object the extinction of the tolls on all the bridges in London. Waterloo Bridge and the Charing-cross Railway Footbridge have already been made free. The tolls will this day be extinguished on five other bridges, and before the end of the year it is hoped that there will be none but free bridges over the Thames throughout the metropolitan area. The metropolis and its inhabitants have received many proofs of the interest which your Royal Highnesses feel in their welfare, and of the encouragement which you are always ready to give to those who are engaged in promoting that welfare. Your presence upon this occasion is a further proof of the interest you feel, and we offer your Royal Highnesses our sincere thanks for the honour you have done us.

> Signed, on behalf of the Metropolitan Board of Works,
> J. M. M'GAREL HOGG, Chairman of the Board,
> May 24, 1879.

The Prince of Wales spoke in reply as follows:

Sir James Hogg and Gentlemen—I thank you in my own name and that of the Princess of Wales for your address, and I can assure you that it gives us both sincere pleasure to take a part in this day's proceedings. The opening of the five bridges westward of Westminster is an important event in the annals of the metropolis, and I rejoice that you should have chosen the Queen's Birthday to declare them free. It is a source of great gratification to us to hear your announcement that the other bridges will, before long, be equally open to the public. A free communication across the Thames is an incalculable boon to all classes of the inhabitants on both sides of the river, and it is our earnest hope that you will be enabled to carry your promised work into effect within the specified time. Let me state in conclusion that the Princess and myself are always ready to assist in advancing any object which identifies us with the population of London, and which tends to promote the interests of the public. The Prince then, amidst loud cheers, exclaimed, 'I declare this bridge open and free for ever.'"

Twenty carriages were devoted to the Members of Parliament, Members of the Metropolitan Board and the Officials the twentieth containing Sir James M'Garel Hogg and some ladies and following this came the three Royal carriages. The route being kept clear of traffic and the spectators massed in lines along side by the police—some 1600 were on duty—the arrangements south side of the bridges being in charge of Captain Braynes, while on the north side Colonel Pearson had the directions. His Royal Highness proceeded by way of the Albert Embankment to Vauxhall Bridge, the approach to which was exceedingly picturesque the banks of the Thames fluttering with flags, and the river crowded with boats that followed the *cortège*. The procession crossed and re-crossed Chelsea Suspension Bridge. In the London, Brighton and South-Coast Railway West-end Goods Traffic Yard a Royal salute was given on the arrival of the Prince by the crushing weight of a locomotive named Rennes, No. 130, passing over twenty-one fog signals, an arrangement previously made by Mr. J. Richardson, the effect of which gave general satisfaction. The west side of the Victoria Railway Bridge which spans the Thames was elegantly decorated from one end to the other by the London, Brighton and South-Coast Railway Company. Festoons and tri-coloured flags representing the colours used for signals on railways were voluntarily displayed in such profusion by Messrs. J. Richardson and Everest as to render the scene quite imposing. In front of Chelsea Hospital were drawn up two hundred warriors of olden times, pensioners in their beaver cocked hats who knowing more about "Brown Bess than the Martini rifle managed to do a salute with tolerable precision." The people assembled in Battersea Park made a rush for Albert Bridge as the procession approached that graceful structure. The Albert Bridge Company was represented by Mr. Ewing Matheson, the Chairman; Mr. Youngman, Manager; Mr. A. C. Harper, Secretary, and Mr. Frederick Stanley, Solicitor. (The Countess of Cadogan presented the Princess of Wales and the Duchess of Edinburgh with handsome bouquets on behalf of the ladies of Chelsea. Button holes of a very choice nature were also presented to the Prince of Wales and the Duke.) Mr. Kingsbury, Chairman of the Chelsea Vestry, had the honour of presenting a silver medal commemorative of the occasion to the Prince of Wales which was graciously accepted. At the north side of the bridge were drawn up the boys of the Duke of York Asylum; at the south side the children of the local schools, all singing with as much gusto as their little lungs would allow "God bless the Prince of Wales." The Pier Hotel and the houses facing the Albert Bridge were gaily and handsomely decorated with flags of all nations, and the balconies at the corner of Cheyne Walk being filled with ladies arrayed in summer toilets, thus lending an additional charm to the *mise en scène*. The military display consisted of guards of honour from the 1st Middlesex Engineer Volunteers and the 2nd (South) Middlesex Rifle Volunteers. The keys of the Albert Bridge were handed over on behalf of the Company by Messrs. Matheson and Stanley and a device swung across the bridge denoting that the latter was "free for ever." On the Chelsea side Mr. Stayton was the designer of the festivities. Passing along the Surrey side of the river the Prince made for Old Battersea Bridge the last of the five to be opened. Here the Surrey Volunteers and the Surrey Artillery mustered in force, and a Salvo of Artillery from the Citizen Steamboat Company announced that the bridge was free. At the approach to the Bridge in Bridge Road stands of evergreens were most tastefully arranged by the employés of Messrs. H. and G. Neal the well-known Nurserymen of Wandsworth Common. At no point in the line of route were greater demonstrations of joy expressed and loyalty manifested than by the Battersea people.

The Royal party returned to Marlborough House—-the other carriages then went to Chelsea Vestry Hall where a banquet was served, and at night there was a display of fireworks at Battersea Park supplied by the Crystal Palace Pyrotechnists, T. Brock & Co., the expense being borne by Earl Cadogan to wind up the eventful day's proceedings.

At the foot of Chelsea Suspension Bridge a board is erected on which is written the following: *Notice, Metropolitan Board of Works. No Traction Engine, Steam Roller, or any load exceeding 5 tons on each pair of wheels, must be taken over this bridge. By order of J. E. Wakefield, Clerk to the Board, May,* 1879.

Shortly after the freeing of the bridges the "bars" were removed, and the old toll house at the foot of Battersea Bridge entirely demolished.

The Stupendous Railway Bridge across the Thames.

The stupendous Railway Bridge across the Thames at Battersea from Battersea Park Railway Pier to Grosvenor Road Station is said to be *the Widest Railway Bridge in the World*. It consists of four arches each one hundred and seventy-five feet span in the clear, with a rise of seventeen feet six inches. The immense ribs which support the superstructure are formed throughout of wrought iron, and are firmly attached to massive cast-iron standards which are placed over the piers; the whole of the frame-work is thus made continuous throughout. On each side of the river is a land arch of seventy feet span, making the entire length of the bridge eight hundred and forty feet. The abutments were put in by means of coffer-dams, and the foundations are carried down thirty feet below Trinity high-water mark. The piers are built upon the same principle as that which was first applied by the late Charles Fox to the building of the Bridge at Rochester, Charing Cross, and Cannon Street, Railway Bridges. The bridge was first erected by Mr. J. Fowler. In 1865-6 it was enlarged by the late Sir Charles Fox.

The spot where Cæsar and his legions are stated by some antiquarians to have crossed the river.

Some antiquarians have stated that about fifty yards westward of Chelsea Suspension Bridge, Cæsar and his legions crossed the river Thames by a ford when in pursuit of the Britons who were retreating from the Romans. The ford is described at low water as a shoal of gravel not more than three feet deep, sufficient for ten men to walk abreast, except on the Surrey side where it has been deepened by raising ballast, and the causeway from the South bank may yet be traced at low water. Others think that the place of crossing was higher up the river, either at Chertsey or Kingston; the latter was anciently called Moreford, or the Great Ford. However, landing at Deal, it is natural the Romans would cross the river at some ford nearest that point.[37]

---

[37] The distance of Chertsey (Surrey) from London is about nineteen miles. Here, says

We would suggest that the next Monolith brought to this country from the and of the Ptolemys or Cæsars be erected on this spot, similar to that of Cleopatra's Needle on the Victoria Embankment.

Watermen and others who navigate the river have observed how very shallow the water is at this spot. Sir Richard Phillips says "the event was pregnant with such consequences to the fortune of these Islands, that the spot deserves the record of a monument; which ought to be preserved from age to age, as long as the veneration due to antiquity is cherished among us. Who could then have contemplated that the folly of Roman ambition would be the means of introducing arts among the semi-barbarous Britons, which in eighteen hundred and forty years or after the lapse of nearly sixty generations, would qualify Britain to become mistress of Imperial Rome; while one country would become as exalted, and the other be so debased, that the event would excite little attention, and be deemed but of secondary importance? Possibly after another sixty generations, the posterity of the savage tribes near Sierra-Leone, or New Holland may arbitrate the fate of London, or of Britain, as an affair of equal indifference."[38]

We shall not attempt to speculate as to what is within the range of human possibilities knowing as all history teaches us how transient is the glory of sublunary things. We believe that while England is true to herself and true to God such a state of things concerning Britain as that depicted by Sir Richard will never be realised. The overthrow of dynasties, of nations and of empires is the result of moral degeneracy—the effect of national and individual sins. "Righteousness exalteth a nation but sin is a reproach to any people. By the Almighty who doeth according to His will in the armies of heaven and among the inhabitants of the earth, kings reign and princes decree justice, He putteth down one and setteth up another." However, while reading the fore-mentioned quotation we were forcibly reminded of Macaulay's New Zealander sitting upon a broken arch of London Bridge contemplating o'er the desolation of England's chief city, or some other traveller from the Antipodes who shall stand on the broken arches of Westminster Bridge, and gazing on a horizon of ruin, cry "Here stood the Metropolis of a Mighty Empire!"

Camden, Julius Cæsar crossed the Thames when he first attempted the conquest of Britain; but Mr. Gough, in his addition to the "Britannia," has advanced some arguments against this opinion. The passage some believe to have been effected at Coway Stakes, about a quarter of a mile below Chertsey Bridge, where Julius Cæsar crossed the Thames when he led the Roman army into the kingdom of Cassivellaunus, who had encamped his forces on the opposite shore. The Britons did everything in their power to prevent the Romans from crossing by driving stakes into the bed of the river and fencing the banks with wooden palisades. Obstacles of this kind were lightly estimated by the bold legionaries. The cavalry at once entered the river; the infantry crossed with their heads only above water, and panic-struck at the sight of Roman intrepidity, the barbarian warriors fled from their post without an effort to maintain it. Bede, who lived in the beginning of the eighth century, tells us, that some of the stakes were then to be seen, and were as big as a man's thigh. Mr. Milner says some of these stakes have been found at a recent period, hard as ebony, each being the body of a young oak tree.

[38] "A Morning's Walk from London to Kew," by Sir Richard Phillips, pp. 26-27, published 1817.

Many years ago a person wrote a note to the Rev. John Brand, Secretary to the Antiquarian Society, to say that as he was passing through Battersea Fields he saw some labourers dig up a leaden coffin, in which was a skeleton and near it there were three more human skeletons. There is no date but it is addressed to Mr. Brand, at Northumberland House, which he left about 1795.

A haunted house.—Battersea Fields.—Duel between the Duke of Wellington and Lord Winchelsea.

About sixty-five years ago there was a house situated in the middle of Battersea Fields which remained for a long time uninhabited on account of the strange and weird stories related and circulated about it. Ignorant and uneducated people said it was "haunted." Nobody would live in it. At midnight "lights" it was said were to be seen "flitting about the rooms," and "dismal groans of one in extremes, at the point to die" were to be heard, and so many believed in "old bogies" and tales of "hobgoblins" so their minds pictured the most frightful and hideous spectres imaginable. At length the house like other old buildings in the neighbourhood was demolished. The Rev. John Kirk, who wrote a Biography of the Mother of the Wesleys, says: "The legendary literature of the world teems with wonderful stories of haunted houses where invisible spirits were believed to utter mysterious sounds, to perform extraordinary pranks, and sometimes communicate revelations of the future, or disclose the dread secrets of the hidden world. These beliefs though strongest and most prevalent where the Gospel is unknown or least influential, are not peculiar to generations 'of old time' or to any particular nation under heaven." Certainly the present generation do not appear to have improved much more than their forefathers in this respect when there is so much nonsensical talk about communicating with the invisible world by means of "spirit rappings," "table turnings," etc. Surely the age when men shall give heed to seducing spirits and doctrines of demons has come!

Battersea Fields, within the Manor along the Thames, were long notable as a marshy tract producing a great variety of indigenous plants; and were the scene on March 21st, 1829, of the duel between the Duke of Wellington and Lord Winchelsea.[39] Battersea Fields were reputed as a place for duelling and prize-fights but are now partly disposed in a fine Public Park, and partly covered with streets and buildings. A lane from Nine Elms past Tuggy's Mill and Rock's Tea Gardens, by the poplar trees led to the Red House which faced the river near the foot of the

[39] The Roman Catholic Emancipation Bill passed the Commons by a majority of 320 to 142, March 30, and was carried on the third reading in the Lords by 313 to 104, April 10. The Bill met with determined opposition from the Marquis of Winchelsea who said some things which the Duke regarded as a personal insult. This led to the hostile meeting at Battersea Fields. It was fashionable in those days for gentlemen to settle their friendly differences with a yard of cold steel or a bullet from the muzzle of a pistol—happily as the result of this duel no blood was shed—the Duke with a directed aim sent a bullet through the hat of Winchelsea, whereupon the Marquis fired his pistol in the air, advanced towards the Duke and made an apology, the Duke of Wellington politely bowed to his political antagonist and then separated. Wellington Road, near Battersea Bridge, marks the locality and derives its name from this circumstance.

South side of Chelsea Suspension Bridge since erected. Here in front was a tall flag-staff with flag waving in the breeze on which were letters denoting the sign of the house. Seats and ale-benches, embowered with clusters of elm trees with wide-spreading branches overhead, were placed for the accommodation of persons who resorted thither for refreshment. The space here embanked and enclosed with an iron palisade formed a kind of jetty, divided in the centre by a flight of steps from the river as well as having a flight of steps at both ends where watermen landed their passengers or took up their fares. There was a ferry here to the "White House" on the opposite side of the Thames.

The Red House.

The "Red House" was built of red bricks with white pointings, wide but not high in elevation. It had one story above the basement with slanted slated roof, and contained in all fourteen rooms. Each of the windows on the ground-floor had wooden shutters hung on hinges painted green, which, when closed or folded, fastened inside with bolts. The windows did not project from the general face of the building except the refreshment bar and the upstairs dining room. This apartment and the long room adjoining commanded an extensive and pleasant prospect of the river. A large lamp, supported by means of an iron branch fastened to the wall, projected over the middle door. The Royal Humane Society's drags were always kept here in readiness in case of emergency, and notice was written on a board suspended outside the west end of the house to that effect. The gardens were laid out in small arbours decorated with Flemish and other paintings and fancifully formed flower-beds. In the centre of the garden was a fish-pond; the walks were prettily disposed; at the end of the principal one was a painting, the perspective rendered the walk in appearance much longer than it really was. The shooting ground was about 120 yards square, and inclosed by palings. Beyond the east end of the house was situated a range of "boxes" or alcoves—seven in number—which at night were illuminated with oil-lamps. Each "box" had a table in the centre with seats all round so that twelve persons could sit inside very comfortably. Of a morning several of the Guards were in the habit of arriving here by water from Whitehall stairs to enjoy their "Flounder breakfast" at ten o'clock. And certain noblemen dignified with their presence and patronage the annual "Sucking Pig Dinner," which generally took place in the month of August.

"Gyp" the Raven.—Billy the Nutman.—Sports.

Mr. Wright, who at one time was proprietor of the "Red House," had a Raven that he called "Gyp" that used to talk. Sometimes as if hailing a waterman from the river the bird would cry out "boat ahoy!" "What's o'clock? what's o'clock?" it would hurriedly repeat as if anxious to know the hour. At another time "Gyp" would call "Rock! over!" "Over!" as if to intimate that somebody requested to be ferried over to the other side. Many a scull has been deceived by the mimic cries of this black-feathered rascal. One day Rock the ferryman was so irritated, having been twice deceived that day by the call of "Gyp," that he took up a quart pewter pot and threw it at his head. "Gyp" narrowly escaped uninjured. Mr. Wright remonstrated and said he would not have the bird hurt at any price. The raven was deliciously fond of picking bones. On one occasion a gentleman accidentally dropped his spectacles; presently, on looking up, he discovered his lost property in the beak of the raven perched on a bough with all the gravity of a sexton. "Gyp" had an incurable antipathy to dogs. If perchance a dog passed by, in an instant he would pounce upon its back, hold on by his claws and peck at it most unmercifully, while the dog thus attacked ran away yelping and howling. When dislodged, "Gyp's" pinions bore him swiftly away from the reach of the teeth of his canine adversary. "Gyp" was of a jealous disposition and did not like to see other birds petted. He has been known to kill a magpie and a raven. It was dangerous to put money down in the presence of "Gyp" for "Gyp" had the propensity of picking it up and of flying away with it. On one occasion he seized a sovereign which a customer put down. As "Gyp" had several hiding places where he deposited "stolen articles," as spoons, knives, forks, etc., diligent search was made but the valuable coin was never discovered. The last account we heard of "Gyp" was that he was taken down to Shropshire and that the poor bird died. Mr. W. Puttick, to whom we are indebted for some curious pieces of information, says, "One of the notabilities at the Red House beside the Raven whose bites I have often experienced was a half-witted man who went by the name of 'Billy' the nutman. He used to carry a bag of nuts and a dial, people paid a penny and turned a hand and had nuts for their money. I have often seen this man stand in the water and let the pigeon shooters shoot at him for a few pence, his gesticulations and grotesque movements at the same time exciting from the spectators shouts and roars of laughter."

Mr. Wright took the house of Mr. Swaine, but after Mr. Wright left, the house was taken by a man of the name of Ireland.

James Rock, a respectable ferryman and lighterman, whose house was hard by, was accidentally drowned in the river Thames, August, 1874. His son, George Rock, is now Pier-master at Battersea Park Railway Pier.

The "Red House" was famed for aquatic sports. Adjoining the premises were grounds for pigeon and sparrow-shooting, and the performance of athletic feats. Pigeons were there sold to be shot at, at 15s. per dozen; starlings at 4s., and sparrows at 2s. The place attained a notoriety not surpassed by the number of excursionists who in summer visit Rye House. Subsequently the Red House with its shooting ground and adjacent premises was purchased by the Government for £10,000.

"The Old House at Home."—Sabbath Desecration.

"The Old House at Home" was a small thatched hut, kept by Farmer Hall, where beer was sold direct from the cask, to be drunken on the premises. It answered the six-fold purpose of shop, dormitory, fowl-house, pig-sty, stable and cow-shed. Within this hovel were gathered pigs, fowls, cats, dogs, singing-birds, ducks, cows, horses and donkeys, which, together with the landlord and his customers who regaled themselves here, constituted a "happy family!" This was a famous place for "egg flip," which consisted of new-laid eggs taken from the hens' nests, beat up in hot ale or porter, sweetened with sugar, and sold to persons who preferred roaming about at mid-night or in the small hours of the morning.

On the Lammas land, in the summer months, gipsies pitched their encampments. On Sundays the place presented the aspect of a pleasure fair, lawlessness, Sabbath desecration, immorality, and vice were rampant. At length the place became a scandal and a public disgrace, and even now, notwithstanding the vast improvements in the neighbourhood, Battersea, as a Parish, to a certain extent is ignored, and persons would no more have smiled at Battersea Park being called Lambeth Park than they do now at Clapham Junction being called by that misnomer, and so with other parts of the parish. A great boon was conferred upon the inhabitants of the South-west of London when this infamous locality was converted into a public park. The intolerable nuisance complained of did not take place previously to the year 1835, after Lord Spencer's first sale when the land fell into the hands of small proprietors. Irrespective of social propriety, public decency and order, horse-racing, donkey-riding, fortune-telling, gambling, cock-shying, swings, roundabouts, boxing, and all the paraphernalia of a pleasure fair with its concomitant evils were the constant scenes witnessed here on Sundays. Mr. Thomas Kirk (now Curate of St. George's) who was for many years a Missionary in Battersea, in his report published in the "London City Mission Magazine," September 1, 1870, states, "that which made this part of Battersea Fields so notorious was the gaming, sporting, and pleasure-grounds at the 'Red House' and 'Balloon' public-houses, and Sunday fairs, held throughout the Summer months. These have been the places of resort of hundreds and thousands, from royalty and nobility down to the poorest pauper and the meanest beggar. And surely if ever there was a place out of hell which surpassed Sodom and Gomorrah in ungodliness and abomination this was it. Here the worst men and the vilest of the human race seemed to try to outvie each other in wicked deeds. I have gone to this sad spot on the afternoon and evening of the Lord's day, when there have been from 60 to 120 horses and donkeys racing, foot-racing, walking matches, flying boats, flying horses, roundabouts, theatres, comic actors, shameless dancers, conjurers, fortune-tellers, gamblers of every description, drinking booths, stalls, hawkers, and vendors of all kinds of articles. It would take a more graphic pen than mine to describe the mingled shouts and noises and the unmentionable doings of this pandemonium on earth. I once asked the pierman 'how many people were landed on Sunday from that pier?' He told me that according to the weather, he had landed from 10,000 to 15,000 people! This influx was besides that by the various land roads by which hundreds of thousands used to come, till the numbers have sometimes been computed at 40,000 and 50,000."

Her Majesty's Commissioners empowered by Act of Parliament to form a Royal Park in Battersea Fields.—Wild Flowers.—Battersea Park.

Mr. Thomas Cubitt, in 1843, suggested to Her Majesty's Commission for Improving the Metropolis the advisability of laying Battersea Fields out as pleasure-grounds, and this design was subsequently pressed upon their attention by the Hon. and Rev. Robert John Eden. An Act of Parliament passed in 1846 empowered Her Majesty's Commissioners of Woods to form a Royal Park in Battersea Fields. Acts to enlarge their powers were passed in 1848, 1851 and 1853, by which a Commission, incorporated as the Battersea Park Commission was appointed with power to sell, demise or lease lands not required for the park. Mr. (afterwards Sir) James Pennethorne's plan was approved, by which 320 acres were to be enclosed at an estimated cost of £154,250. The fields were entirely overflowed by the river at high water, until about three hundred years ago when an embankment was raised, and the land reclaimed.[40] Brayley referring to this period says, "The land reclaimed went to the Lord of the Manor, but was subject to some ill-defined rights of inter-commonage exercised by the inhabitants of Battersea at stated periods of the year. From various causes these rights have been nearly extinguished and

---

[40] It was a miserable swamp, said to have been gained for the parish of Battersea by the act of charitably burying a drowned man there who had been refused sepulture in the adjoining parish. This act was held in a subsequent law-suit to prove a right of ownership, and thus a good deed was amply recompensed.

On the northern side of the river Thames is conspicuously situated that grand national asylum for decayed and maimed soldiers known as Chelsea Hospital. This Hospital was begun by Charles II., carried on by James II., and completed by William III. in 1690. The first projector of Chelsea Hospital was Stephen Fox, grandfather to the Hon. Charles Fox. "He could not abear," he said "to see these soldiers, who had ventured their lives, and spent their strength in the service of their country, reduced to beg." And with the munificence of a philanthropist, he subscribed £13,000 towards the establishment of the Hospital. It was built by Sir Christopher Wren, at a cost of £150,000, on the site of an old theological college escheated to the Crown. In 1850 there were 70,000 *out* and 539 *in pensioners*. The body of the Duke of Wellington lay here in state 10-17 Nov., 1852. Ranelagh Gardens lay at the northern foot of Vauxhall Bridge, a portion now forming the pleasure-grounds of Chelsea Hospital, and were formerly the gardens of Lord Ranelagh's Mansion. They were opened 1733. The amusement were masquerades, illuminated and day-light fêtes, dancing, music, and promenading, which was continued until the end of the century. The grand rotundo, which somewhat resembled the Pantheon of Rome, had an external diameter 185 feet, the internal 150. It was taken down in 1805. In Cheyne Walk was a famous Coffee-House, first opened in 1695, by one Salter a barber, who drew the attention of the public by the eccentricity of his conduct, and furnished his house with a large collection of natural and other curiosities. Admiral Munden and other officers who had been much on the Coast of Spain enriched it with many curiosities and gave the owner the name of Don Saltero, by which he is mentioned more than once in the "Tatler," particularly in No. 34. This coffee-house was frequented by Richard Cromwell and many of the wits and authors of that day. "The Folly," a gilded barge where music and dancing and other amusements delighted the beaux and belles of the day of the Restoration, was moored in the Thames not far from the Modern Cremorne. Adjoining Chelsea Hospital is the Physic Garden belonging to the Company of Apothecaries, which was enriched with a great variety of plants, both indigenous and exotic, and given in 1721 by Sir Hans Sloane, Bart., on condition of their paying a quit-rent of £5, and delivering annually to the Royal Society fifty specimens of different sorts of plants of the growth of this garden till the number amounted to 2,000. In 1733 the Company erected a marble statue of the donor, by Rysbrack, in the centre of the garden, the front of which was conspicuously marked toward the river by two noble cedars of Lebanon, the first ever planted in England, of which only one remains. Sir Hans Sloane was born at Killileagh in the north of Ireland, in 1660, of Scottish extraction. He retired at the age of eighty to Chelsea, to enjoy a peaceful tranquillity, the remains of a well-spent life. He died Jan. 11, 1752. He

most of the land is now held by different proprietors, and partly let for building and other uses." Wild flowers grew abundantly in Battersea Fields.[41] A learned botanist in the last century compiled a flora of Battersea, and many of the plants that luxuriated in these fields were not to be met with elsewhere, except at places much farther from London. Its surface was raised by a million cubic yards of earth published the "History of Jamaica" in 2 vols. folio. In the churchyard is the monument of Sir Hans Sloane, Bart., founder of the British Museum; and on the south-west corner of the church is affixed a mural monument to the memory of Dr. Edward Chamberlayne, with a punning Latin epitaph, which for its quaintness, may detain the reader's attention. In the church is a still more curious Latin epitaph on his daughter; from which we learn, that, on the 30th of June, 1690, she fought, in men's clothing, six hours against the French, on board a fire-ship under the command of her brother. The Chelsea Embankment extends along the north bank of the river from Chelsea Hospital to Albert Suspension Bridge; it was opened 9th May, 1874, by the Duke and Duchess of Edinburgh, Lieut. Col. Sir James Magnaghten Hogg, M.P., Chairman of the Metropolitan Board of Works; Sir Joseph Bazalgette, C.B., Engineer. A beautiful view of Chelsea Embankment with its adjacent buildings may be had from the broad Boulevard running along the river-side in Battersea Park; including the lofty spire of St. Luke's Church, Old Chelsea Church, the Gardens of the Apothecaries' Company, the fine old trees and picturesque Dutch-like houses of Cheyne Walk, the Gardens and Buildings of Chelsea Hospital, the New Barracks beyond, and the lofty Pumping Station and Tower near Grosvenor Road Station.

[41] We are acquainted with an aged gentleman well skilled in medical botany who in the early part of his professional experience used to have gathered certain choice herbs for therapeutic purposes which grew abundantly in this locality.

The following are the names of some of the indigenous plants:—

Circea intetiana—Enchanter's Night Shade (in the lane from the fields to the Prince's Head, Battersea, uncommon in shady lanes). *Valeriana dioica*—Small Marsh Valerian. *Fedia olitoria*—Corn Salad (dry banks Battersea Fields and Lavender Sweep). *Panicum Vertiullatum*—Rough Panic Grass (rare). *P. Viride*—Green Panic Grass (near the Red House and Nine Elms). *P. Crusgalli*—Loose Panic Grass (near the footpath). *Bromus diandrus*—Upright Annual Broom Grass (rare, on an old wall near Battersea Church). *Avena flavescens*—Yellow Oat-Grass (not common, in the footpath from Battersea Bridge to Lavender Hill). *Myosotis palustris*—Great Water Scorpion Grass or, Forget me not, (ditches and marshy grounds; plentiful in Battersea Fields). An elegant plant, the emblem of affection among the Germans. *Lithospermum arvense*—Corn Gromwell, (Battersea Cornfields; not common). *Primula vulgaris*—Primrose. *P. Veris*—Cowslip (Fields on Lavender Hill). *Hottonia palustris*—Water Violet, (plentiful in Latchmere). *Scirpus Triqueter*—Triangular Club Rush, rare, (Banks of the Thames between Vauxhall and Battersea). *Lysimachia vulgaris*—Great Yellow Loose Strife. *Samolus valerandi*—(Brook weed, Water Pimpernel). *Chenopodium bonus Henricus*—English Mercury. *C. olidum*—Fetid Goosefoot, (rare). *Cicuta Virosa*—Water Hemlock, (deadly poison to men and cattle). *Conium Maculatum*—Common Hemlock, (a very dangerous plant). *Œnanthe fistulosa*—Water Dropwort. *Œ. crocata*—Hemlock Water Dropwort, (deadly poison to men and cattle). *Œ. Phellandrium*—Fine-leaved Water Dropwort, (a very poisonous plant). *Smymium Olusatrum*—Alexanders, (waste grounds near old houses). *Ornithogalum umbellatum*—Star of Bethlehem. *Rumex Sanguineus*—Blood-veined Dock, (rare, bank of a ditch on Lavender Hill, between the Nursery and the footpath). *R. pulcher*—Fiddle Dock. *R. palustris*—Yellow Marsh Dock. *R. Hydrolapathum*—Great Water Dock. *Triglochin palustre*—Marsh Arrow Grass. *Alisma plantago*—Water Plantain, (ponds and marshes). *Polygonum Bistorta*—Bistort, or Snake Weed. *Butomus umbellatus*—Flowering Rush. *Saxifraga granulata*—White Saxifrage. *S. Tridactylites*—Rue-leaved Saxifrage. *Sedum reflexum*—Reflex Yellow Stonecrop.

from various sources, particularly from the London Docks (Victoria) Extension. The Park comprises 198 acres, was purchased at a cost of £246,517, and laid ou in 1852-58 at a further cost of £66,373. In 1857 planting was commenced. Up to this period the works had been executed under Mr. Pennethorne, Architect of the Office of Works, when the late Mr. Farrow was appointed to take charge and complete the unfinished works. The park has a grass surface of nearly 66 acres. About 40 acres are set apart for cricket and croquet. There are two match grounds, which together, admit of seven matches being played at the same time. On these grounds between 600 and 700 matches are played annually. The spaces are assigned by ballot. There is a practice-ground for organized adult cricket clubs, on which from 70 to 90 cricket clubs practice on different days; and a general practice ground, appropriated to schools and junior clubs, and the public generally. The season for cricket is from 1st May to 30th September. Other large spaces are used for the drill and exercise of troops stationed at Chelsea Barracks. Various volunteer corps as also the district police are drilled here. The park contains one of the richest collections of shrubs and trees in or near London. Its soil is specially suited to the rose, so that visitors who take delight in the queen of the English garden resort to the rosery.

The Sub-tropical Garden opened in August, 1864, is nearly four acres in extent. It is situated at the head of the ornamental water surrounded by sloping banks, parterres and rolling lawns. In this region flourish palms, tree-ferns, plants with large leaves, gigantic grasses, and the climbers and creepers of Equatorial forests and jungles. India-rubber trees, castor-oil plants, Japanese honeysuckle, Chinese

---

Lychnis flos Cuculi—Meadow Lychnis. *Chelidonium majus*—Celandine. *Papaver dubium*—Long Smooth-headed Poppy. *Stratiotes aloides*—Water Aloe. *Thalictrum flavum*—Common Meadow Rue. *Nepeta Cataria*—Cat Mint. *Lamium incisum*—Cut-leaved dead Nettle. *Scutellaria galericulata*—Common Scull Cap. *Prunella vulgaris*—Self Heal. *Pedicularis palustris*—Tall Red Rattle. *Antirrhinum Cymbalaria*—Joy-leaved Snapdragon. *A. spurium*—Round-leaved Fluellin or Snapdragon. *A. orontium*—Lesser Snapdragon, (Cornfields, etc., Battersea Fields). *Cochlearia armoracia*—Horse Raddish. *Nasturtum amphibium*—Amphibious Yellow Cress. *Sisyonbrium irio*—Broad Hedge Mustard. *S. sophia*—Fine-leaved Hedge Mustard. *Erysimum Cheiranthoides*—Worm-seed Treacle Mustard. *Geranium pratense*—Blue Meadow Crane's Bill. *G. Robertianum*—Herb Robert. *G. Lucidum*—Shining Crane's Bill. *G. pyrenaicum*—Perennial Dove's-foot Crane's Bill. *G. rotundifolium*—Soft Round-leaved Crane's Bill, (by the road side near the Prince's Head, Battersea). *Malva rotundifolia*—Dwarf Mallow. *Lathyrus aphaca*—Yellow Vetching. *Ervum hirsutum*—Hairy Tare, (Osier ground near Battersea). *Trifolium fragiferum*—Strawberry-headed Trefoil. *Hypericum humifusum*—Trailing St. John's Wort. *H. pulchrum*—Small upright St. John's Wort. *Tragnopogon pratensis*—Yellow Goat's Beard. *Cichorium Intybus*—Wild Endive; or, Succory. *Onopordum Acanthium*—Common Cotton Thistle. *Bidens cernua*—Nodding Bur-Marygold. *Tusslago Petasites*—Butter Bur. *Orchis morio* and *maculata* are said to have been found in Battersea Meadows. *Listera ovata*—Common Twayblade. *Typha augustifolia*—Lesser Cat's Tail; or, Reedmace. *Sparganium ramosum*—Branched Bur-Reed. *Carex dioica*—Common Separate-headed Carex. *C. remota*—Remote Carex. *C. riparia*—Common Bank Carex. *Sagittaria sagittifolia*—Arrow Head. *Mercurialis annua*—Annual Mercury. *Equisetum limosum*—Smooth naked Horsetail.

See a catalogue of the rarer species of indigenous plants which have been observed growing in the vicinity of Clapham; systematically arranged according to their class and order, with a reference to the figures in English Botany, printed in a deeply interesting work entitled "Clapham and its Environs," by David Batten.

privet, the banana of Abyssinia recalling the expedition to Magdala; the papyrus plant of Egypt, the veritable bulrush of the Nile, the beautiful scarlet foliage of the dragon's blood tree from South America, the large-leaved tobacco plant, the caladium esculentum from the West Indies, the neottopteris australis etc., besides a variety of other vegetable forms from the tropics. Eastward of the Sub-tropical Garden is situated the Peninsula, containing some of the choicest combinations of floral work, resembling in pattern the most exquisite tapestry. The Alpine point gives a miniature representation of the valleys and mountain-peaks of Alpine scenery. Several little hills are so arranged as to show in miniature the ascending zones of vegetation, beginning with the low warm plains with palms, and leading up to snow-clad heights. The snow is represented by gnaphalium tementosum. The lake, rocks, waterfalls and landscapes are truly picturesque, being so arranged as to produce the most pleasing effect.

The ornamental water covers 23 acres of ground, with an average depth of 2½ feet. Ornithological specimens of the web-footed class afford sport for the aged as well as for the young who feed the aquatic birds with cake, biscuit and crumbs of bread. Besides a large colony of Moorhens that have settled down in these friendly waters may be seen Chinese, Egyptian and Barnacle geese, and Carolina and Muscovy ducks; also

> "The Swan, with arch'd neck
> Between her white wings mantling proudly, rows
> Her state with oary feet"

The lark, the linnet, the thrush, the black-bird join in chorus to fill the air with their bird-song. At night passers-by are charmed with the sweet, rich mellow notes of

> "The merry nightingale,
> That crowds, and hurries, and precipitates,
> With fast thick warble his delicious notes,
> As if he were fearful that an April night
> Would be too short for him to utter forth
> His love chant."

Coleridge.

It may not be uninteresting for the naturalist to know that larva of the goat moth (*cossus ligniperda*) inhabits poplars and willows in Battersea Park. This park too is considered famous for the congregation of vast flocks of starlings just before their migration.

Boating here is a safe and enjoyable amusement. Skiffs are one shilling per hour, party boats eighteenpence. In Winter, when the water is frozen over, it is quite an area for skaters.

The lake is an artificial one, and is fed partly from the Thames and partly by a steam engine fixed for the purpose of supplying the park with water for the lodges, drinking-fountains, roads, flower-beds, etc.

The Gymnasium is in the South-western portion of the park. On the adjacent sward Sunday and other schools may hold their annual treats. In the space thus appropriated preaching is allowed and public meetings are permitted.

Nearly at the centre of the Peninsula there is a reservoir which is excavated below the level of the neighbouring springs. The water from this self-supplied source is as clear as crystal; it is pumped into an elevated tank above the engine house which holds 20,000 gallons, from which are laid service pipes for the supply of the park.

The avenue occupies a central position of the park; the trees are the English elm. This affords an enjoyable and shady promenade.

The horse ride or equestrian road, about forty feet wide, nearly encircles the park and is almost two miles in length. Here is also an excellent carriage drive separate from the latter by a row of young plane trees. There are numerous seats in the park for the accommodation of the public. Situated in the centre of the park is a band-stand. The band plays in the Summer and Autumnal months for the entertainment of those who are fond of instrumental music.

There are two refreshment rooms where light refreshments can be obtained at moderate prices. The lodges too are appropriated to the public and offer refreshments and cloak-rooms.

The advantage of a river frontage possessed by Battersea Park is shown by the fact that upwards of 12,000 persons have landed at the Park Pier on fine Summer days. On Sundays, when Chelsea Bridge is free, in fine weather, 40,000 or 50,000 people have been in the park.

The public owe a tribute of grateful respect to the late Mr. John Gibson, of Surrey Lane, whose acquaintance with horticulture and the science of botany was something considerable, who for about fifteen years was Park Superintendent. That gentleman went on a Botanical Mission to India for and at the expense of the Duke of Devonshire. The manner in which portions of the park are disposed was from designs originally his own. The new rock work is by Mr. Pulham, of Broxbourne. Mr. Alexander Rogers is at present Park Superintendent; Mr. E. W. Partridge, Inspector. There are twelve Park Constables, viz., Mr. J. Cook, South-east Lodge; J. Hawkins, South Lodge; Edwin Ashby, West Lodge; George Weedon, Charles Page, William Jones, James Powell, J. Pointer, George Dicks, W. Sheppard, Isaac Chamberlain, William Withers, Mr. Dowly, Foreman of the Gardeners. On an average about forty gardeners are employed in the park. The park is under the Commissioners of Works, No. 12, Whitehall.[42]

The park was opened March 28th, 1858.

In 1862 the Royal Agricultural Society of England held their Annual Show in Battersea Park.

Recently some beautiful villas in Queen Anne's style have been built in Albert road.

---

[42] On Battersea Park Embankment, near where the Albert Bridge now spans the river, lies like some ancient ruin the beautiful Portico of Burlington House. It was when removed from Piccadilly in 1868 to have been re-erected in the Park.

Opposite the Western gate a site has been chosen for the erection of a Chapel-of-Ease to St. Mary's.

At the angle facing the South-western gate two stately mansions have recently been erected contiguous to each other, called Lancaster Tower and Strathedon House.

London, Brighton and South-Coast Railway Company's two Circular Engine Sheds and West-End Goods Traffic Department.

The two Circular Engine sheds, about 90 yards in diameter, belonging to the London, Brighton and South-Coast Railway Company, adjacent to the East-end of the Park, Victoria Road, built about seven years since, show a marked difference to the small wooden shed they erected some eighteen years ago when they had convenience for only four engines. The present sheds are very soundly built, and can accommodate 56 engines which work from the end of the line, there being 63 engines at work when there is no extra traffic, which is not very often the case. The locomotive staff numbers upwards of 300 hands, the major part being drivers, firemen, and cleaners, who muster 200. They have every facility for doing work required in a prompt manner. There is an engine-hoist which will lift an engine of forty or more tons in a very short time. The break-down van stands in one of the sheds ready at a moment's notice for any casualty that might happen. This is fitted up with hydraulic apparatus and every appliance for getting engines and other vehicles on the line quickly. The method of coaling engines is very good. Half-ton trolleys are loaded out of the trucks of coal, which can be moved with ease by one man on the iron-plated coal stage, from which it is shot on the tender of the engine; so that one man can in a few minutes put one or two tons of coal on a tender. Three hundred tons of coal are kept in stock, and the weekly consumption is about five hundred tons. The sheds are remarkably clean, being constantly whitewashed, and the engines, which are kept clean and fresh painted, to use a figurative expression, are perfect pictures. The passenger engines are a light brown color and the goods engines are a dark green. The offices attached to the sheds are at the entrance in one of the railway arches, and suit in every way the requirements of the place, and when inside one would hardly think it was only a railway arch. Other arches have been fitted up as work-shops for the mechanics, and another arch is entirely appropriated for the stores. Also an arch has been utilized so as to form a comfortable mess-room for enginemen and firemen, with cooking apparatus, lockers, and lavatory; adjoining which is a room similarly fitted up for the engine cleaners. Although these works are fraught with many dangers, it is rarely that any serious casualty occurs. District Loco. Superintendent, Albany Richardson, Esq.; Assistant Superintendent, Mr. John Richardson.

There are two gauges known as the Stephenson or narrow gauge, 4-ft. 8½-in., and the broad gauge 7 feet between the rails introduced by the younger Brunel on the Great Western Railway.

The locomotives on the Brighton and South-Coast Railway are constructed for the narrow gauge. The "Kensington," No. 205, belonging to the London, Brighton and South-Coast Railway Company, is a four-wheel coupled engine, designed by W. Stroudley, Esq., Locomotive Engineer. Diameter of cylinders, 17 inches; stroke, 24 inches; diameter of driving and trailing wheels, 6 feet 6 inches; leading wheel, 4 feet 3 inches; wheel base, 16 feet 3 inches; number of tubes, 260; diameter of ditto outside, 1½ inch; length of ditto, 10 feet 11¾ inches; area of fire-grate, 10.25 square feet; pressure of steam, 140 lbs. per square inch; tube surface, 1,125 square feet; fire-box surface, 112 feet; total surface, 1,237. The total weight of this class of engine and tender when loaded is about 50 tons, and will convey a load of 236 tons at a speed of 40 miles an hour.

This class of engine was constructed for running the express traffic, which in the season is very heavy on this line. Cost of engine about £2500.

"A pint of water is converted into two hundred and sixteen gallons of steam by two ounces of coal, and has sufficient power to lift thirty-seven tons; the steam thus produced has a pressure equal to that of common atmospheric air. By allowing it to expand, by virtue of its elasticity a further mechanical force may be obtained, at least equal in amount to the former. A pint of water therefore, and two ounces of coal are thus rendered capable of raising seventy-four tons a foot high. Two hundred feet of steam can be condensed in one second by four ounces of water, and their expansive power reduced to one-fifth."

The first person who sought to apply the expansive force of steam as a motive power to machinery was an Egyptian, Hero of Alexandria, who lived about 15 years before Christ.

In the year 1543, Basco de Garay, a Spanish captain, astonished the world by asserting that he would propel a vessel without sails or oars. The Emperor Charles V. ordered the experiment to be made, and on the 17th of June a vessel called the "Trinity," of 200 tons burden was moved by wheels turned by steam at the rate of two leagues in three hours. To Spain belongs the honour of having invented the first steam vessel.

In the annals of the steam-engine are enumerated the names of Solomon de Caus, Giovanni Branci (1629). Edward Somerset, (1698). Newcomen, Cawley, Humphrey Potter (an engine boy), and Smeaton. But it is to the master spirit and inventive genius of James Watt the mathematical instrument maker who was born at Greenock in Scotland January 19, 1736, that we are indebted for the high state of efficiency to which our modern steam-engine has been brought. Matthew Bolton of Birmingham undertook the enterprise of introducing Watt's condensing engine into general use as a great working power.

Samuel Smiles says, "Many skilful inventors have from time to time added new power to the steam-engine; and by numerous modifications rendered it capable of being applied to nearly all the purposes of manufacture—driving machinery, impelling ships, grinding corn, printing books, stamping money, hammering, planing, and turning iron; in short of performing every description of mechanical labour where power is required. One of the most useful modifications in the engine was that devised by Trevithick, and eventually perfected by George Stephenson and his Son, in the form of the railway locomotive, by which social changes of immense importance have been brought about of even greater consequence, considered in their results on human progress and civilization than the condensing engine of Watt."

The Stockton and Darlington Railway was one of the first examples of locomotive power on a railway for passengers. Mr. Murdock was the first Englishman who in the year 1784 constructed a non-condensing steam locomotive of lilliputian dimensions. It is to be seen at South Kensington, in the Patent Museum.

Battersea Wharf, belonging to the Brighton, and South-Coast Railway Company, close to Chelsea Bridge, combines a water frontage affording facility for discharging cargoes of goods for and from all parts of the Brighton, South-Eastern, London, Chatham and Dover Railways. The traffic during the last ten years has very sensibly increased, and the point itself has become an important place and of great convenience to the public.—Manager, Mr. William Everest.

The London and Brighton Railway was opened 21st September, 1841. In 1873, Number of miles open 345; gross receipts for the same year including 31st December, £1,618,461.

Comparative statement of traffic returns for week ending October 6th, 1877, to corresponding week in 1876. Total miles open 379¾.

RECEIPTS, 1877,	RECEIPTS, 1876,	INCREASE,
£40,425.	£37,210.	£3,215.

Long-Hedge Farm.—London, Chatham and Dover Railway Locomotive Works.

That part of Battersea known as Long-Hedge Farm which was kept by a Mr. Matson and afterwards by Mr. Graham, is now partially inclosed by the London, Chatham and Dover Railway Locomotive Works. The land originally purchased by the Railway Company was about 75 acres, and nearly one-half this space is appropriated to the Locomotive Department and Goods traffic yard.

The Works were built by Messrs. Peto and Betts, from designs furnished by Joseph Cubitt, Esq., engineer, and finished in the year 1863, (two years ago the erecting shop was enlarged). The name, however, is still retained and the Works are called Long-Hedge Works. These Works are surrounded with a wall ten feet high. There are six gates, but the principal entrance to the Works is at the gate by the time-keeper's office; the other five gates are used for shunting purposes. Within this enclosure no person is allowed to go except on business, and this rule is strictly carried out. There are the boiler-shop, the tender-shop, erecting shop, copper-smiths' shop, fitting-shop, brass-finishers' shop, pattern-makers' shop, smiths' shop, boiler-house with three large boilers, which drive the large stationary engine. The whole of these buildings, which consists of a series of ranges, are substantially built of brick, with walls of immense thickness. On the south side is the stores department. At the east-end of the turnery is the Superintendent's office, clerks' offices, etc. The area between each shop has an intersection of rails communicating with the line.

The lower turnery is 250 feet long and 44 wide. It has twenty-five windows on either side; the dimensions of each window is 12 feet by 3, and a third portion of each window can be opened or closed at pleasure for ventilation; also three pairs of double doors of the same height as the windows, and wide enough to admit a truck or carriage. There are lines of rails laid parallel with the building, both on the outside and through the centre. Opposite each of the large doors, both inside and out, are turn tables to connect the shops with any part of the yard. The floor is laid with blocks of wood about five inches square. Around large steam-pipes are laid on either side of the shop to add to the comfort and convenience of the men. The shaft which gives motion to the machinery passes through the centre of the shop and the machinery on each side. Towards one extremity of this range of building is the engine house, in which are two beautifully-finished high and low pressure horizontal engines of one hundred horse power, which drive all the machinery and fan-blasts for smiths. There are three boilers, each thirty feet long, and six feet in diameter, having pressure of forty pounds upon every square inch. The shaft belonging to the stationary engine is forty-seven yards high.

In the lower turnery there is a double-headed slot-wheel, three large wheel lathes, and two small wheel lathes; the small are for carriage wheels. There are also three fifteen-inch lathes, two crank lathes for turning crank axles, two twelve-inch lathes, two large boring machines — one of these is a radial machine for boring tube plates; one boring machine for cylinders, also one large planing machine for the same purpose, and one hydraulic press for taking off axles. On the same basement with the turnery is the Loco. Manager's office.

Leaving the turnery we ascend a broad and substantial staircase of wood over-laid with sheet-lead, leading to the fitting-shop which is over the turning shop. On the same story is the brass-finishers' and pattern loft. The fitting-shop is light, clean, well ventilated, and comfortable. Here, as in the shop below, the shafting runs through the centre with a continuous branch of counter shafts on one side, extending the entire length of the building. The whole machinery is propelled by the same engine as that below. In this shop there is one large planing machine, nine shaping machines, six drilling machines, three slotting machines, one double-headed slot drill for cutting key-ways in axles, one twelve-inch lathe, four ten-inch lathes, four eight-inch lathes, two six-inch lathes, one ten-inch break lathe, six small planing machines of different sizes, four screwing machines, one nut-cutting machine, two grindstones, one hoist, twenty pairs of vices, etc., etc. In the brass-fitters' shop are four six-inch lathes in use for cocks, plugs, injectors, etc. Length of fitting, brass and pattern shops (inclusive) 406 feet.

The boiler shop is 200 feet in length and 48 feet in width. It has a stationary engine with machines for punching, drilling and bending the boiler-plates; also a powerful travelling crane, arranged for conveying boilers from one end of the shop to the other. The second building on the left-hand-side and facing the turnery is the erecting shop, 380 feet in length and 100 feet wide. This shop has a travelling table which runs from one end to the other, and is worked by a small engine. The use that is made of the table is to convey those engines which need repairing to the different pits. There are 42 pits in this shop with room for 42 engines. There are two travelling cranes above which run on girders; these are worked by the hand and are employed for engines. There is also a small stationary engine for driving drilling machine and grindstone, and each side has a row of vice-benches extending from one end of the shop to the other.

Not an uninteresting department is the smithery. Its length is 306 feet and it is 48 feet wide. On entering one seems to have got into a region where Vulcan and his Cyclops are at work, not forging thunderbolts for Jupiter, but giving shape and form to bars of half-molten iron, which shall afterwards be used in the structure of steam-engines and for other practical purposes. The scene is grand, and might supply a study for such painters as West, Stothard, Conway and Northcote. In the back ground is a depth of gloom, sombrous and murky which is relieved at intervals by the fierce glare of thirty fires. At as many anvils strong, athletic, Titan-like figures, with uplifted arm and heavy stroke scatter "as from smitten steel," sparks like brilliant stars, in all directions. Here are thirty smiths' forges, and the tools used by the smiths, as tongs, hammers, swages, etc., are arranged in racks against the walls. Here also are two steam-hammers, one fifteen tons, the other five tons. Either can be most scrupulously adjusted by aid of a small lever. Here also are furnaces, a stationary engine with fan, grindstone, and powerful shears for cutting bar-iron. Lines of rails run throughout the shop, so that the coal and iron can be conveyed to any part where it is required.

A Second Shop for Carriages, Waggons, etc., is being erected at an estimated cost of nearly £14,000.

The carriage shop is 370 feet long, 150 feet wide, 30 feet high in the centre, and is capable of containing 80 railway carriages. It is divided longitudinally into three parts by the two rows of iron pillars which support the roof. The central division is forty feet wide and is occupied by the traversing table which is used for shifting the carriages. The two side divisions are the parts for vehicles under repairs, and are also occupied by the workmens' benches, etc. The roof is composed of a light but strong iron framing covered first with deal boards, and with slates over all except the central part, which is composed almost entirely of glass. The floor consists of wood bricks, laid on a solid foundation of concrete, and is intersected by the iron rails for the carriages and traverser. At the south end are the offices, with the trimming shops above them. The shop is well and efficiently ventilated, and is furnished with a system of heating apparatus consisting of a double row of large steam-pipes passing all round under the windows. Water is laid on in ample quantities, and one of the regulations carried out with unvarying rule, is to fix hose pipes in two separate parts of the shops every night with stand pipes ready for instant use in case of fire. There are 130 windows in the shop exclusive of the roof. Most of the carriages are made of teak instead of mahogany, as being more durable as well as economical and not so likely to split when exposed to the heat of the sun.

The saw-mills are used for cutting the timber, with rack and vertical saws. It is then prepared by eleven other different machines, such as general joiner, rabbeting, grooving, tenoning, mortising, boring and moulding machines, of every description. The timber is first cut out with the hand-saw, and then shaped by a

large shaping machine 5 feet 4 by 2 feet 10, with two perpendicular spindles performing upwards of 1200 revolutions a minute. The saw-mills are well arranged,
the driving wheel and shafting being all underneath. Next to the saw-mills is an
engine-house in which is a horizontal engine of forty horse power with two large
boilers, sixty pounds pressure, made by Walter May and Co., Chelsea.

At the west end, and near "Long-Hedge House," is a small building containing the gas-meter; this, like the water-meter in the traffic yard, has its index taken
every morning to show the amount of gas that has been consumed in the works.

The stores department consists of a large building, with various offices for
the store keeper, clerks, and warehousemen. One half is upstairs which is fitted
up with shelves, tables and pigeon-holes for the various articles kept in stock. The
lower part is arranged for heavier goods, such as brass, copper, steel, and iron.
There is a large yard for goods of different descriptions, and for the purpose of
receiving goods brought by carriers, etc. The design of this department is to keep
for immediate use almost every article used on a railway, to supply all the departments with materials for the making and keeping of the line in good condition,
and to forward the goods as required to their destination on the line, and the quality of the goods is there determined before received for use.

In the running sheds engines are cleaned and running engines kept repaired,
etc.[43] There are 82 locomotives, 65 of which are daily running on the line. Since
the opening of the Ludgate Station on the London, Chatham and Dover Railway
Metropolitan Extension Line a very considerable portion of the Goods traffic is
carried on at Blackfriars.—Locomotive Superintendent, W. Kirtley, Esq.; Works

---

[43] Since the above was written, the semi-circular Engine Shed has been pulled down
and a very large quadrangular Engine Shed constructed in its place. The former shed was
inconveniently small and not at all adapted to the present emergency. It has been demonstrated by Mr. Kirtley that the system which has been so popular (with Locomotive Superintendents) in the early days of railways of using a turn-table or revolving platform for
turning locomotives into the direction required in sheds where they undergo repairing,
cleaning, etc., was at all times liable to cause not only delay in the departure of one engine,
but in the event of mishap to the turn-table itself, the whole stock of engines would be
locked up; hence the erection of the splendid new engine shed at the London, Chatham and
Dover Railway Locomotive Works, which is said to be one of the finest and most commodious of its kind in England. It stands upon about 1¾ acres, and some idea of its magni-
tude may be realized from some of the principal materials used in its construction: name-
ly, 40,000 cubic yards excavation; 6,000 cubic yards concrete; about 3½ million of bricks,
besides 250,000 blue paving bricks of the Staffordshire hard manufacture which form the
flooring; 30,000 feet of glass; 60,000 feet of slating, 260 tons of iron, and over three acres of
boards which form the roof, and the newly-invented steam and smoke conductors designed
by Messrs. Mills and Kirtley. There are also offices for the foremen of each department, and
separate mess-rooms for the men of various grades employed, wherein their every comfort
has been carefully studied, with lavatories, cooking apparatus, etc. Besides boiler-house
and standing engine for driving machinery, etc. Also a tank of enormous capacity, made by
Spencerlayh and Archer, of Rochester, to supply the engines with water from a well of considerable depth in case of failure of the regular supply from the Water Company's Works.
There is also a new coal stage, built upon an entirely new principle, from which engines can
be loaded with the necessary supply of coals in less than half the time previously occupied,

Manager, Mr. G. Leavers; Manager of Carriage Department, Inspector, etc., Mr. C. Spencer; Superintendent of Stores Department Mr. John Ward.

FOREMEN, (*Locomotive Department*).		FOREMEN, (*Carriage Department*).	
Erecting Shop	J. Fletcher.	Painters' Shop	W. Banks.
Fitting "	W. Siddon.	Coach-builders' "	G. Faulkner.
Turning "	T. Eaton.	Fitters' "	W. Churchill.
Smith "	R. Allen.	Trimmers' "	J. Gallop.
Boiler "	W. Benton.	Saw-mill "	C. Picton.
		Waggon "	F. Laraman.

The number of operatives employed inclusive of drivers and firemen is about 600. The men are intelligent and orderly; they, with myriads of their fellow-countrymen, are assisting in carrying out the great practical issues of civilization. Of such a class of noble-minded, generous-hearted, skilled mechanics and artisans, England may well be proud.

"What says each true workman, where'er he may toil
As bravely he joins in life's busy turmoil,
With each sinew brac'd stoutly by duty and love,
And the gaze of his soul fixed on heaven above.
Oh I'm king of a line of long renown,
And the sweat of my brow is my diamond crown;
I toil unrepining from morn till night,
For I bear in my bosom a heart brave and light,
And my labour no matter how hard it may be,
Brings ever a joy and a blessing to me."

The London Chatham and Dover Railway was opened 29th of September, 1860. Number of miles open 141. Gross Receipts including 31st December, 1873, £904,509.

The first railway train (London, Chatham and Dover) entered the City of London over the new Railway Bridge, Blackfriars, 6th October, 1864.

Adjacent to the Railway Viaduct and facing the south-eastern gate of Battersea Park is Sargent's Carpet Ground. Here during the Summer and Autumnal months a Gospel tent is pitched wherein Special Religious Services for the people are con-

---

with a similar diminution of labour. Another great feature in the approach to these Works is that the roads, sixteen in number, all lead from one line of rails. Each road, with pit in the engine shed, will hold five main-line locomotives or seven tank engines. The whole building will hold between eighty and ninety locomotives. The Works have been designed by Mr. W. Mills, C.E., and carried out by Mr. Charles Dickinson, the Contractor, and his Agent, Mr. D. Stubbings, and under the immediate superintendence of Mr. R. S. Jones, C. E., the engineer in charge of the works. Although nine months have only elapsed from the time of the demolition of the former structure to the erection of the New Engine Shed, etc., it is gratifying to state that under a merciful Providence no casualty such as might have been expected considering the number of locomotives running in and out daily has occurred. Mr. W. Wilkinson is foreman of this Branch of the Locomotive Department.

ducted by Messrs. Simmonds, Swindells, Waller, Rigley, Harris, Smith, Hewett, Crosby, Turpin, Twaites, Kirby, Reeve, Thompson, Eveleigh, Lane, and other well-known Christian workers.

Extracted from the Kensington News. — Amidst the various styles of ecclesiastical architecture which our modern amalgamation of various civilizations has produced, none strikes one as so peculiar as that which is called the preaching tent. Associated as this moveable structure is with the wandering life of the Eastern Arab, its consecration to purposes of modern Christian evangelization is a proof of the intense catholicity and energy of our modern religious life. While thousands of our home heathen never enter the sacred precincts of our churches or chapels, it is a blessing to find that they enter by hundreds inside the temporary canvas walls of our consecrated gospel tents. Very often the surroundings of the locality where these places are erected, the kind of services held in them, and the earnestness, homeliness, humanity, and appropriateness of the illustrations of the preachers who discourse at them, have beyond question, great attractions for the class of our Metropolitan inhabitants just mentioned. It calls for no surprise to find gigantic temporary structures of this kind erected amidst the uncultivated and populous "East" for the purposes of religious worship, but we hardly expect to find their tapering canvas roofs amidst the luxury of the "West."

A Canvas Cathedral.

But in these days of change, and strange things, we are not easily surprised, and consequently we passed by gospel tents at Kilburn and Kentish Town without expressing much wonder. Having a desire to see how the un-church and un-chapel going population of this mighty metropolis spent their Sunday out doors, we strolled to the classic ground of Chelsea and found ourselves on the north side of the bridge. This spot has been for several years the scene of rather unclassical and disorderly debates, and open air preaching. This arena of intellectual life was rather dull on this occasion; there was only the ordinary open air service and a few groups of the usual unintelligent and sceptical wranglers. Seeing nothing worthy in what we witnessed to detain us at this place, we strolled over the bridge, towards the canvas cathedral, which has lately been erected there. Having reached the middle of the bridge, the floating banners in the distance clearly indicate the locality where this place of public worship rears its canvas walls, and as we approach nearer we find the well known words "God is Love" neatly inscribed on one of them. At this portion of the road our attention is arrested by a few of the church-going population outside the entrance to Battersea Park, gathered round some open air preachers. At last we reach the south-eastern gate of Battersea Park, opposite which is the front of the canvas cathedral a substantial tent, capable of holding about 300 people. (The tent will seat 200). We were very much surprised to find at one of the entrances a well-executed and coloured diagram of the famous Babylonish temple of the Seven Spheres. We saw from the crowded nature of the audience that the service on this occasion was a very special one, for not only was the tent full but large groups of people surrounded the entrances. A small bill informed us that Mr. G. M. Turpin, a gentleman in connexion with the Christian vidence Society, was to preach this evening on Modern Discoveries and the Bible, llustrated with diagrams. As we entered the interior of the cathedral, we noticed hung behind the preacher a number of nicely drawn and strikingly coloured diagrams representing views of Nineveh, Babylon, Nimroud, slabs discovered in heir ruined palaces, a page of the annals of an Assyrian monarch, representations of a besieged city, and a copy of the Moabite stone.

The service was very simple in its character. It consisted of a few devout extempore prayers, reading a portion of Scripture, and the singing (accompanied with an harmonium) of some of Sankey's hymns. As may be imagined, our curiosity was excited as to how the preacher could make a sermon containing anything spiritual profitable to his hearers out of the pictures behind him. The portion of Scripture selected for his text only stimulated our curiosity for it was the beautiful words of our Lord contained in John c. 17 v. 17, "Sanctify them through thy truth; Thy word is truth." One felt inclined to say "Sanctification and pictures; a great deal of sanctification the preacher will get out of them for his audience." No sooner, however, has the preacher got into his introduction than the connection between his diagrams and his text is clearly apparent, for he was evidently going to talk about the truth of God's word as contained in the Bible. The text was divided into two parts; first the assertion that God's word was truth; secondly, the instrument of His people's sanctification. In treating of the first division of his discourse the preacher gave forth some very clear ideas on some of the most difficult topics, for revelation, the instrument through which it ought to come and the form by which it was to be transmitted to humanity in after ages, were all noticed, and men as the media, and the book as the written record, and not oral tradition, were shown to manifest the wisdom and condescension of God. "The Christian Church," said the preacher, claims that in the Bible they have a revelation of God's will, and the sublime idea of God in the possession of the Jews plainly proved that it came from God's own revelation. But objectors exist, and modern doubt cast suspicion on the sacred records. What then is the voice of modern discoveries? Is it for or against the credibility of the sacred record? In favour of reposing trust in its statements, for modern science and discovery and exploration have proved the truth of all the historical and geographical details of the Bible, removed many of its historical difficulties, and by its identification of sites of cities which were the subject of prediction, proved its fulfilment and thus borne testimony to the supernatural in the Bible. These propositions were supported by a vast array of facts drawn from the traditions of mankind, the newly-discovered palaces and libraries of Assyria, and the scholar's translation of its clay and stone records.

When the preacher treated the second portion of his theme, the intensely practical nature of his mind was clearly shewn in the way in which while asserting God's truth to be the instrument of the sanctification, he appealed to all present in a most solemn manner to put the important question—"Were they sanctified?" "If you are not you will never tread the golden streets of the New Jerusalem, but while your friends are passing in you will be shut out." Mr. Turpin evidently had the whole of his audience in his mind, for at the end of his discourse he pressed home on the juvenile portion of his audience the beauty of early piety by a contrast between the dying chimney-sweep and Lord Byron in which the character of the sweep shone to the disadvantage of the celebrated poet. Another hymn and prayer closed the interesting canvas cathedral service. Those present, both old and young, evidently enjoyed the service, for they listened with breathless attention for the 100 minutes which the preacher had occupied in delivering his glowing discourse. A brief prayer meeting closed this instructive Sunday evening, which if we may judge from the expressions of some of the audience, will not soon be forgotten. As we retired we felt that many such canvas cathedrals, with able preachers and hearty singing, would lay hold of large numbers of those who are at present outside ordinary religious influences.

The tent was purchased expressly for this object by Basil Wood Smith, Esq., a warm and devoted friend of the working classes and who is a member at present of the Parent Committee of the London City Mission. The tent was originally erected on the triangular piece of ground outside the south-eastern gate of Battersea Park before the roads were completed, with the sanction of Lord John Manners when his Lordship was in office as Chief Commissioner.

Among other respectable firms in the building trade within the Parish may be mentioned the firm of Messrs. Lathey Brothers, Builders, 1, St. George's Road, New Road. Messrs. Lathey Brothers were the builders of St. George's Vicarage House, Christ Church Schools and Residences, Infant School in Orkney Street, St. Saviour's Church, the enlargement of St. George's Church, and the enlargement of St. George's National Schools. Also a Mortuary built in 1876 in the Churchyard of St. Mary's from designs by Mr. W. White, Architect, and the re-interment of all coffins, 1875, in the vaults or crypt under the church 424 in all. Some of these coffins were brought here from St. Bartholomew's Church, Royal Exchange, in the city of London, in 1840. A Record was made of the Inscriptions on all the coffins which were re-interred. This document, which is in the possession of Messrs. Lathey Bros., would form an interesting Obituary if published.

H.P. Horse Nail Company's Factory.

The H.P. Horse Nail Company's (Limited) Factory, New Road, has at present machinery capable of turning out one million nails per day. With the exception of a few mechanics most of the employés are young women. Of late years horse nails have become an important branch of industry and a leading article in trade, the consumption, indeed, being very large; and when it is considered that each horse has in its four hoofs 28 or 30 nails, and that these nails are wearing out all day and all night, and require renewing about every month, and that in Great Britain and Ireland there are at the present time not less than 3,000,000 horses, representing a demand exceeding a thousand million nails per annum the trade is entitled to rank with others in importance and influence. Mr. J. A. Huggett, the inventor of the Patent Machinery employed at this factory for the manufacture of horse nails, has hit the right nail on the head, the quality of the nails having met with the general approval of veterinary surgeons, farriers, and ironmongers. The quality of the iron of which the nails are manufactured has its perfection attributed to three causes:—First, it is the best Swedish charcoal iron; secondly, it is heated in the Siemens furnace; and lastly, which certainly is not the least important, it passes through a rolling-mill worked by steam power, each roller weighs about ten cwt.—Manager, Charles Moser, Esq.

Hugh Wallace's Vitriol Works were situated in the New Road; Schofield and Co.'s Steam Saw-Mills and Stone Works, Stewart's Lane. The saw frames are worked by fly wheels and connecting shafts so constructed that the frame is always level be it ever so high a block sawing; this is done by lengthening or shortening the shaft. By some persons the frames are considered the easiest working ones in London. The moulding machines are by Hunter, Queen's Road, Battersea, specially adapted for string courses and steps. About eighty men and boys are employed at these works.

ST. GEORGE'S CHURCH.

St. George's Church, its clergy, its graveyard, epitaphs and inscriptions (St. Andrew's Temporary Iron Church).

ST. GEORGE'S CHURCH, Battersea—The following particulars respecting this Church may not be uninteresting. The living is a vicarage of the yearly value of £240 with residence in the gift of Trustees.

The Chapel-of-Ease, as St. George's was called, in Battersea Fields, was built partly by a rate and partly by grant from the Parliamentary Commissioners at a cost of £2,819; it is a neat building in the style of English architecture, by Edward Blore, Esq., Architect. Its erection began September 18, 1827. It was consecrated August 5th, 1828, by Dr. Sumner, Lord Bishop of Winchester, and the first church his Lordship consecrated in his diocese. The Rev. J. G. Weddell was the first clergyman appointed. He held the living twenty-five years: died June, 1852. Within this hallowed sanctuary the venerable, esteemed and truly honoured servant of Christ the Rev. John Garwood, late Secretary of the London City Mission, laboured as curate in charge for nine years previous to Mr. Weddell's death. The Rev. H. B. Poer was appointed in 1852. It was made a District Church in 1853. The churchyard was closed as a burial ground in 1858. The Rev. E. S. Goodhart was appointed in 1859: he remained ten months. The Rev. Burman Cassin was appointed in 1860: he resigned and was instituted at St. Paul's, Bolton, 1872: he preached his last (valedictory) sermon December 31, 1872, at a watch-night service.

The Rev. John Callis was appointed January, 1873. During his time the Church underwent alterations. These were begun August 24, 1874, when the side galleries were removed and the church enlarged by the addition of two aisles at the cost of £1,700. The church will accommodate 800. The church was re-opened by the Right Reverend Harold Browne, Lord Bishop of Winchester, November 21st, 1874, at 4 o'clock p.m. The Rev. John Callis left for South Heigham, Norwich, July, 1875.

The Rev. Thomas Lander, M.A., now holds the living, he was appointed August, 1875. The Rev. T. Kirk ordained and appointed Curate to St. George's, September 24th, 1876. Previously to his ordination he had laboured for twenty-six years in connection with the London City Mission, and was much beloved and respected in the district among the people to whom he has been and still is so much blessed.

The population of the Ecclesiastical parish in 1871 was 16,172.[44] The register dates from the year 1858. The area is 443 acres.—John Gwynn, Samuel Lathey, Churchwardens.

According to the census of 1881, the inhabited houses and population of Bat-

---

[44] St. Andrew's Temporary Iron Church, Patmore Street, was opened on St. Andrew's Day, Saturday, Nov. 30, 1878, by the Bishop of Guildford, late Dr. Utterton. The persons who took part in the service were Canon Clarke, Revs. Lander, Hamilton and Kirk. Rev. G. Hamilton is the Mission Clergyman. Some few years ago a gentleman offered to put up a Church in South London. St. George's Parish, Battersea, was named as being in need of one. A short time after the promise was made the gentleman died. His widow anxious to carry out her deceased husband's intentions, set apart the amount for the purchase and removal of the Iron Church, which then stood in Chelsea.

tersea were as follows:—

	Number of Inhabited Houses.	Number of Inhabitants.
St Mary's	3758	24595
Christ Church	2011	14404
St Peter's	1183	8919
St John's	1068	7069
St Saviour's	1747	14172
St Philip's	2444	17428
St George's	2380	20612
Total	14591	107199

"I love her gates, I love the road;
The church adorned with grace
Stands like a palace built for God
To show his milder face."

—*Watts.*

At the east end of the interior and south of the pulpit a white marble tablet mounted on a dark marble slab has recently been erected. Within a wreath of virgin marble most artistically executed is the following epitaph engraved. "In memory of Elizabeth Maria Graham, of Clapham Common, died December 14, 1874, aged 79, through whose devoted and indefatigable labours this Church, the Vicarage, and Mission-room were built and the St. George's Schools were founded. 'The love of Christ constraineth us.'—2nd Cor. v. 14. 'The harvest truly is great but the labourers are few, pray ye therefore the Lord of the harvest, that He would send forth labourers into His harvest.'"—Luke x. 2.

"They that feared the Lord spake often one to another; and the Lord hearkened and heard it, and a book of remembrance was written before him for them that feared the Lord, and that thought upon his name. And they shall be mine saith the Lord of Hosts, in that day when I make up my jewels; and I will spare them, as a man spareth his own son that serveth him."—Malachi iii. 16-17.

In St. George's Churchyard the ground has been levelled and the hillocks have disappeared to make it resemble more a garden or field with flat grassy surface studded here and there with shrubberies than a receptacle of the dead, there are however some "sacred memorial," a few grave stones etc., which indicate to the passer-by that this was formerly used as a place of interment. We will just pause to read some of the inscriptions. At the east-end of the churchyard is the vault of the Rev. John Grenside Weddell, twenty-five years pastor of this flock, who died the 23d of July, 1852, aged 75 years.

"I have sinned but Christ hath died."

Also in the same vault are the remains of Caroline the beloved wife of the Rev. J. G. Weddell, who died the 22nd of December 1839, aged 64 years.

"Whose faith follow, considering the end of their conversation. Jesus Christ the same yesterday, and to-day, and for ever." — *Hebrews xiii. 7.*

A few yards from this spot a head-stone is erected "Sacred to the memory of Mrs. Ann Puttick of Nine Elms, who departed this life Oct. 5th, 1855, aged 64 years. Also of Henry her beloved husband, interred at the Cemetery, Battersea. 'Even so Father for so it seemed good in thy sight.'"

Here is a vault sacred to the memory of Leonora the wife of John Charles Mc-Mullens, Esq., of Lavender Hill, in this parish, who died 24th June, 1813, aged 35 years. The epitaph states,

> "Faithful and meek she bore the will
> Of Him who to a troubled sea,
> In powerful words said 'peace be still,'
> My grace sufficient is for thee."

Also that of her husband, J. C. McMullens, Esq., who died 30th September, 1855.

On the west-side of the gravel walk leading to the entrance of the church a stone slab covers the grave of all that was of Louisa, wife of Mr. J. A. Michell of this parish, who died in child-bed on the 24th November, 1834; aged 23 years.

> Far, far remote from objects dear,
> A virtuous wife here rests;
> Who ever studied while on earth,
> To comfort and caress.
> Her husband, and her parents dear,
> Now mourn departed worth,
> Affections was her constant theme,
> While she had breath on earth.
> In child-birth first her troubles rose,
> Her babe on earth abides;
> Extreme her grief, extreme her pain,
> Delivered, and she died.
> Her husband now consoles himself
> With hopes not found in vain,
> That as her happy soul's at rest,
> His loss will be her gain.

Also of Sarah Gywnn, wife of James Gywnn, who died May 28, 1850, aged 67. And also of James Gywnn, who died January 28, 1851, aged 77.

Hard by is another grave-stone sacred to the memory of Mrs. Elizabeth Stewart, widow of the late Lieut. James Stewart, R.N., who departed this life on the 10th of — — aged 60 years. The letters on this slab are so eaten away by the tooth of time that we could not decipher the date.

A head-stone marks the grave of Margaret Young, who died August 13th, 1855, aged 58 years. Added to this inscription are the words:

> "For now shall I sleep in the dust;

And thou shalt seek me in the morning,
But I shall not be."—The book of Job vii. 21.

The epitaph on another slab is as follows: "Blessed are the dead who die in the Lord"—so died on the 24th of May, 1829, aged 56 years—Mary, the beloved wife of B. Jonathan Broad, late Chief Secretary at the Rolls. Also beneath this stone are deposited Barber Jonathan Broad, Esq., many years an inhabitant of this parish, who died the 10th of July, 1831, aged 61 years.

On another grave-stone is an inscription sacred to the memory of Alice Buckney, daughter of Thomas and Charlotte Buckney, of this parish, who died 9th August, 1830, aged 16 days.

Against the west wall in the rear of the houses in Ceylon Street is a head-stone erected sacred to the memory of Elizabeth Dicker, the beloved wife of Job Dicker, who departed this life May 6th, 1858, in the 55th year of her age. At the bottom of this epitaph are inscribed the lines so familiar to us and which all have seen in many a churchyard:

Afflictions sore long time I bore;
Doctors were in vain!
Death and disease—and God did please
To ease me of my pain.

Weep not for me, my children dear,
Nor shed for me a single tear:
In heaven I hope we all shall meet,
Then all our joys will be complete.

Here is a stone in memory of Richard, third son of Henry Roston and Amelia Bowker, who died Sept. 18th, 1849, aged 6 years. His dying words were: "Suffer little children to come unto me, and forbid them not." Also Elizabeth, who died Sept. 23rd, 1849, aged 1 year 3 months. Also Alfred, who died Oct. 18, 1849, aged 4 years. Also Mr. Henry Roston Bowker, father of the above children, who died July 23rd, 1852, aged 40 years. Also at the foot of this grave lie the remains of Mr. William Robbins, grandfather to the above children, who departed this life July 1st, 1858, aged 71 years. "Boast not thyself of to-morrow, for thou knowest not what a day may bring forth."

Near the wall at the south-side of the burial ground stands a solitary head-stone sacred to the memory of Sarah Fisher, relict of Jonathan Roundell Fisher, late of Cumberland and Otley, Yorkshire, who departed this life 17th September, 1854, aged 67. The memory of the just is blessed.

Near the entrance to the church at the south-side stands a plain head-stone with no adornment, sacred to the memory of Elizabeth Clunie, during 40 years the beloved friend of Mrs. Graham's family, of Clapham Common. Born at Hull, August 29th, 1793. Died at Clapham Common June 22nd, 1853. Carefully trained by pious parents and by faith engrafted in youth into Christ the living vine. She brought forth throughout her whole life the precious fruits which spring from that all important union, and abiding in Him her end was peace.

Scripture Readers, Mr. F. Vellenoweth, 62, St. George's Road; Mr. C. Brooks, 9, St. George's Road; City Missionary, Mr. H. Langston; London Mission Bible Woman, Miss Hulbert, 1, Ceylon Street.

CHRIST CHURCH is a composition of the early Lancet style, consisting of chancel, nave, aisles and north and south transepts, with tower and spire built of Kentish rag and Bath stone, raised by subscriptions at a cost of £5,556, with sittings for 900. Interiorly it has two small galleries. It was designed by Mr. Charles Lee, and repaired, decorated and re-heated under the superintendence of Mr. E. C. Robins. The first stone of this elegant church was laid by the Bishop of Sodor and Man, on May the 27th, 1847. The living is a vicarage in the gift of the Vicar of St. Mary's. The income is derived from the pew rents. The area is 408 acres and the population of the Ecclesiastical parish in 1871 was 18,720. The Rev. Samuel Bardsley was the first Vicar of Christ Church but not the first minister. For some years it was a Chapel-of-Ease and was supplied by the Vicar of the Mother Church. The Rev. Samuel Bardsley was there from 1861 to 1867. The schools, the Vicarage, and the school in Orkney Street were built during his time. He resigned the living to become Rector of Spitalfields, and was succeeded by the Rev. Edward Cumming Ince, M.A., of Jesus College, Cambridge. In May, 1877, Mr. Ince resigned having suffered from enfeebled health, amid the painful regrets of his beloved flock, who for ten years had listened to his thorough evangelical discourses and had profited so much under his faithful ministry.

Christ Church, its clergy.

The Rev. Stopford Ram, M.A., Secretary of the Church of England Temperance Society, Instituted (Hospital Sunday) June 17th, 1877, left on account of ill health, July, 1880, and died at Bournemouth, May 22nd, 1881, and buried on Ascension day.

"There remaineth, therefore, a rest for the people of God."

> He has gone to his rest, like the bright summer sun
> As it sinks in the west when its day's work is done,
> But only to leave us a little while here,
> To shine in another and far distant sphere.
>
> He has gone to his rest—the journey is o'er,
> And safely he lands on that bright, blissful shore,
> Where banished for ever is sorrow and pain,
> 'Mid the harps that are tuned to a holier strain.
>
> He has gone to his rest—no longer to roam,
> The Master has called His dear labourer home;
> Triumphant he enters the mansions of bliss,
> And welcomes the change from a world such as this.
>
> He has gone to his rest—the race has been run,
> And vict'ry accomplished through Jesus the Son.
> Unwearied by conflict, he knew no defeat;

His trophies are laid at our Great Captain's feet.

He has gone to his rest—we shall miss the dear voice
Which so often on earth made our spirits rejoice.
Yet mourn we? Ah, no! If in Jesus we reign
To-morrow we all shall be meeting again.

He has gone to his rest—that sweet Zion to share
With some of his flock awaiting him there;
Like him let us labour, the right to uphold;
Brave, patient, enduring, true-hearted, and bold.

Alfred Sargant.

The Rev. H. Guildford Sprigg, M.A., the present Vicar, commenced his duties, September, 1880.

"Holy, holy, holy: Lord God of Sabaoth.
Heaven and earth are full: Of the majesty of thy glory.
The glorious company of the apostles: Praise thee.
The goodly fellowship of the prophets: Praise thee.
The noble army of martyrs: Praise thee.
The holy church throughout all the world: Doth acknowledge thee."

— Te Deum laudamus.

"Serve the Lord with gladness: Come before his presence with singing."— *Psalm c.* 2.

Mr. Lowres, of Plough Lane, an energetic City Missionary, has laboured in Christ Church district for nearly twelve years, and his local Superintendents were the Rev. S. Bardsley and the Rev. E. C. Ince.

Mr. Warren, in an adjoining district, is another devoted Missionary.

ST. JOHN'S CHURCH.

St. John's Church.

ST. JOHN'S CHURCH, Usk Road, was completed from the designs of Mr. E. C. Robins, selected in competition. It is a remarkably inexpensive church. It provides accommodation for about 750 persons at a cost of £4 10s. per head. The church received a grant from the Incorporative Society for Building Churches upon one-third of the sittings being made free. It is designed in the early English style, with nave, north and south aisles and apsidal chancel, a small western gallery and two bell turrets. Messrs. Sharpington and Cole were the builders, who executed the work for the sum of £3,300. (St. John's Parsonage was built by the same architect). The foundation stone of St. John's was laid August 6, 1862. The consecration and opening took place May 5th, 1863. The living is a Vicarage in the gift of the Vicar of St. Mary's. The area is 157 acres, and the population of the Ecclesiastical parish in 1871 was 7,839. The district assigned to the church was formed out of the parishes of St. Mary's Battersea, and St. Anne, Wandsworth, by an Order of Council bearing date July 27, 1863—(the register dates from this period). The new parish was legally constituted and named the Consolidated Chapelry of St. John, Battersea. The first Vicar of the new parish was the Rev. Edwin Thompson, D.D., who from beginning his work with services in a room in Price's Candle Factory, afterwards, lived to be instrumental in building the two Churches of St. John and St. Paul, together with the Schools in Usk Road, erected 1866, and Parsonage House, Wandsworth Common; a noble monument of his untiring energy and zeal. He died suddenly February 2nd, 1876, aged 51 years. The present Vicar of St. John's is the Rev. William John Mills Ellison, M.A., Wadham College, Oxford.

The windows in the chancel representing John the Baptist, St. Peter, St. Andrew, St. John; the last supper and the ascension to the glory of God, and in memory of Daniel Watney, departed March 16, 1874, aged 74, are erected by his son John Watney.

On the south side of the church the Memorial Windows representing David and Samuel to the glory of God, and in memory of W. H. Hatcher, at rest August 2nd, 1879, aged 58. Erected by Friends and Sunday Scholars. "Their works do follow them." — *Rev. xiv.* 13.

On the north side the Memorial Windows representing St. Paul and St. Barnabas, in loving memory of a dear mother, Martha Colden, who died August 25, 1880. Erected by her only child M. A. B. S. Estimated cost of each window £15 15s. Guard and fixing to each £2 2s.

"Know ye that the Lord he is God: it is he that hath made us, and not we ourselves; we are his people, and the sheep of his pasture." — *Psalm c.* 3.

St. Paul's Church.

ST. PAUL'S situated on St. John's Hill, is a Chapel-of-Ease to St. Mary's Battersea, designed by Mr. Coe for the late Rev. Dr. Thompson. It is a stone structure consisting of chancel, apsidal, nave, aisles and tower with spire. It was built at a cost of about £6,300.

"Those that be planted in the house of the Lord shall flourish in the courts of our God." — *Psalm xvii.* 13.

St. Philip's Church.

ST. PHILIP'S CHURCH, Queen's Road, is a Gothic stone building consisting of chancel, nave, aisles and transept with tower, built from the designs of Mr.

James Knowles, Junr., at a cost of £13,000. A considerable portion of this sum was given by P. W. Flower, Esq., the remainder was raised by public subscriptions. The church will accommodate nearly 1,000 persons. The living is a Vicarage, yearly value £200, in the gift of the Bishop of Winchester, and held by the Rev. John Hall.

A Mission in connection with the Bishop of Winchester's Fund was commenced in the month of June, 1869, in a house lent by the proprietor for the purpose, in Queen's Road, Battersea Fields. Services and Parochial Institutions were then established, which have become the foundation of those now in active operation.

On July 13th, 1870, the New Church of St. Philip was finished, and consecrated by Dr. Samuel Wilberforce, Bishop of the diocese, and who also held his Trinity Ordination at the Church of St. Philip the year before he died.[45] On May 16th, 1871, a District formed out of the Parishes of St. Mary, St. George, and Christ Church, Battersea was attached to the Church, and published in the "London Gazette." On the 6th July, 1871, an Endowment of £200 per annum, which had been promised by the Ecclesiastical Commissioners, was legally secured to the Cure of St. Philip, and published in the "London Gazette" on the 26th of the same month. The payments were to date from the day on which the District was assigned (viz., May 16th, 1871), and the first payment was to be made on November 1st, 1871. The seats are free and the expenses of the church have to be defrayed by the weekly offertory.

A New Organ has been built by Messrs. Hill and Son and placed in the north chancel aisle; the cost with the platform is £516 1s. 11d. If, when the Church of St. Philip was erected, the original design of having a lofty spire with flying buttresses had been carried out, St. Philip's Church would have been the most magnificent Ecclesiastical structure in Battersea.—Churchwardens, W. G. Baker, A. W. Wilkinson.

"They continued stedfastly in the apostles' doctrine and fellowship, and in breaking of bread and in prayer."—*Acts ii.* 42.

"Blessed is the man that heareth me, watching daily at my gates, waiting at the posts of my doors."—*Proverbs viii.* 34.

> We'll crowd Thy gates with thankful songs,
> High as the heavens our voices raise;
> And earth with her ten thousand tongues
> Shall fill Thy courts with sounding praise.
> Wide as the world is Thy command,
> Vast as eternity Thy love;
> Firm as a rock Thy truth must stand,
> When rolling years shall cease to move.

> —*Watts.*

The construction of Queen's Road, etc., on Park-town, Battersea Estate, cost

---

[45] Bishop S. Wilberforce, born September 7th, 1805, died 19th of July, 1873, through a fall from a horse.

Mr. Flower about £3,000.—C. Merrett, Clerk of the Works for the Estate.

A New Railway Station has been erected in the Queen's Road, on the South-Western Line.

St. Mark's Church.

ST. MARK'S, Battersea Rise, is a Gothic building, and consists of chancel, nave, aisles, transept with porch, and western vestibule and handsome crypt. The corner-stone was laid by the Right Rev. Dr. Harold Browne, Bishop of Winchester, November 11th, 1873, and it was dedicated by his Lordship September 30th, 1874. The Architect is Mr. William White, F.S.A., and the total cost has been £6,500. It is seated for 600, with backs and kneelers throughout. Mr. T. Gregory, of Battersea, builder. The living is a Vicarage, in the gift of the Vicar of St. Mary's.

"The rich and the poor meet together; the Lord is the Maker of them all." — *Proverbs xxii.* 2.

The dedication festival of this church, in which the late Philip Cazenove took so warm an interest, was agreeably marked by the placing of a stained window of two lights, representing St. Philip and St. James, in the north transept. The name of Mr. Cazenove is inscribed on the tablet of a glass mosaic, set in alabaster, and sunk in the brick-work of the wall beneath the window. The tablet is a material much used for church purposes by the executants, Messrs. Powell, Whitefriars, and called "opus sectile." The design is simple and chaste, as befitted one whose unostentatiousness was one of his leading characteristics. The window was placed in the transept by his two daughters. — *South London Press*, May 15th, 1880.

St. Luke's Chapel-of-Ease.

ST. LUKE'S CHAPEL-OF-EASE, Nightingale Lane, is a pretty Iron Church, originally erected on Battersea Rise in 1868, was moved in September, 1873, to the adjacent plot, and used by the congregation while St. Mark's was being built. On November 14, 1874, having been once more removed to its present site it was dedicated anew in the name of St. Luke by the Bishop of Guildford.

"O come let us worship and bow down, let us kneel before the Lord our Maker." — *Psalm xcv. 6.*

ST. MATTHEW'S, Rush-hill Road, Lavender Hill, is a Chapel of Ease to St. Mary's, it is built in the Early English Style of Architecture, has vaulted roof and sacristy, seats 550, and cost about £3,000. Mr. W. White, F.S.A., Architect; Mr. W. H. Williams, Builder. The Dedication Service was conducted by the Right Reverend J. S. Utterton, D.D., Bishop Suffragan of Guildford, on Saturday, 28th of April, 1877, at 3 p.m. The Rev. W. B. Buckwell is the Officiating Minister.

"Blessed are they that dwell in thy house; they shall be still praising thee." — *Psalm lxxxiv. 4.*

St. Saviour's Church.

ST. SAVIOUR'S CHURCH, Lower Wandsworth Road, now called Battersea

Park Road, erected by Messrs. Lathey Brothers at a cost of £4,000 from the designs of Mr. E. C. Robins. It accommodates 700 persons and is designed in the early French Gothic style faced with Kentish rag and Bath stone dressings. It consists of a nave with clerestory, north and south aisles and rectangular chancel with small western gallery over the entrance lobby. There is a bell turret at the east end. The chancel has been decorated in color by Messrs. Heaton and Butler. The glazing is of cathedral glass. The living is a vicarage in the gift of the trustees. The population of the district is about 11,500. The foundation stone was laid by H. S. Thornton, Esq., January 4th, 1870. The consecration of the church on the 19th October, 1871, by the late Samuel Wilberforce, D.D., Lord Bishop of Winchester. The offertory amounted to the sum of £40, which was added to the Church Building Fund. The Petition to consecrate was read by the Rev. C. E. Ince, Vicar of Christ Church, Battersea, and the deed of conveyance was presented to the Bishop by W. Evill, Esq., one of the most generous and zealous friends of the undertaking. The litany was read by the Rev. J. MacCarthy. At the evening service an appropriate sermon was preached by the Rev. E. C. Ince, and at the opening services on Sunday, the 22nd, the morning sermon was preached by the Rev. J. MacCarthy, and that in the evening by the Rev. E. Daniel. The Rev. J. MacCarthy was the first Vicar.

The institution of the present Vicar, the Rev. Samuel Gilbert Scott, M.A., Magdalen College, Oxford, took place on Sunday, April the 29th, 1877. The Bishop of Guildford instituted the Vicar after the Nicene Creed. At the close of the sermon the Bishop celebrated Holy Communion; there were 55 communicants. The offertory on the day amounted to nearly eight pounds. Curate, the Rev. W. J. Harkness, B.A., Emmanuel College, Cambridge. Churchwardens, John Elmslie, John Merry. Lay Readers, with Episcopal sanction, Mr. Hussey, 32, Chatham Street; Mr. Hann, 2, Millgrove Street. Mission Women, Mrs. Wootton, 23, Warsill Street; Mrs. Collins, 5, Chatham Street.

"Enter into his gates with thanksgiving, and into his courts with praise: be thankful unto him, and bless his name for the Lord is good; his mercy is everlasting; and his truth endureth to all generations." — *Psalms c.* 4-5.

Mr. Crosby, a Missionary in this district, held Evangelistic Services at a Mission Hall in Arthur Street, Battersea Park Road.

St. Peter's Church.

ST. PETER'S CHURCH, Plough Lane, is a beautiful Gothic structure built of red brick, with chancel, nave, aisles, and lofty tower with spire pointing like a finger to the sky as if to remind man that when the Saturday night of this world shall arrive and earth's trials are o'er "there remaineth a rest for the people of God." — *Hebrews iv.* 9.

In the tower are four illuminated dials, by Messrs. Gillett & Bland of Croydon. The Church has sittings for about 820. The top-stone of the spire of St. Peter's Church was laid about 5 p.m., on the 24th of April, 1876, by Mr. Toone, in the presence of Mr. White the Architect, Mr. Carter the Builder, Mr. Williams the Clerk of the Works, and a few others, with the formula "In the faith of Jesus Christ and to he glory of His Holy Name we lay the top-stone of this spire of St. Peter's Church, n the Name of the Father, and of the Son, and of the Holy Ghost, Amen." A crowd of well-wishers below watched the ceremony with interest. The corner-stone of this church was laid by the Bishop of Winchester, on St. Peter's Day of 1875, and on the same festival, June 29th, 1876, it was Consecrated by the same prelate. At the Consecration Service the Bishop of Guildford read the Gospel, the Rev. S. Cooper Scott the Epistle, and the Bishop of the Diocese preached the Sermon from the words of the Gospel "Thou art Peter and on this rock I will build my Church." There were 120 communicants. The Bishop of Guildford preached in the evening to an overflowing congregation.

The interior of St. Peter's Church is spacious. The rich carving of the capitals has been executed by Mr. Harry Hems, of Exeter, as also the pulpit and font. The pulpit is of stone with alabaster figures introduced in the panels representing St. Peter, St. Paul, St. John, Isaiah, King Solomon, Moses and Noah. The bowl of the font is also of alabaster supported by angels carved in the same material. The pavement is beautifully tessellated and has several scriptural illustrations. The seats are fixed—these and all the internal wood-work are varnished. The cost of erection was about £10,500. The belfry at present contains one bell only, a tenor of six, it cost £120, and cast with the words on it, *When I do call, come serve God all!* It was rung on St. Peter's day, 1876. The Register dates from 1876. The living is a Vicarage, in the gift of the Vicar of St. Mary, and held by the Rev. John Toone, B.A., of St. John's College, Cambridge.

"I was glad when they said unto me let us go into the house of the Lord. Peace be within thy walls, and prosperity within thy palaces." —*Psalm cxxix.* 1-7.

St. Peter's Temporary Church and School-room was completed in 1874, at a cost of £1,200. St. Peter's Vicarage was formerly the residence of Mr. Burney.

Temporary Church of the Ascension.—St. Michael's Church.

TEMPORARY CHURCH OF THE ASCENSION, Lavender Hill.—A permanent church adjacent is now in course of erection, and being raised by voluntary contributions. The Rev. J. B. Wilkinson is the Officiating Minister. The foundation stone of this church was laid by the Earl of Glasgow, 1st of June, 1876. This structure is being built of Bath stone and red bricks, and is groined throughout with stone ribs and brick panels. The foundation stone is situated under the "altar." James Brooks, Architect, 35, Wellington Street, Strand; Mr. Chessam, Builder, Shoreditch.

"A day in thy courts is better than a thousand; I had rather be a door-keeper in the house of my God, than to dwell in the tents of wickedness." —*Psalm lxxxiv.* 10.

ST. MICHAEL'S CHURCH, Chatham Road, Bolingbroke Grove, Wandsworth Common—the Memorial to the Rev. H. B. Verdon and Mr. Philip Cazenove, the eminent and successful merchant. The Temporary Iron Mission Church which for the last nine years had been used as a Chapel-of-Ease to the Mother Church of St. Mary, Battersea, and the site on which the present edifice is erected were the gifts of the latter gentleman. Henry Boutflower Verdon was born December 8, 1846.

Himself the son of an excellent clergyman was educated at the Clergy Orphan School, Canterbury, from which he went to Jesus College, Cambridge, as Rustat Scholar and took his degree in 1868. After a period of study at Cuddensdon Theological College he began clerical work as a curate under the Rev. Aubrey Price, M.A., Vicar of St. James', Clapham, where the poor speak in affectionate terms of his memory. In the Spring of 1872 he became curate of Battersea, a few weeks after the appointment of the present Vicar. From the first Mr. Verdon took special interest in the district known as Chatham Road, Bolingbroke Grove, and the residents there were very much attached to him. The Sunday evening services and Sunday Schools held in St. Michael's Chapel were objects of his unremitting care. He acted as the Secretary of the Committee during the time St. Mark's Church was being built. He was an active member of the Charitable Organization Committee—he promoted the work of the Royal Society for the Prevention of Cruelty to Animals and established a mission Branch in Battersea. His marriage in January, 1879, to Miss Wheeler, was the cause of much congratulation; but before the expiration of many months this conjugal relationship was to be severed. Had he lived the Incumbency of St. Mark's Church would have been transferred to him. He died of a rapid consumption October 10, 1879.

The two Memorial Stones were laid in the Chancel of the Church (which is now completed) by the Archbishop of Canterbury. "The Archbishop after tapping them with the mallet saying at each 'In the faith of Jesus Christ we place this stone for a memorial of thy faithful servant whose name is written thereon and in the name of the Father and of the Son and of the Holy Ghost,' and the choir chanting Amen. The stone on the south side of the chancel bore the inscription carved in antique on a gilt ground, 'Henry Boutflower Verdon, M.A., Æt. 33 obt. X. Oct. A.D. 1879,' and that on the north side, the words, 'In mema. grata Philip Cazenove, Æt. 81 obt. XX. Jan. A.D. 1880.' After laying the stones the Archbishop delivered a short address in the course of which he said that the two servants of God whose names were on the memorial stones worked hand in hand together for good though separated from each other by fifty years of life; one dying almost in his prime and the other living on to a long old age but each dedicated to the service of God, one ministering in the sanctuary and daily officiating in the house of God, the other taking part during a long life in the trade and exchange of this great city, busy with the arrangements by which human industry is promoted. Both different yet wonderfully alike, and both judicious servants bearing the stamp of their heavenly Master and serving Him bravely, faithfully and laboriously. Let them be thankful that this space of fifty made no difference in the two men. As we got old we began to think that wisdom and goodness were with the old only, but he thanked God that in His Church there never had failed and never would fail a succession of faithful servants century after century to carry on the work which the Lord loves and which will make the world at last ready for His second coming. The name on the one stone might be little known beyond his own neighbourhood or the name of the other beyond the city of London, but they were known to their heavenly Master whom they served faithfully, and in His book are the names of both written. The memory of the young man whose name was on the one stone would linger long among those whom he loved and the poor and the sick to whom

e had endeared himself and for whom he faithfully laboured, but for the speaker
his thoughts and friendship were with the old man whose name was on the other
tone. Five and twenty years ago when the speaker entered on the laborious work
of the See of London, the first to welcome and assist him was Mr. Cazenove. He belonged to the noble band who helped Bishop Bloomfield from the very first. Those
five and twenty years had been as laboriously spent in doing good as the years
that had gone before. When those men first entered on the work how different was
his suburb of London to what it is now. Great wars had absorbed the attention
of men, and a large population had grown up before people knew it, and before
men had thought of the duty of meeting the spiritual wants of the new suburbs. If
t had not been for the noble band who gathered round Bishop Bloomfield what
a different account would have had to be rendered now. Let us trust and believe
that when all of us have passed away it will be found that God has raised up a
succession of faithful servants; men of every business and profession who will still
regard the profession of Jesus Christ as the most noble of all, for no profession was
more noble than the service of the Heavenly King. Let us trust that with dangers
around us the spirit of vigorous Christianity may continue to be triumphant as it
had been in so many instances already. Let us trust to the good work begun and
carried forward during the last fifty years will flourish with God's blessing for
many years to come."

"The new church is a plain Gothic structure built of red and stock bricks, and
is 90 feet long by 70 feet wide. It consists of a nave, chancel, and two aisles, surmounted with a timber roof of three spans covered with red tiles. There are two
entrances, one in Chatham Road and the other in Darley Road; the former surmounted by a figure of St. Michael in conflict with the serpent. There is also a small
tower containing a bell weighing 2 cwt. There is a commodious crypt beneath the
chancel. The latter contains three rows of stalls for the clergy and choir, and is
lighted by six small windows of stained glass, in each of which there is an angel
exquisitely executed from the Studio of Messrs. Lavers, Barraud and Westlake. It
is also intended to place a reredos of white marble here. The altar is approached
from the nave by nine steps. The nave communicates with the aisles by large Gothic arches supported on octagonal pillars of 'granolith'—a material composed of
granite chips and Portland cement. The floor is of blocks of wood and the building
is 'pewed' with open benches to accommodate about 750 worshippers. The pulpit
(a memorial gift by Mr. Verdon's widow) is of carved oak with a base of Caen
stone, and is reached by a short flight of stone steps. Behind the pulpit in the south
aisle is the organ, which has been brought from St. Luke's church, Derby, and was
built by Mr. Abbott of Leeds. At the west end of the church is a font (which is in
memory of a loved grandchild of Mr. Cazenove) of veined marble supported by
nine columns of polished granite and Caen stone. It is surmounted by a polished
oak cover and is a gift 'to the glory of God and the memory of Philip Henry Hes-
sey.' The church is warmed with hot air. It has been erected by Mr. J. D. Hobson,
from the designs of Mr. White, F.S.A. The total cost is £4500, which (with the exception of £800 unpaid at the commencement of the dedication services) had all
been contributed by the relatives and friends of the late H. B. Verdon and Philip
Cazenove. The church is provided with prayer books, hymn books, and kneelers

throughout."

The Dedication of St. Michael's Church was on September, 10, 1881, by the Right Rev. The Lord Bishop of Rochester—the service commenced at 11.30 a.m.

> Lord of hosts, to thee we raise
> Here a house of prayer and praise!
> Thou thy people's hearts prepare
> Here to meet for praise and prayer.
>
> O King of glory come,
> And with thy favour crown
> This temple as thy dome,
> This people as thy own!
> Beneath this roof, O deign to show,
> How God can dwell with men below.
>
> Here may thine ears attend
> Our interceding cries,
> And grateful praise ascend,
> All fragrant to the skies!
> Here may thy word melodious sound,
> And spread celestial joys around!
>
> Here may thy future sons
> And daughters sound thy praise,
> And shine like polish'd stones,
> Through long succeeding days!
> Here Lord, display thy sov'reign power,
> While temples stand, and men adore!

All Saints' Temporary Iron Church.—Rochester Diocesan Mission, St. James', Nine Elms.

ALL SAINTS' TEMPORARY IRON CHURCH, is situated in Victoria Bridge Road, near the south-eastern gate of Battersea Park. It will accommodate 200 persons. All seats free and unappropriated. It was opened for Divine Service Saturday, Sept. 6th, 1879, at 3.30 p.m. The Rev. Canon Clarke, Vicar of Battersea, and Rural Dean, preached the first sermon. His text was:—"Nevertheless the foundation of God standeth sure, having this seal, The Lord knoweth them that are his."—II. Timothy ii. 19. An income of £200 a year from the Rochester Diocesan Fund has been granted to the clergyman of the district, the Rev. A. E. Bourne, formerly Curate of St. Peter's, Battersea. The new provisional district of "All Saints," Battersea, has been formed out of three parishes, viz., St. Mary's, St. Saviour's and St. George's, to meet the requirements of the rapidly increasing population of the neighbourhood. Roughly speaking the boundaries of the new district are the London, Chatham and Dover Railway from the river to the London and South Western Railway, along the London and South Western Railway to Park Grove; down Park Grove, across the open land to the Park round the north corner. The only exceptions are the streets between Queen's Road and Russell Street which remain

part of St. Philip's parish.

"God is greatly to be feared in the assembly of His saints and to be had in reverence by all them that are about Him."

> Let us then with gladsome mind
> Praise the Lord for He is kind;
> For His mercies shall endure
> Ever faithful, ever sure.

ROCHESTER DIOCESAN MISSION, St. James', Nine Elms. Clergyman in charge, Rev. William George Trousdale, B.A.—The Mission Buildings situated in Woodgate Street and Ponton Road, Nine Elms Lane, have lately been enlarged by the Misses Baily of Esher, at a cost of over £1200. The church contains sittings for 250. There are in connection with the Mission, Sunday Schools, two Mothers' Meetings, Girls' Bible Class, Girls' Sewing Class, Recreation Room for Girls, Provident Club, Penny Bank. It is also proposed to establish shortly a Working Man's Club and a Crêche, for which there is ample accommodation in the Mission Buildings. Services—Sunday at 11 and 7, Wednesday Evening at 8, Children's Service the 3rd Sunday in the month at 3.

St. Aldwin's Mission Chapel.—The Church of our Lady of Mount Carmel and St. Joseph.

ST. ALDWIN'S MISSION CHAPEL, (Rochester Diocesan Society) Poyntz Road, Latchmere Road, was opened on Sunday, 12th September, 1880, at 7 p.m. It will comfortably seat 300 persons. St. Aldwin's district is formed partly out of St. Saviour's and partly out of Christ Church parish—the latter ceded the Colestown Estate, the former handed over Latchmere Street and Road, and the cluster of streets which is surrounded by the triangle of railways. Mission Curate—Rev. T. B. Brooks, M.A., 2, Nevil Villas, Albert Road. Mission-woman—Mrs. Monk, Mission House, 25, Poyntz Road.

"Both young men and maidens, old men and children; let them praise the name of the Lord."—Psalm cxlviii. 12-13.

"Blessed is the people who know the joyful sound: they shall walk O Lord, in the light of thy countenance."—Psalm lxxxix. 15.

> "Thy power to save!" thrice happy they
> Who taught of Thee delight to pray,
> Rejoicing in Thy love:
> Now clothed in righteousness divine,
> The heirs of glory,—soon to shine
> In realms of joy above.
>
> A pastor's warning voice!—"Take heed,
> Whilst by the sunny banks you feed
> Of England's good old Church!
> Live close to Jesus;—not on forms,
> Lest, unprepared for coming storms,

You founder in the lurch!

Heed well the Word—the joyful sound,
The Gospel of our God—still found
To point straight up to heaven:
Beware of sounds of 'yea and nay,'
For God's own 'yea' is man's sure stay,
Not Pharisaic leaven."

The presence of the Lord is found
Where love, and joy, and peace abound,
Fruits of the Spirit's Word;
Where Christian hearts unite in prayer
In Jesus' Name—the Lord is there,
Jehovah, Jesus, God.

There are two Roman Catholic places of worship in Battersea, viz.:—

THE CHURCH OF OUR LADY OF MOUNT CARMEL AND ST. JOSEPH, situated in Battersea Park Road, was built by a lady of the name of Mrs. Boschetta Shea (of Spanish extraction, and whose husband was an Irish Protestant) in 1868, and put under the management of the late Very Rev. Canon Drinkwater, who retained the control of the church and adjacent buildings, including the Convent of Notre Dame and Girls' School, the St. Joseph's Boys' School, and the New Church lately erected. The Duke of Norfolk gave £500 towards the building fund for the new church.

Within the grounds adjoining the Convent are kitchen and flower gardens with a gravel walk and a very compact grotto.

In the month of May, the month dedicated to the Blessed Virgin Mary, there are processions in the grounds every Sunday afternoon in which boys and girls take part, singing hymns in honour of "our Lady." The Boys' School is of an oblong shape, and is governed by the Xaverian Brothers, including several pupil teachers. Subjects taught: reading, writing, arithmetic, grammar, English, Roman and Grecian history, geography, mathematics and the Roman Catholic religion.

Church of the Sacred Heart.—The Old Baptist Meeting House, Revs. Mr. Browne, Joseph Hughes, M.A., (John Foster), Edmund Clark, Enoch Crook, I. M. Soule, Charles Kirtland.

CHURCH OF THE SACRED HEART, Trott Street, is an Iron building with turret and cross, opened 10th of October, 1875. It was built by the Countess of Stockpool at a cost of £700. The freehold site of land including one acre cost £1,000. Priest, Rev. McKenna. New Schools have lately been erected.

THE OLD BAPTIST MEETING HOUSE, York Road, Battersea, was erected in 1736, but a church was not formed for sixty-one years afterwards. About the year 1755 the Rev. Mr. Browne became Officiating Minister, and for forty years preached to a small congregation, but as his age and infirmities increased the number of attendants on his ministration diminished till he had not more than four or five persons to hear him; enfeebled and disheartened he resigned, and in 1796 a young man, then a Student at Bristol Academy, afterwards well known as the Rev. Joseph Hughes, M.A., supplied the pulpit with so much acceptance that in 1797 a church was constituted, and he, in the 29th year of his age, was elected to be the pastor. The constitution and order of the church thus formed may not be uninteresting, it reads as follows:—

"We, the undersigned, desirous of the privilege connected with religious fellowship and a stated ministry, having already sought the Lord, and we trust, chosen Him as our Sovereign and Friend, do hereby give ourselves afresh to each other, according to the Divine Will, that being united in a Christian Church, we may render mutual aid, as fellow-travellers from earth to heaven; and, though we firmly embrace the sentiments peculiar to the Baptists, yet, espousing with equal determination the cause of evangelical liberty, we welcome to our communion all who give evidence of a change from sin to holiness; who appear to love our Lord Jesus Christ, who are willing to be accounted learners in His school, and who wish to be enrolled in connection with us. And we hope it will be our united endeavour, and the endeavour of such as may hereafter be added to us, by all means to keep the unity of the Spirit in the bond of peace; to mingle faithfulness, spirituality and affection in our intercourse; strictly to regard the Divine Ordinances—so far as we know them; and to walk before the Church, our families, and our God, worthy of our heavenly calling."

Under the Rev. Joseph Hughes's ministry the work of God took deep root here and greatly flourished. By his energy, learning and eloquence, and his connexion with different local societies for the promotion of religious worship, he was brought acquainted with Mr. Wilberforce, Mr. Vansittart, and Mr. Perceval, by whose aid he established the "Surrey Mission Society." At a meeting of the Religious Tract Society he afterwards promulgated the idea of an institution for supplying not only the inhabitants of the British Isles, but *the whole world*, with copies of the Holy Scriptures; and hence arose the Bible Society, of which Mr. Hughes was joint Secretary until his death. Mr. Hughes expired on Thursday evening, October 3, 1833, in the 65th year of his age. His mortal remains were interred in Bunhill Fields.

"John Foster derived much spiritual benefit from his friendship with Mr. Hughes of Battersea Chapel with whom after he left Chichester he resided for a time, and it increases not a little the debt of gratitude due from the Christian community to that excellent man, that though his own authorship was limited to a few pulpit productions, and his sphere of duty was one of action rather than of meditation, he performed the noble office of stimulating the exertions and cherishing the piety of one of the most original and influential religious writers of his age."

Mr. Foster says "the company who made sometime since an establishment at Sierra Leone in Africa, have brought to England twenty black boys to receive European improvements, in order to be sent when they are come to be men to attempt enlightening the heathen nations of Africa. They have been placed in a house at Battersea for the present till some kind of regular and permanent establishment shall be formed, and I have been requested, and have agreed to take the care of them for the present." — *Foster's Life and Correspondence*, Vol. I. p. 58-60, edited by J. C. Ryland, A.M.

The Rev. Edmund Clark held the Pastorate from Spring of 1834 to Mid-Summer, 1834 — three months. He was succeeded by the Rev. Enoch Crook, who was two years and a half Pastor of the Church, viz., from Mid-summer, 1834, to 1837. A tablet to his memory is placed on the wall in the vestry of the chapel. Subsequently from January, 1838, it was the scene of the labours of the Sainted Israel May Soule, who for thirty-six years was Pastor of the Church of Christ assembling here; he faithfully discharged his ministerial duties; his doctrine was truly evangelical; his services unremitting and his deportment exemplary — beloved by his flock and highly esteemed by Christians of other denominations for his large liberal-heartedness, sound judgment and unsectarian spirit. It was he who first conceived the idea of enlarging the Old Chapel and had a model in his study to represent the style of alteration which his own mind suggested with a view to meet in some humble measure the growing and increased spiritual wants of the neighbourhood. However, instead of enlarging the Old Chapel a second time, he used strenuous efforts and succeeded in having the Old Chapel demolished and a commodious place of worship erected on its site. The Chapel was enlarged and repaired in 1842 and the freehold purchased and put in trust at a total cost of £1,000. In 1868 the requisite land for further enlargement of the Chapel was purchased. The present handsome Chapel involved an outlay of £5,000, erected in the Romanesque style from the designs of Mr. E. C. Robins. The accommodation on ground-floor and galleries is for 900 worshippers. The open timbered roof is one span, and the building is faced with white bricks with Bath stone dressings. It was constructed by the late Mr. John Kirk. The same architect has recently enlarged East Hill Chapel, Wandsworth. The memorial stone of the New Chapel was laid by Field Marshal Sir G. Pollock, G.C.B., G.C.S.I., on the 8th of June, 1870, being the 33rd year of the Rev. I. M. Soule's ministry; the building was completed by the end of the year, so that Mr. Soule had the pleasure of conducting the opening services January 1st, 1871. Previously to his coming to Battersea Mr. Soule for seven years had been Pastor of the Baptist Church, Lewes, Sussex. He was born Dec. 25, 1806, died unexpectedly Nov. 8, 1873, having preached with his usual energy on the previous Sunday, when in the morning he took for his text Rev. xxii. 14, and afterwards administered the Lord's Supper. The funeral service was conducted Nov. 15th, by the Rev. D. Jones, B.A., of Brixton, assisted by the Rev. Edward Steane, D.D., the Rev. Robert Ashton and other ministers. At the grave, in the presence of about 7,000 persons, the Rev. Samuel Green delivered an address. On the following day, Sunday, November 16, Funeral Sermons were preached in Battersea Chapel to overflowing congregations, in the morning by the Rev. D. Jones, in the evening by the Rev. Dr. Angus.

His mortal remains lie interred at St. Mary's Cemetery with those of Amelia his wife, where in token of fond affection to his memory a beautiful obelisk of grey polished granite has been erected. The epitaph states "that he consecrated himself in early life to the service of God; that he received during a long and faithful ministry signal tokens of Divine favour in the number who through his instrumentality were brought to a knowledge of the Saviour. His earnest constant labours to the last for the education and welfare of the young are of untold benefit, while rich and poor alike have lost in him a kind and sympathizing friend, whose loving and Christian spirit will long be remembered in Battersea." A monumental tablet to his memory is about to be erected in the Chapel.

> "Servant of Christ well done,
> Rest from thy loved employ,
> The battle fought, the victory won,
> Enter thy Master's joy."

In a small room under the south gallery is erected a beautiful marble tablet *in memoriam* of the Rev. Joseph Hughes, M. A. Also under the north gallery are erected tablets in affectionate remembrance of Henry Tritton, Esq., for many years a resident in the Parish of Battersea, and whose mortal remains lie buried under the Chapel. He died 20th of April, 1836, aged 48 years. Also Amelia, his wife, third daughter of Joseph Benwell, Esq., died March 28, 1855, aged 64 years.

April, 1874, Mr. Soule was succeeded by the Rev. Charles Kirtland, who still continues to fill the pastoral office.

> Let strangers walk around
> The city where we dwell;
> Compass and view the holy ground,
> And mark the building well.
>
> The orders of Thy house,
> The worship of Thy court,
> The cheerful songs, the solemn vows,
> And make a fair report.

"God is a Spirit: and they that worship him must worship him in spirit and in truth." —*John iv.* 24.

Deacons—G. Lawrence, Cubbington Cottage, Battersea Rise; H. M. Soule, St. John's Hill, Battersea Rise; W. H. Coe, York Road, Battersea; G. Mansell, 1, Cologne Road, St. John's Hill; Philip Cadby, 24, St. Peter's Square, Hammersmith; Thomas Sadler, 88 Spencer Road. Chapel-keeper—D. Rayner, 31, Verona Street, York Road.

Baptist Temporary Chapel, Surrey Lane.

BAPTIST TEMPORARY CHAPEL, Surrey Lane. This building having stood beyond the time allowed by Government was condemned by the Board of Works. The Church which formerly worshipped there have removed to the Lammas Hall until a permanent building can be raised. A fund is established which progresses slowly. A. Peto, Esq., The Boltons, South Kensington, is the Treasurer to the Building Fund. Rev. C. E. Stone is the Pastor. Deacons, J. Weller and F. T. Ashfield. It is worthy of note that this was the second Baptist Church formed in Battersea.

"I have set my affections to the house of my God." — *I. Chron. xxix.* 3.

> "Christ is the Foundation of the house we raise;
> Be its walls salvation, and its gateways praise!
> May its threshold lowly to the Lord be dear;
> May the hearts be holy that worship here!"

Battersea Park Temporary Baptist Chapel.

BATTERSEA PARK TEMPORARY BAPTIST CHAPEL was erected in 1869, at a cost, including the purchase of freehold land, of £2,000. In 1872 a front gallery was added which cost £175. In 1876 a piece of ground was bought at the back of the Chapel for £105, and new class-rooms and vestries erected at an additional cost of £420. The grand object of the London Baptist Association next to the promotion of spiritual work, is the extension of their bounds by the erection of at least one new Chapel in each year. The Rev. C. H. Spurgeon, the third President (1869), had the pleasure of seeing a chapel erected in this region where the poor would be gathered. He was able to purchase and give to the enterprise this fine freehold site in Battersea, and leaving the front portion thereof for a future chapel, he expended the grant of the Association in erecting a school-chapel, seating 630 persons, which was put in trust without incumbrance. The neighbourhood being too poor to bear the burden of debt, and no wealthy friends being forthcoming this was thought to be the wiser course. The Rev. W. J. Mayers commenced his pastorate in the beginning of the year 1870. Upon his resignation he was succeeded by the Rev. Alfred Bax, who for two years or more preached with much acceptance. On the 2nd of April, 1877, the Rev. T. Lardner became the officiating minister. Deacons of the Church—J. S. Oldham, William Weller, W. Chaplin.

In 1866, Mr. E. Carter shoemaker by trade, residing at 16, Henley Street, commenced holding a Sunday School in his own hired house.

One Sunday Afternoon, two young students from the Metropolitan Tabernacle, called at his residence to see if they could hold religious services there, but it does not appear that they at that time succeeded. Afterwards the School was removed to 32, Russell Street, then to 53, Arthur Street, where Mr. Rees, a young man from the Metropolitan Tabernacle conducted Morning and Evening Services regularly every Lord's day. Subsequently he was succeeded by Mr. William Wiggins of the Rev. C. H. Spurgeon's College who on account of the place "being too strait" made arrangements to open Norton Villas, Battersea Park Road, for Sunday School and regular Sunday Religious Services, and at stated times on Week Evenings. Norton Villa, was opened as a place of Worship, October 20th, 1867. In 1868, a Baptist Church was formed by the late Rev. I. M. Soule of Battersea Chapel and Mr. Wiggins was recognised as the Pastor, the Church consisted of forty members and a Congregation of about a hundred persons besides a Sunday School of one hundred and twenty Children; this place however, became too small to accommodate the persons desirous of attending. It was proposed therefore, to erect an Iron Chapel on a site near York Road Station. But those friends who made the proposition, on hearing that the Baptist Association had an intention to build a permanent Chapel in Battersea Park Road, abandoned the idea of purchasing and erecting an Iron Chapel so in 1870, when the present Chapel was completed, the Baptists who had met at Norton Villa for worship, (Mr. Wiggins, having resigned his pastorate there) united with the Church at Battersea Park Chapel, under the Pastoral care of the Rev. Walter J. Mayers.

"Not forsaking the assembling of ourselves together, as the manner of some is; but so much the more, as ye see the day approaching." —*Hebrews x.* 25.

"Great the joy when Christians meet,
Christian fellowship, how sweet!
When, their theme of praise the same
They exalt Jehovah's name."

—*Burder.*

"Truly our fellowship is with the Father, and with his Son Jesus Christ." —*I. John i.* 3.

Baptist (Providence) Chapel.

BAPTIST (PROVIDENCE) CHAPEL, Meyrick Road, is a brick building—seats 350. It is intended to have galleries when it will then accommodate 500. The memorial stone was laid by Mr. H. Clark, October 5th, 1875, on which are engraved the words "The fear of the Lord is the beginning of wisdom." —*Psalm cxi.* 10. Cost of Chapel including the purchase of freehold land on which the Chapel is erected £2,400. G. G. Stanham, Esq., Architect; Messrs. Turtle and Appleton, Builders, Battersea. Officiating Minister, Mr. Philips. Deacons, H. Clark, S. Stiles, Joseph Palmer.

"Philip said (to the Eunuch), If thou believest with all thine heart thou mayest (be baptised); and he answered and said, I believe that Jesus Christ is the Son of God." —*Acts viii.* 37.

"For we are all partakers of that one bread." —*I. Cor. x.* 17.

"Come in, ye chosen of the Lord,
And share the bounties of His house;
His dying feast, His Sacred word,
Our joys our hopes, and solemn vows.

Come share the blessings of that board,
Which Jesus for His Saints has spread;
Receive the grace His ways afford,
Commune with us and Christ our Head."

—*G. Smith.*

Baptist Chapel, Chatham Road.—Wesleyan Methodist Mission Room and Sunday School.—United Methodist Free Church, Church Road, Battersea.—The United Methodist Free Church, Battersea Park Road.

THE NEW BAPTIST CHAPEL, Chatham Road Bolingbroke Grove.—A suitable plot of ground was obtained at a cost of £150; cost of Chapel, about £850.

Services were conducted by Charles and Thomas Spurgeon. The building will seat 258 persons.

The cause was commenced about fourteen years ago in a very humble way by Mr. G. Rides, a working man, who, previously to the erection of the above place of worship, held meetings in his own hired house, Swaby Street. William Higgs, Jun., Architect; Higgs and Hill, Builders.

WESLEYAN METHODIST MISSION ROOM AND SUNDAY SCHOOLS, Everett Street, Nine Elms, opened 1871. Mr. John Farmer, Steward and Superintendent. Now closed.

UNITED METHODIST FREE CHURCH, Church Road, Battersea.—The Memorial Stone was laid by James Wild, Esq., May 25th, 1858. Another stone was laid by Mrs. Bowron, Sept. 22, 1864, when the Chapel was enlarged. S. J. Stedman, Architect.

THE UNITED METHODIST FREE CHURCH, Battersea Park Road.—The School-room at the back of the Chapel in Landseer Street was built in 1865, at a cost of £500, and it was used as a preaching Station. In 1871-2 the present Chapel was built, at a cost of £2,200. Seats about 600. Has a Lecture-room and Schools underneath the Chapel. The freehold was purchased in 1876 and cost £400. Rev. James Whitton is now Resident Minister in connexion with the 7th London Circuit.

"The brotherly covenant."—*Amos i. 9.*

"One in heart, and one in hand,
One for all, and all for one;
Love shines through this Christian band,
Kindled from the heavenly sun."

—*Edmeston.*

In the District known as New Wandsworth, near the Bolingbroke Grove, Wandsworth Common, is a large and increasing population which presents an opening for Christian enterprise.

The Free Methodists of the 7th London Circuit have undertaken this work. Preaching has been commenced in a room No. 89, Bennerly Road, and a society of twelve members have been formed.

A suitable freehold site has been secured in the Mallinson Road at a cost of £400, and it is proposed to erect a Chapel and Schools thereon.

The whole scheme will involve an outlay of £4,000, but at present it is only intended to build the School, which is estimated will, with the ground, cost nearly £1,200.

Primitive Methodist Chapel, New Road.

PRIMITIVE METHODIST CHAPEL, New Road, was built in 1874. The Chapel including the purchase of freehold, cost about £1,030. Seats 200. Mr. Murphy, Architect; Mr. Stocking, Builder.

Now a new and much more commodious Chapel is erected. Respecting it origin the following account may not be uninteresting.

About twelve years ago the friends of Hammersmith Station decided to Mis sion this neighbourhood. First of all they opened two small parlours at 32, Rus sell Street, Battersea Park Road, as a Preaching Station and afterwards secured premises in Stewart's Lane, which they converted into a small Chapel, and here for several years, were numbers of conversions; but, like all small and out-of-the way places, it became a feeder to other churches. It was at last decided to secure a suitable site and build. First a lease of a piece of land in the New-Road, and eventually the freehold was secured, and a small school-room was erected on part of the site, which has since been used for school and preaching services. The building being altogether inconvenient, it was decided, after prayerful and mature deliberation, to build a Chapel which should be more in harmony with the requirements of the neighbourhood. Mr. A. J. Rouse, the Architect, was consulted, plans were prepared, and tenders invited. The contract was let to Mr. J. Holloway, builder, Wandsworth, for £2000, which, with the debt of £690 on the school-room and Architect's fees, will bring it up to £2800. The building is plain, neat, and substantial, with stone facings. It will accommodate about 600 persons; there are two aisles, a gallery on the sides and at one end, with a back gallery for the organ. Adjoining the chapel is a large class-room capable of holding sixty children. Externally, the building is one of the most imposing and attractive in the neighbourhood, and one of the cheapest in London.

On Whit-Monday, 1878, the memorial-stones were laid. The opening address was delivered by Mr. G. Harris. It was practical, earnest, and eloquent. Stones were laid by R. Burns, R. Adams, and R. Morton, Esqs., and Messrs. J. J. Flux, W. Bayford, W. Gibbs, Rev. T. Penrose for G. Palmer, Esq., M. P., Mr. S. Fortune, Circuit Steward, for the Sunday-schools, Mesdames W. and H. Baker, and Miss Whiting.

At the end of the Chapel is a Tablet in memory of Alfred James Rouse, Architect, who met with his death in the collision between the Princess Alice and the Bywell Castle on the Thames, September 3rd, 1878. Life is short but Art is long.

"Therefore be ye also ready for in such an hour as ye think not the Son of Man cometh. *Matt*. 24. 44."

The first Primitive Methodist preachers were, William Cowes and Hugh Borne, in 1807. When the first Primitive Methodist Church was formed it consisted of ten members; now it numbers over 180,000 and employs more than a 1,000 ministers.

"Where two or three are gathered together in my name, there am I in the midst of them." —*Matthew xviii*. 20.

Primitive Methodist Chapel, Grayshott Road.—Primitive Methodist Chapel, Plough Lane.

PRIMITIVE METHODIST CHAPEL, Grayshott Road, was erected in 1875. The stone was laid by J. T. Hawkins, Esq., M. A., for the Right Hon. Earl Shaftesbury, K. G., November 21, 1874. Rev. J. Toulson, Superintendent, 7th London Circuit.

Another Stone was laid by a Shareholder of the Artizans, Labourers and General Dwelling Company Limited. Rev. W. E. Crombie, Minister. Mr. A. J. Rouse, Acting Architect; J. Lose, Builder. The Chapel seats 400, and cost about £2,600. The entrance to the Chapel is up a flight of steps; the Schools are underneath the Chapel.

"Jehovah, Shammah." *Ezek. xlviii.* 35. "Allelujah!" *Rev. xix.* 1.

In the Wandsworth Road, near Grayshott Road, is an old milestone which marks the space between that and the Royal Exchange five miles, and Whitehall four and a half miles.

PRIMITIVE METHODIST CHAPEL, Plough Lane,—In the year 1855, a few Primitive Methodists, residing in the neighbourhood of York Road, with the view of having their hearts knitted more closely together in holy love by Christian fellowship and prayer, met from house to house for this purpose to worship God—In this way they continued to meet till the year 1858, when the Firm of Orlando Jones & Co. gave them the use of their Reading Room. Here as elsewhere they preached the Gospel of Jesus Christ and their numbers steadily increased. In 1870, a piece of land was secured in Knox Road, and the firm above mentioned, helped them to erect an Iron Chapel with a School-room underneath. This building having stood beyond the time allowed by Government was condemned by the Board of Works. It was opened in June 1871, and was finally closed in September 1880. About this time the Estate of the Late Rev. I. M. Soule was sold, and an effort was made to secure a plot of land thereon, situated in Plough Lane. The freehold site selected, was purchased, and a substantial brick Chapel with School-room underneath erected at a cost of £2,300. The Chapel will accommodate 400 worshippers. It was opened October 24th, 1880, on which occasion Sermons were preached by the Rev. J. Baxter. I will command My blessing upon you—Lev. 25. 21.

> Command Thy blessing from above,
> O God on all assembled here:
> Behold us with a Father's love
> While we look up with filial fear.
>
> Command thy blessing Jesus, Lord,
> May we thy true disciples be;
> Speak to each heart the Mighty Word,
> Say to the weakest, follow me.
>
> Command thy blessing in this hour,
> Spirit of Truth and fill the place
> With wondering and with healing power,
> With quickening and confirming grace.
>
> With Thee and these forever found,
> May all the Souls who here unite,
> With harps and songs Thy throne surround,
> Rest in Thy love, and reign in light.

St. George's Mission Hall.—Battersea Congregational Church, (Inde-

pendent), Bridge Road.

ST. GEORGE'S MISSION HALL, Stewart's Lane, formerly belonged to the Primitive Methodists, and was used by them as a chapel.

"Glory, honour, praise and power
Be unto the Lamb for ever;
Jesus Christ is our Redeemer,
Hallelujah! Amen."

"Walk about Zion, and go round about her: tell the towers thereof. Mark ye well her bulwarks, consider her palaces; that ye may tell it to the generations following. For this God is our God for ever and ever: he will be our guide even unto death."-*Psalms xlviii.* 12-14.

BATTERSEA CONGREGATIONAL CHURCH (Independent), Junction of Bridge Road and Surrey Lane South, fifteen minutes' walk from Clapham Junction and York Road Stations, ten minutes' from Battersea Station; is an edifice constructed of Kentish rag with Bath stone dressings, and has a tower with spire at the north end of the building. The interior is spacious and lofty; the pews are made of pitch-pine, varnished, and will accommodate, including the seats in the south gallery, 600 persons. Cost of erection £4,500. H. Fuller, Architect; F. W. Sawyer, Builder. With respect to its history, this is the first Congregational Church in Battersea. It owes its origin to the Surrey Congregational Union, under whose directions services were held in the Lammas-Hall previous to the erection of the previous Church building. The Foundation Stone was laid by the Rev. J. G. Rogers, B. A., of Clapham, September 17th 1866. It was opened Tuesday, October 12th, 1867, and the Dedication Service was conducted by the Rev. Samuel Martin, of Westminster. The present is the third pastoral settlement, the first minister being the Rev. J. Scott James, of Cheshunt College, who commenced his ministry in Battersea. In 1870 the Rev. J. S. James resigned to take the Pastorate of the Church at Stratford-on-Avon, and was succeeded April, 1871, by the Rev. Joseph Shaw, of Boston, Lincolnshire. In 1878 the Rev. Joseph Shaw resigned and was succeeded by the Rev. Thomas Jarratt, the present Pastor.

The Sunday School and Lecture Hall, with class-room adjoining, was opened in April, 1874. The entire cost of the building, furnishing, heating, lighting, and fencing the ground was £510, the whole of which was discharged July, 1875. Of this amount a generous friend gave £300 through the Rev. Joseph Shaw; and thirty-two pounds were contributed by the Sunday School Children. The room will seat 300 persons.

The "Church Manual" for 1870 states "This is Congregational, we regarding the New Testament as the only infallible guide in matters of Church order, and learning from it that each Church is authorized to elect its officers, receive and dismiss its members, and act authoritatively and conclusively upon all questions affecting its purity and administration. We recognize the Lord Jesus Christ as our King and Sole Ruler in spiritual things, and His Word as our Statute-Book and only Standard. The membership. We believe this should be composed only of regenerated persons who are received into the Church on profession of their faith in Christ, or by letters from sister Church. Members of other churches, acting on this principle, are also received on their producing proper certificates. Candidates for membership should make their application direct to the Pastor. Deacons, Mr. John Allen, Mr. Thomas C. Tabor; Treasurer, Mr. Samuel James Roberts; Secretary, Mr. Edwin John Eason."

The seats are free, not sold or rented, but are allotted for family convenience and to preserve order. The revenues of the Church are chiefly derived from the weekly free-will offerings of the church and congregation.

"How amiable are thy tabernacles, O Lord of Hosts."-*Psalm lxxxiv.* 1.

> "The Hill of Zion yields
> A thousand sacred sweets,
> Before we reach the heavenly fields
> Or walk the golden streets."

Stormont Road Congregational Church, Lavender Hill.

STORMONT ROAD CONGREGATIONAL CHURCH Lavender Hill.

The Schools are in connexion with the above place, where the worship is at present conducted. They are built from designs by J. H. Vernon Esq., and are capable of accommodating 450 scholars. There are eight class-rooms, and there is every convenience for carrying on Sunday School work.

The site, which is freehold, as is also the adjoining one for the future Church was the gift of the London Congregational Union. The cost of the school buildings was £2820. The foundation stone was laid on July 27th, 1878, by J. Kemp Welch Esq., and the buildings were opened on February 18th 1879, when Sermons were preached by the Revs. R. W. Dale of Birmingham, and Dr. Raleigh. A Church is now being formed under the Pastorate of the Rev. R. Bulmer, late of Whitby, who commenced his ministry on Sunday the 2nd of October, last. It is proposed to commence the building of the Church as soon as possible. The building according to plans will seat 850. The whole of the Christian work in connection with the above place is in a very active state, and include Band of Hope, and Improvement Societies.

Wesleyan Methodism in Battersea.

WESLEYAN METHODISM IN BATTERSEA.—It is not easy to determine the time of the first appearance of Methodism in Battersea. From Mr Wesley's Journal it appears that in his later years he was accustomed to pay an annual visit to this neighbourhood, including Chelsea, Wandsworth and Balham. In the absence of any definite record of the matter we may assume that some persons in Battersea came under his influence. A half century elapsed before the Methodist Society found a local habitation in Battersea, even then, not destined to be a permanent one. A small Chapel, chiefly at the cost of the late Rev. J. Partes Haswell, was erected on the site of the present one in the Bridge Road West in 1846; the foundation stone being laid by the late Mr. Scott of Chelsea, and the works being executed by Mr John Sugden, Builder, of Bermondsey New Road.

The building was let to the late Mr. J. Boughton and others, for the use of the Wesleyan Society by Mr. Haswell, and it continued in their occupation until 1855. The agitations which disturbed the Wesleyan Connexion in 1851 and following years were felt with great severity in Battersea. The congregation and Society were so weakened by the separation that took place, that the Lessees, after allowing the Chapel to be occupied for a time by the seceding party, finally surrendered their lease into Mr. Haswell's possession again.

In the meantime, however the Wesleyan Society, began to recover from the great depression into which it had fallen; and in 1858, on their behalf, Messrs. Bell and Molineux, with the late Mr. Holloway of Battersea, took the former Chapel on a short lease from the persons into whose hands it had passed; and ultimately it was purchased by a duly appointed body of Trustees in 1862.

In 1864, aided by a munificent donation of £425 from Mr. J. Steadman of South Lambeth, and by other liberal contributions, the Trustees were enabled greatly to enlarge the building, nearly doubling its former area; and finally in 1871, it was brought to a state of completion, by the erection of a Gallery and an Organ, with other minor improvements. It now furnishes accommodation for 700 people.

The usual congregation amounts to about 500, of whom more than 300 are members of the "Society."

The Rev G. Bowden, and the Rev. E. Hawken, are the present circuit ministers, he latter being resident in Battersea, and taking special charge of the Wesleyan Church there.

The usual times of service on Sundays are, 11 o'clock in the morning, and 6.30 in the evening. There are also Weekly Prayer Meetings on Sunday mornings at 7 a.m.; and on Monday evenings at 7 p.m.; and a Week-night service on Tuesday evenings at the same hour.

In 1870, in view of the growing Educational necessities of the Wesleyan Body, the General Wesleyan Education Committee decided on the establishment of another Training College, in addition to that which they had in Westminster. Circumstances led to the placing of this on the Southlands estate, near the Battersea High Street Railway Station. It furnishes accommodation for 110 female Students, who are under training for the Office of Teachers; and who in due time are employed in all parts of the kingdom in Schools under Inspection. They constitute, it need hardly be said a very interesting portion of the congregation. The Rev. G. W. Olver, B.A., is the Principal, and Mr. James Bailey the Headmaster of the College.

A Sunday School with 280 Scholars in average attendance meets twice on each Sunday, and is conducted with more than the usual efficiency. There are also the customary benevolent and religious agencies maintained by the Wesleyan Church here; and Day Schools for Girls and Infants are connected with Southlands Training College.[46]—W.S.

> O happy souls that pray
> Where God delights to hear!
> O happy men that pay
> Their constant service there!
> They praise thee still; and happy they
> Who love the way to Sion's hill.
> They go from strength to strength,
> Through this dark vale of tears,
> Till each o'ercomes at length,
> Till each in heaven appears:
> O glorious seat! Thou God, our King,
> Shall thither bring our willing feet.

We know for certain Battersea on one occasion was honoured with the preaching of the Rev. John Wesley as recorded in one of his Journals, dated November 4, 1766, wherein this indefatigable servant of Christ states, "I preached at Brentford, *Battersea*, Deptford and Welling, and examined the several societies." His Journals state that he preached repeatedly at Wandsworth, as the following extracts

[46] In olden time this place was called the "Retreat," a spacious mansion, stuccoed, situated in the midst of an extensive pleasure ground and shrubbery it belonged to Valentine Morris, Esq.—but when Sir George Pollock became the occupier he changed the name to that of Southlands, jocosely punning at the same time upon its former name by saying that he *never made a retreat*. Afterwards Sir George Pollock removed to Clapham Common. Near it stood Manor House the seat of Richard Morris Esq. Son of Valentine Morris Esq. a large brick edifice in the style of George the First's reign.

will show. Wednesday, November 16, 1748. "In the afternoon I preached to a little company at Wandsworth who had just begun to seek God; but they had a rough setting-out, the rabble gathering from every side, whenever they met together throwing dirt and stones, and abusing both men and women in the grossest manner. They complained of this to a neighbouring Magistrate, and he promised to do them justice; but Mr. C. walked over to his house, and spoke so much in favour of the rioters, that they were all discharged. It is strange, that a mild, humane man could be persuaded by speaking quite contrary to the truth, (means as bad as the end) to encourage a merciless rabble in outraging the innocent! A few days after Mr. C., walking over the same field, dropped down and spoke no more! Surely the mercy of God would not suffer a well-meaning man to be any longer a fool to persecutors."

Tuesday, January 17, 1758, "I preached at Wandsworth, a gentleman come from America, has again opened a door in this desolate place. In the morning preached in Mr Gilbert's house. Two Negro servants of his, and a Mulatto, appear to be much awakened. Shall not his (God's) saving health be made known to all nations?"

Thursday, 8th February, 1770, the Rev. John Wesley writes, "I went to Wandsworth. What a proof we have here that 'God's thoughts are not our thoughts! Every one thought that no good could be done here; we had tried for above twenty years, very few would even give us the hearing, and the few that did seemed little the better for it. But all of a sudden crowds flocked to hear; many are cut to the heart; many filled with peace and joy in believing; many long for the whole image of God. In the evening, though it was a sharp frost, the room was as hot as a stove, and they drank in the word with all greediness, and also at five in the morning, while I applied 'Jesus put forth his hand and touched him, saying I will: be thou clean!'"

Previously to the erection of the present commodious Wesleyan Chapel in Bridge Road West, the friends of the Wesleyan Communion met for worship in a large upper room over a carpenter's shop in King Street. Subsequently they removed to premises now belonging to Mr. G. King, Ironmonger, in the vicinity of Surrey Lane.

John Cullum, an artist by profession, who resided in Battersea, was connected with the Wesleyan-Methodists. He was a zealous Open-air Preacher and Temperance Advocate. It is said that he was the first person who introduced *Teetotalism* in Battersea and held meetings for that object. He died in 1852, aged 51 years.

This good man kept a record of important events which had transpired in Battersea. From a manuscript of his, entitled "The Antiquities of Battersea," the following extract is taken—it will be read with interest.

"There is also a Wesleyan Chapel and Society here, which originated at a small house in Bridge Road, near the Bridge, after which it was removed to Mr Steadman's yard, in which a large room was fitted up for Divine Worship, and a School formed under the fostering care of Mr. Lark and Mr. Bridge, assisted by other zealous female teachers. In conformity with the principles of Mr. Wesley the Society has, under God's blessing, increased from one Class to three Classes, besides a Sunday School which is in a flourishing condition. Mr. T. Boughton, the present Superintendent, is assisted by twelve male and female teachers who still persevere in the good work of instructing the young. The present Chapel was built in King Street and was considered necessary both from the fact that there was not room for the persons who assembled for worship and other circumstances relative to the Society at that time. The Chapel was opened by three sermons being preached on Sunday, October 11, 1840, by the Rev. W. Atherton, Rev. J. P. Haswell, and the Rev. J. Scott. And on Monday evening, October 12, a meeting of the Friends connected with the Chapel was held, at which the Rev. J. P. Haswell presided, one of the chief friends to the cause at this place. The object of the meeting was to excite a spirit of enquiry with respect to the ministry of the Word and Christian instruction of youth in order to benefit the morals of the neighbourhood and salvation of souls.

"There is connected with this Chapel a Stranger's Friend Society, whose object is to search out the most forlorn and distressing cases of poverty and sickness. Its plan is carried out by Visitors who read to the sick a portion of the Holy Scriptures and engage in prayer with them, and by conversation and tracts endeavour to instruct so as to lead the heart to the Saviour, and relieve their temporal wants by affording them food, &c. rather than money. Many instances of good have been the result, and the conversion of some to the truth. Its founders were Messrs. Cooper and Stanley, Wandsworth; its present officers, Messrs. Stedman and Evans, Secretary and Treasurer, Cullum, Bridge, Winter, &c., Battersea. There is a small Branch of the Wesleyan Missionary Society carried on here—a Tract Society, &c. May the Lord prosper the work that many may be enlightened by the Gospel of Jesus Christ and made partakers of his great Salvation."

Methodistic Chronology.

1703, June 17. The Rev. John Wesley born.

1725, Sept. 19. Mr. Wesley ordained by Bishop Potter.

1735, Oct. 14. Mr. Wesley sailed as a Missionary for America.

1739. The Wesleyan-Methodist society established.

1744, June 25. The first Methodist Conference held in London.

1751, April 24. Mr. Wesley preached his first sermon in Scotland, at Musselburgh.

1769. Messrs. Boardman and Pilmoor sailed for America.

1784. The "Deed of Declaration" enrolled in the Court of Chancery.

1785, Aug. 14. The Rev. John Fletcher died.

1786. The Methodist Missions in the West Indies established.

1788, Mar. 29. The Rev. Charles Wesley died.

1791, Mar. 2. The Rev. John Wesley died.

1814, May 3. Dr. Coke died on his passage to Ceylon.

1821, Feb. 16. The Rev. Joseph Benson died.

1832, Aug. 26. Dr. Adam Clark died.

1833, Jan. 8. The Rev. Richard Watson died, in the 53rd year of his age.

1834. The Wesleyan Theological Institution established.

1838. Members in the Methodist society, 1,062,427.

1839. Centenary of Wesleyan Methodism.

The first Œcumenical Methodist Conference held in London September, 1881.

Wesleyan Chapel, Queen's Road.

WESLEYAN CHAPEL, QUEEN'S ROAD.—The following is a brief account of the rise and progress of Wesleyan Methodism in this neighbourhood. In the year 1871, in the order of God's providence, a good man and his wife removed from the Great Queen's Street Circuit to Frederick Street, now known as Newby Street, Wandsworth Road. On October 17, 1871, they very kindly opened their houses for a class meeting, to be held in connexion with the Society of which they were members. Here on Sunday, December 3rd of the same year, the first preaching Service was conducted. As the room became inconveniently crowded at the Sunday Services it was felt that a more suitable place was needed, so after a short time a Billiard Room capable of holding 150 persons, situated at No. 588, Wandsworth Road, was secured, and on April 21, 1872, was opened for Public Worship. On June 2nd, about 30 children were garnered in and a Sunday School commenced. Notwithstanding the unsuitableness of the place and other difficulties which had to be surmounted, the work of the Lord was carried on in this place until February, 1879; in the meanwhile however, strenuous efforts were made in order to obtain an eligible piece of ground on which to erect a more commodious building. In 1878, the freehold site situated in Queen's Road, was purchased for £1,140, and a temporary Iron Chapel erected, with seats for 500, at a cost of about £600, this temporary Sanctuary was opened February 14th, 1879. This Structure while making ample provision at first was soon found to be inadequate to meet the requirements of a neighbourhood where the population was large and rapidly increasing, hence the Trustees and Friends endeavoured to raise £4,000, by means of grants and loans from the late Sir Francis Lycett's Fund, the Metropolitan Chapel Fund, etc., towards the entire outlay of about £7,000, (the estimated cost of the permanent building etc.) leaving about £3,000, to be raised by funds in the Lambeth Circuit. On August 28th, 1881, the New School-Room which holds about 320 persons, was opened for Public Worship and Sunday School purposes. The Iron Chapel having been sold to make way for the New Chapel now in course of erection which is expected to be opened for Divine Service about May 1882.

On Friday July 15th, 1881, the Memorial Stone was laid at 3 o'clock, by Lady Lycett, when the Rev. G. W. Olver, B. A., gave an address.

By express desire of the Local Committee the Italian Style has been adopted, and the building will be erected in Bath Stone and Picked Stocks—Sitting accommodation for 1,000 will be provided, on the ground floor 650, and in the galleres 350. Adjoining the Chapel large School-Rooms have been erected with Vestry, Class-Rooms, and the usual offices. The Architect is Mr. James Weir, of the Strand. James Holloway, Builder, Marmion Road, Lavender Hill. *"That thine eyes may be open upon this house day and night."* 2. *Chron. vi.* 20.

Christ is our corner stone,
On him alone we build;
With his true saints alone
The Courts of heaven are filled;
On his great Love Our hopes we place
Of present grace and joy above.

O! then with hymns of praise
These hallowed courts shall ring;
Our voices we will raise
The Three in one to sing;
And thus proclaim in joyful song,
Both Loud and Long, that glorious Name.

Here gracious God do Thou
For evermore draw nigh;
Accept each faithful vow,
And mark each suppliant sigh,
In copious shower on all who pray
Each holy day Thy blessing pour.

Here may we gain from heaven
Thy grace which we implore:
And may that grace once given,
Be with us evermore:
Until that day, when all the blest
To endless rest are called away.

Free Christian Church, Queen's Road.

FREE CHRISTIAN CHURCH, Queen's Crescent, Queen's Road. Some 6 years or more ago, Mr. Crosby began the above work in Arthur Street Mission Hall, a small Hall situated in the lowest part of Battersea, and the work under his super-intendence has been so manifestly owned and blessed of God, that it was some time since deemed imperative on his part as the Lord's steward, to seek further to extend this effort in His cause. As far as the means of himself and friends al-lowed, and in the exercise of much consecrated faith and self-denial, a plot of land was secured, and an iron building erected adjacent to the most needy part of the neighbourhood, where the extended work is now carried on. The building, however, is of a temporary character, the Board of Works granting a license only of two years on iron buildings, and according to an agreement entered into in faith of the Lord's continued favour, a brick building must be erected in the course of 4 years. The present building, owing to the speedy growth of the work is even now too small. An effort is being made to purchase the freehold, and erect a building capable of holding about 700 persons, at an estimated cost of £2,750. W. Crosby, Pastor, E. V. Kelly, Treasurer.

Trinity Mission Hall, Stewart's Lane.—Plymouth Brethren.

In addition to other lay helpers (including Scripture Readers and Bible Women) there are six agents at work in Battersea connected with the London City Mission. This is an excellent Institution, having for its object the Evangelization of the poor of London. Mr. David Nasmith founded the London City Mission May 16, 1835. The general business of the London City Mission is conducted at the Mission House, Bridewell Street, Blackfriars, by a Committee consisting of an equal number of members of the Established Church and of Dissenters; and the Examiners of Missionaries consist of an equal number of Clergymen and Dissenting Ministers, all of whom, with the Treasurers, Secretaries and Auditors and Members of the Committee, ex-officio. These gentlemen give practical illustration of the purest ideal of Christian unity by showing, notwithstanding the peculiar church organization to which each may be attached, how harmoniously they can work together on one common platform under the guidance of their Divine Head for the extension of the Redeemer's Kingdom by bringing back wanderers from God to the fold of the one Great Shepherd, Jesus Christ. The number of City Missionaries engaged in the Metropolis is about 450.

The Corner Stone of Trinity Mission Hall, Stewart's Lane, promulgated and subscribed to by the members and adherents of Trinity Presbyterian Church, Clapham Road, was laid Wednesday, June 20, 1877, by the Rev. David Macewan, D.D. in the presence of a very large concourse of people. It is estimated that the Hall will accommodate about 400 persons; and in addition to the Hall there is a School-room which will probably accommodate 150 to 200 scholars The building cost about £2,500. The land, which is freehold, has been purchased for £400. The Hall is built of brick with box stone dressings. W. H. Robbins, Esq., Architect; B. E. Nightingale, Builder. Mr. Cameron is the Minister.

The handsome edifice belonging to the Presbyterian Church of England, Clapham Road, cost about £12,000, built through the unremitting energy and pious zeal of the late Dr. John MacFarlane and was for many years the scene of his earnest, faithful and successful pastoral labours.

PLYMOUTH BRETHREN.—A body of Christians calling themselves "The Brethren" came into existence about 1830-1835 in Plymouth, Dublin, and other places in the British Islands, extended throughout the British Dominions, and in some other parts of the continent of Europe, particularly among the Protestants of France, Switzerland, and Italy, and also in the United States of America. Many of the first religious communities found in Plymouth and elsewhere, were retired Anglo-Indian officers, men of unquestionable zeal and piety and those communities began to appear almost simultaneously in a number of places. Mr. Darby, regarded as an influential member, afterwards separated from them with many adherents. Mr. Darby was previously a Barrister, moving in the highest circles of Society, and under deeply religious impressions became a Clergyman of the Church of England, lived for some time in a mud-hovel in the County of Wicklow evoting himself to his work. The Plymouth Brethren object to National Churches s too Latitudinarian, and to other Dissenters as too Sectarian; their doctrines however agree with those of most Evangelical Protestant Churches, but they recognize o ordination of minister; their tenets may be stated thus:—Original Sin, Predestination, the efficiency of Christ's Sacrifice, the merits of his obedience, the power f his intercession, the gracious operations of the Holy Ghost in Regeneration and anctification; they also generally maintain millenary views, usually practise the Baptism of believers without regard to previous infant baptism, they acknowledge he Sacrament of the Lord's Supper and administer it to one another in their meetings usually every Sunday, or first day of the week. In 1851, they had 132 places f Worship in England and Wales. This year 1879, the (exclusive) Brethren have rected a small place of Worship in High Street, near Battersea Railway Station.

A Railway Arch in Latchmere Road, has been utilized for a Gospel Hall where he (Open) Brethren meet for worship.

"The Little Tabernacle."—Thomas Blood.

Situated in the rear of Lawn House Laundry, Orkney Street, is a small place of worship called the "*Little Tabernacle*" erected at the sole expense of Mr. John Strutt, where meetings for Bible Readings, Breaking of Bread, Exhortation, and Prayer are held every Lord's day.

THOMAS BLOOD, generally known by the appellation of *Colonel Blood*, was a discarded officer of Oliver Cromwell's Household; he was notorious for his daring crimes and his good fortune. He was first distinguished by an attempt to surprise he Castle of Dublin, which was defeated by the vigilance of the Duke of Ormond, and some of his accomplices were executed. Escaping to England he with his confederates meditated revenge, and actually seized the Duke of Ormond one night in his coach in St. James' Street, intending to hang him, and had got him to Tyburn, where, after struggling with his would-be assassins in the mire, the Duke was rescued by his servants, 6 Dec, 1670. Blood afterwards in the disguise of a clergyman, attempted to steal the crown and regalia from the Jewel Office in the Tower, 9th May, 1671. He was very near succeeding, for he had bound and wounded Edwards the keeper, and was making off with his booty, but was overtaken and seized with his associates. Blood, who was accused as being the ringleader in this conspiracy, when questioned he frankly owned that he had taken part in the enterprise, but refused to discover his accomplices, "the fear of death (he said) should never induce him to deny a guilt or betray a friend." All these extraordinary circumstances made him the subject of general conversation. Charles II. moved by the influence of popular excitement, or from idle curiosity, granted him a personal interview. Blood confessed to the king that "he had been engaged with others in a design to kill him with a Carbine (said to be in the vicinity of Battersea Priory) where His Majesty often used to bathe (beneath the garden belonging to the Priory was a Subterranean passage leading to the river-bank); that the cause of this resolution was the severity exercised over the consciences of the godly, in destroying their religious assemblies; that when he had taken his stand among the reeds on the other side of the river full of these bloody resolutions he found his heart checked with an awe of Majesty; that he not only relented himself, but diverted his associates from their purpose; that he had long ago brought himself to an entire indifference about life, which he now gave for lost; yet he could not forebear warning the king of the danger which might attend his execution; that his associates had bound themselves by the strictest oaths to revenge the death of any of their confederacy and that no precaution nor power could rescue any one from the effects of their desperate resolution." Yet notwithstanding these and other offences, the King not only pardoned but granted him an Estate of £500 per annum, thus this man who had been regarded as a monster became a kind of favourite. He lived to enjoy his pension about ten years, till being charged with fixing an imputation of a scandalous nature on the Duke of Buckingham, he was thrown into prison, where he died August 24, 1671.

Battersea Priory.—Alien Priories.

Battersea Priory is a castellated building reported to have been a Convent for Ursuline Nuns.

PRIOR was the Ecclesiastical title formerly given to the head of a small Monastery, to which the designation of Priory was applied. The Prior ranked next in position to the Abbot. Similarly the term Prioress was applied to the head of a female convent. The title of Grand Prior was given to the Commandants of the Grand Military Priories of the Orders of John of Jerusalem, of Malta and of the Templars.

Alien Priories were cells of the religious houses in England which belonged to foreign Monasteries. The whole number is not exactly ascertained; the Monasticon has given a list of 100. Weever, p. 338, says 110. The houses belonging to the several religious orders which obtained in England and Wales, were, Cathedrals, Colleges, Abbeys, Priories, Preceptories, Commandries, Hospitals, Friaries, Hermitages, Chantries, and free Chapels. These were under the direction and management of various officers; the dissolution of houses of this kind began as early as 1312, when the Templars were suppressed; and in 1323 their lands, churches, advowsons, and liberties, here in England were given by Ed. II., st. 3, to the prior and brethren of the hospital of St. John at Jerusalem.

In the years 1390, 1437, 1441, 1459, 1497, 1505, 1508, and 1515, several other houses were dissolved, and their revenues settled on different Colleges in Oxford and Cambridge. From the year 1312 in the reign of Edward the 2nd to the close of the reign of Henry VIII, 1547, the number of houses and places suppressed from first to last as far as any calculations appear to have been made were 23, 4; besides the friars' houses and those suppressed by Wolsey, and many small houses of which we have no particular account. Henry VIII founded six new bishoprics of which Westminster was one, which was changed by Queen Elizabeth into a Deanery with twelve prebends and a school.

Persons desirous of obtaining information respecting Monasteries should consult Dugdale's *Monasticon Anglicanum*, (Lond. 1655, 1661, 1673). Also a new and greatly Enlarged Edition by Bandinel, Caley and Ellis, published in 1817, 1830, and reissued in 1846.

Ursulines.

URSULINES, or Nuns of St. Ursula: a sisterhood founded about the year 1537, by Angela Merici at Brescia, the community numbering at that time, as many as six hundred. St. Angela was born in 1511, at Desenzano, on the Lago de Garda, and died at Brescia, 21st March, 1540. The institution was formally approved of and confirmed by Paul III., in 1544, and it was on this occasion that the name of Ursulines was given to the order after the famous St. Ursula; a Virgin Martyr of the Roman Catholic Calendar especially honoured in Germany, and especially at Cologne, which is the reputed place of her Martyrdom. The Legend substantially, in its present form, can be traced as far back as the end of the 11th or beginning of the 12th Century, as it is to be found in the revised Edition of the Chronicle of Sigebert of Gemblours (Pertzs Rerum Germanicarum Scriptores VIII. 310) which was made between 1106 and 1111. "According to their writer, Ursula was the daughter of the British King, Deonatis; and on account of her distinguished beauty, was sought in marriage by the son of a heathen Prince who was originally named Holofernes, but afterwards when a Christian was named Ætherius. Her father was forced to yield to the demand; but Ursula made it a condition that her suitor should become a Christian, and that she should be allowed the space of three years, during which she proposed, in company with her maidens to each of whom should be assigned a thousand companions and a three-oared galley to convey them, to make a voyage of pious pilgrimage. The conditions were accepted; the maidens to the number of 11,000 were collected from all parts of the world, and at length the expedition set sail from the British Coast. Arriving at the mouth of the Rhine they sailed up the river to Cologne, and thence upwards to Basel, where leaving their galleys, they proceeded by land to visit the tombs of the Apostles at Rome. This Pilgrimage accomplished, they descended the river to Cologne, which however, had meanwhile fallen into the hands of an army of Hunnish invaders under the headship of a Chief, who although not named is plainly the Attila of history. Landing at Cologne in ignorant security, the pious Virgins fell into the hands of these barbarous heathens by whom they were all put to the sword with the exception of Ursula, who for her beauty sake was reserved as a prize for the chief. She too, however, as well as another maiden, who had at first concealed herself in terror, demanded to join her companions in Martyrdom and then the full number of 11,000 victims was made up. Heaven, however, interposed a host of Angel Warriors who smote the cruel Huns; Cologne was again set free; and in gratitude to their Martyred intercessors the citizens erected a church on the site still occupied by the Church now known under the name of St. Ursula." Soon after the Reformation this legend became the Subject of a most animated controversy "on one hand the Centuriators of Magdeburg exposed its weak points with unsparing severity, on the other a Jesuit father, Crombach devoted an entire folio volume to the vindication of the narrative." Secular writers deny that the Legend has any foundation in historical facts; they trace no reverencing of Virgins in the Martyrologies and missals till the latter half of the 9th Century. Many suggestions have been offered by way of explanation of its startling improbability viz., the alleged number of the Martyred victims 11,000. One of these is that the belief arose from the name of a Virgin who was really the companion of Ursula's Martyrdom called according to the legend and

according to a Missal which belonged to the Sorbonne, Undecimilla for a number
The Roman Martyrology mentions the Saint and her Companion, without stating
their number. St. Ursula was the Patroness of the Sorbonne. The record of the Mar
tyrdom in the Calender thus begins. "*Ursula et Undecim Milla* V. V." Ursula and
Undecimilla Virgins was easily mistaken for "Ursula et *Undecim Millia* V. V. Ursu
la and *Eleven thousand Virgins*." Respecting further remarks concerning this Leg
end, suffice it to say, "that while the most learned of the Catholic hagiographers
putting aside the idea of a directly and unintentionally invented narrative, hav
traced the origin of the legend to a real historical massacre of a very large numbe
of Christian Maidens, which took place during the invasion of Attila, and soo
after the celebrated battle of Chalons in 451, all the modern writers of that Churcl
are agreed in regarding the details of the narrative, the number, the pilgrimages to
Rome, the interposition of the heavenly host, etc, as legendary embellishments o
the Medieval Chroniclers."

Young as Angela was she had been elected the first Superior of her Order and
had ruled it well for the two or three years she lived.

At first the Ursulines practised charity and devoted themselves to the edu
cation of Children without being bound to the rules of Monastic Life. In 1571-
Pope Gregory XIII. made the Society a religious order, subject to the rule of St
Augustine, at the solicitation of Charles Borromeo the additional privileges thus
conferred were afterwards confirmed by Sextus V. and Paul V. "They add to three
religious vows a fourth to occupy themselves gratuitously in the education of their
own sex. The order is under the Superintendence of the Bishops. In the 18th Cen
tury, it had 350 Convents. Many governments which abolished Convents in gen
eral, protected the Ursulines on account of their useful labours, particularly in the
practice of Christian Charity towards the sick. The *Dictionnaire de Theologie* pub
lished in 1817, says that 300 Convents of these sisters existed at that time in France
their dress is black with a leather belt, and a rope for the purpose of self-scourging
Their congregations however did not universally accept the Monastic rule; and in
France and Italy, there were Societies, the members of which only took the vow
of Charity, and gave instruction like their sisters. Their dress was that commonly
worn about 200 years ago by widows." In some countries however, their dress
appears to have been white, and to have varied in other respects as well as colour.
The Ursuline Sisters have several Educational Establishments in Ireland, in En
gland and the United States.

Battersea Grammar School, St. John's Hill.

BATTERSEA GRAMMAR SCHOOL, St. John's Hill. Founded under the Trust
of Sir Walter St. John A.D. 1700. Scheme revised A.D. 1873. Governors:—William
Evill, Jun., Esq., Robert Hudson, Esq., Rev. Evan Daniel, M.A., W. G. Baker, Esq.,
John Costeker, Esq., *Treasurer*, Rev. Canon Clarke, M.A., James H. T. Connor, Esq.,
Richard Hadfield, Esq., Thomas D. Tully, Esq., Charles Few, Esq., James Stiff, Esq.
Head Master:—Rev. E. A. Richardson, M.A., late Scholar of Queen's College, Ox
ford. Assistant Masters:—W. H. Bindley, B.A., late Scholar of Emmanuel College,
Cambridge, M. Michael, Bachelier-es-Lettres, University of Paris, C. P. Martinnant,

University of London, Mr. Badel, Writing Master, Serjeant Major Doberty, Drill Master.

Scheme of Instruction. RELIGIOUS INSTRUCTION, (according to the principles of the Church of England) forms a regular part of the teaching of each class. Those boys are excepted from the teaching of the Church Catechism and Prayer Book, whose parents, (being Dissenters), express a desire to that effect, in writing to the Head Master. THE COURSE OF STUDY comprises the English, Latin, Greek, French and German Languages; Writing, Arithmetic, Book-keeping and Mathematics. History and Geography; Natural Science and Drawing. French is taught throughout the School; German in the three highest classes only. DRAWING, (Freehand, Model and Landscape), is taught in all classes. TECHNICAL DRAWING, (including Practical Geometry, and Perspective), and Painting are taught only in the two upper classes. SCIENCE, (comprising Physics, Chemistry and Botany), is taught only in the upper classes. Vocal Music is taught.

School Term and Holidays. The period of instruction is divided into three terms, as nearly equal as possible. The holidays are four weeks at Christmas, three weeks at Easter, and six weeks at Mid-summer, commencing about the 1st of August.

1st Term commences September 7th; ends December 7th.

2nd Term commences January 8th; ends March 29th.

3rd Term commences April 23rd; ends July 31st.

Tuition Fees. The annual payment for boys above 12 years of age, £12; for boys under 12, £10. The fees are to be paid terminally and in advance.

Regulations for Admission. Application for admission must be made either in person or by writing to the Head Master. No boy will be admitted, who shall be found on examination unable to read English, to write correctly and legibly from dictation and to work sums in the first four rules of arithmetic. The boys must attend at the school for examination on the first day of each term, at two o'clock p.m. The Governors require a term's notice to be given on the removal of a boy, or the payment of the terminal fee.

The Southlands Practising Model Schools.—St. Peter's Schools.—St. Saviour's Infant.

THE SOUTHLANDS PRACTISING MODEL SCHOOLS.—Girls' School, seven years and upwards, 6d. per week. Infants' Boys and Girls to seven years, 3d. per week.

ST. PETER'S SCHOOLS. Fee, 9d. per week.

ST. JOHN'S, Usk Road. Boys 1st, 2nd, and 3rd classes, 4d. per week, the rest 3d. Girls 1st class 3d., the rest 2d. Infants 2d. per week.

ST. SAVIOUR'S INFANT. Infants 2d. Girls 3d. over 10 years of age 4d. per week.

Christ Church National Schools.—St. George's National Schools.— Voluntary Schools.

CHRIST CHURCH NATIONAL SCHOOLS, Grove Road, Falcon Lane, were erected from designs of Mr. C. E. Robins, selected in competition, and were built by Messrs. Lathey Brothers at a cost of £3,000. Accommodation is given for 200 boys, 200 girls and about the same number of infants. There are two residences, one for the Master and the other for the Mistress. The buildings form a picturesque group facing the roads on three sides with intermediate play-grounds for each sex. Mr. Robins was also the Architect for the British Schools at Wandsworth and other Educational Buildings in the Parish, as the Walter St. John's Upper Schools and the extension of the Training College, the Chapel of which was decorated by him some seven years since. The office of E. C. Robins, F.R.I.B.A., etc., is No. 14, John Street, Adelphi.

ST. GEORGE'S NATIONAL SCHOOLS, built in 1857 from designs furnished by Joseph Peacock, Architect, Bloomsbury Square. Cost about £4,500 including a Parliamentary Grant of £1,500. The Schools were enlarged in 1870. The Infant Schools were established in 1826. The following text of Scripture is engraved on a stone outside the buildings.

"From a child thou hast known the Holy Scriptures, which are able to make thee wise unto Salvation through faith which is in Christ Jesus."—*II. Timothy iii.* 15.

Boys and Girls 4d. per week for one in a family, 6d. for two brothers or sisters, and 7d. for three in a family, Infants 2d.

Erected outside St. Mary's Schools, Green Lane, is a tablet bearing the following inscription:—"National Schools for Girls and Infants. These buildings were erected by Miss Champion on land granted by Earl Spencer, and opened April 10th, 1850, for the education of the children of the poor on Scriptural principles." This tablet is placed by order of the Parishioners in Vestry assembled in Grateful Remembrance of her Munificent Charities to the Parish of Battersea.—Rev. J. S. Jenkinson, M.A., *Vicar.* W. H. Wilson, John Hunt, *Churchwardens,* 1855.

Within the Parish of Battersea there were in the year 1879, Fourteen Voluntary Schools, viz.:—

	Accommodation.
SIR WALTER ST. JOHN'S Up-stairs Middle-class for Boys. Terms, 15s. to 25s. per quarter.	
Ditto Ground-floor Public Elementary School for Boys. Payments, 6d. and 9d. per week. Head Master, Mr.Taylor; Assistants, Mr. Jones, B.A., Mr. E. Mills, Mr. Oliver, and Mr. Blackman.	489

St. Mary's, Green Lane. Girls; Mistress, Miss Keene. Infants' Governess; Miss Paul. Boys: Master, Mr. T. Ryder. Fees, Boys and Girls 4d. a week, of which at the year's end 2d. a week will be returned to all who have attended more than 250 times. Infants 3d. a week, of which 1d. a week will be returned to regularattendants at the year's end.	606
Christ Church, Grove Road. Master, Mr. Weston. Mistress, Miss Paton. Infants, Miss Kemp.	590
St. John's, Usk Road. Head Master, Mr. Henry Smith. Mistress, Miss Hook. Infants' Governess, Mrs. Hughes.	658
St. Peter's, Plough Lane. Head Master W. F. Normon. Assistant, W. Beasley.	180
St. Mark's, Battersea Rise. Infant Schools, Miss E. Townsend. 4d. per week.	99
St. George's, New Road. Head Master, Mr. John Douthwaite. Mistress, Miss Salter. Infants' Governess, Miss Holding.	609
St. George's Girls and Infants' Schools, Ponton Road, Nine Elms. Mistress, Miss B. Smith. Infants' Governess, Miss A. E. Basnett.	184
St. Saviour's, Orkney Street. Mistress, Miss Merrett.	201
Wesleyan Model, High Street.	557
St. Michael's, Bolingbroke Grove, (mixed). Mistress, Mrs. M. Watson. 3d. per week.	152
Grove Boys' British, York Road, Established 1799, Enlarged 1840. Master, Mr. James Hammond.	196
Girls' British, Plough Lane. Mistress, Miss Mansell. Assistant, Miss Willett.	297
St. Joseph and St. Mary, Battersea Park Road.	466
Total	5284

London Board Schools.

In 1879 there were Nine Board Schools in Battersea:—[47]

[47] Since the First Edition of this Work was published, Tennyson Road School has been enlarged in order to accommodate 400 Scholars. Landseer Street Board School is held in the large room under the Chapel and accommodates 200 boys. J. R. Ayris, Head Master. Ponton Road Board School, Nine Elms, opened for girls 9th June, 1879, and for boys August 18th, the same year, has accommodation for 350, Master, Mr. Chase. Mistress, Miss Nutcher. On the South side of Battersea Park Road, between Lockington Road and Havelock Terrace a

Name of School.	Builder.	When Opened.	Boys' Master.	Girls' Mistress.	Infants' Mistress.
Bolingbroke Road.	Mr. Spinks, Clapham Junction.	Dec. 1, 1873	Mr. Pink.	Miss Deacon.	Mrs. Pink.
Battersea Park.	Mr. Sheppard, Bermondsey.	April 14, 1874	Mr. Stokes.	Mrs. Cox.	Mrs. Parker.
Winstanley Road.		Jan. 6, 1874	Mr. Vince.	Miss Gale.	Miss Blackburn.
Sleaford Street.	William Higgs, South Lambeth.	Aug. 10, 1874	Mr. Wheaton.	Miss Pook.	Miss Browett.
Gideon Road.	Wall, Bros., Kentish Town.	May 16, 1876	Mr. Lee.	Miss Dunn.	Mrs. Pyle.
Mantua Street.		Sept. 1876	Mr. Mansell.	Miss Spalding.	Miss Spalding.
Holden Street.		Feb. 1877	Mr. Morris.	Miss Macleod.	Miss Marshall.
Tennyson Road.	Mr. Tyerman.	Feb. 1877	Mr. Philips.	Miss Davis.	Mrs. Lower.
Belleville Road.	Mr. Thompson, Camberwell Green.	Aug. 13, 1877	Mr. Barter.	Mrs. Christopher.	Mrs. Watson.

N.B.—There are Sunday Schools connected with the different places of Worship some of which are held in Board Schools.

London School Board, Lambeth Division.

LAMBETH DIVISION LONDON SCHOOL BOARD.—Accommodation Area and Cost of New Permanent Schools.

large Board School has been built to hold about 1,400 children. Christ Church Schools, Falcon Grove, have passed for the present into the hands of the School Board for London. It is in contemplation to erect four more Board Schools in Battersea.

Name of School.	Children Accommodation.	Area sq. feet.	Cost of Site.	Cost of Building.
Sleaford Street	1,055	23,000	£2543 1s. 4d.	£8399 19s. 3d.
Tennyson Road	837	28,000	£2376 18s. 6d.	£7590 9s. 1d.
Gideon Road	776	19,700	£3404 18s. 3d.	£9921 7s. 5d.
Holden Street	1,101	26,887	£3074 14s. 1d.	£10305 1s. 7d.
Battersea Park	1,334	32,670	£2378 5s. 5d.	£7442 12s. 9d.
Bolingbroke Road	792	54,426	£768 5s. 5d.	£5980 15s. 10d.
Mantua Street	1,105	32,670	£2334 5s. 4d.	£11337 1s. 1d.
Winstanley Road	1,127	17,792	£3152 5s. 5d.	£7948 4s. 7d.
Belleville Road	828		£1661 6s. 2d.	£10165 19s. 11d.
	8,955			

The first building erected for the London School Board, situated in one of the most densely crowded localities of the East-end, was opened in July, 1873, and since that time no fewer than 152 large Schools have been completed with a total accommodation for about 182,000 children, and an average accommodation for 872 children each. In addition to these, between 30 and 40 schools are now in course of erection, and about 50 other schools have been determined upon, thus the Board is most active in providing for the educational requirements of the Metropolis. Mr. E. R. Robson, F.R.I.B.A., is the Architect of this Board.

The Board School in Winstanley Road accommodates about 1130 children, the site is the shape of a rhomboid, and the School has been skilfully planned to make the most of it.

Gideon Road Board Schools, the boys and girls' departments are built upon arches to form covered play-grounds underneath. As the site contains sufficient area, the infants' department has been erected as a separate building.

The Board Schools are elaborately fitted up. Books, slates, pencils, etc., for the scholars are provided. The terms for tuition at the Board Schools in Battersea are:—Bolingbroke Road, boys, girls, and infants 2d. each. Battersea Park, Mantua Street, Winstanley Road, Tennyson Road, and Sleaford Street, boys and girls 3d. each, infants 2d. Gideon Road and Holden Street on the Shaftesbury Park Estate, boys and girls 4d. each, infants 3d. each.

School Board Visitors in Battersea:—Mr. Armstrong, Mr. Dalton, Mr. Myland, Mr. Fane, Mr. Chamings and Miss Sydney.

London Ratepayers' School Board Association Established 8th October, 1870.

London or Metropolitan School Board elected 29th Nov., 1870.

Regulations for School Boards issued 21st December, 1870. First election of Metropolitan School Board (Lord Lawrence, Chairman). Arrangements for erecting or adapting buildings for New School Board, December, 1871.

London School Board Education Scheme proposed 23rd June, 1871.

The London School Board occupied their new buildings on Victoria Embankment, 30th September, 1874.

Second Metropolitan School Board elected; religious party strongest. Sir Charles Reed, M.P., Chairman, November, 1878.

Sir Charles Reed, Chairman of the School Board for London, died March 25, 1881. Was interred at Abney Park Cemetery, Wednesday, March 30, 1881.

Fourth Metropolitan School Board elected, 1879.

E. N. Buxton, Esq., Chairman of the London School Board.

LONDON SCHOOL BOARD, LAMBETH DIVISION.[48]

MISS HEN. MULLER,	REV. G. M. MURPHY,
T. E. HELLER, ESQ.,	JAMES STIFF, ESQ.,
CHAS. R. WHITE, ESQ.,	STANLEY KEMP-WELSH, ESQ.

The Elementary Education Acts.—Regulations affecting Parent and Child.

The Elementary Education Act of 1870 aims at the compulsory supply of school accommodation in those districts in which there is a deficiency. The general survey under the Education Act of the School provision of every Parish in England did not commence till the 1st of May, 1871.

By virtue of the Elementary Education Act, 1876, and of the Bye-Laws of the School Board for London, the following will be, on and after the 1st January next, the state of the law as regards children, their parents and employers within the Metropolis.

I.—REGULATIONS AFFECTING PARENT AND CHILD. The term "parent" includes guardian, and every person who is liable to maintain, or has the actual custody of the child. The parent of every child between the ages of 5 and 14 must cause such child to receive efficient elementary instruction in reading, writing, and arithmetic.[49] A.—By the Bye-Laws of the School Board, which continue in force, the

[48] The Division of Lambeth is thus defined: The Division of Lambeth shall include the Parliamentary Borough of Lambeth, all the parts of the Parishes of Lambeth and Camberwell outside the Boundary of the said Borough and the Wandsworth District, as described in Schedule B. and Part I. of the Metropolitan Local Management Act, 1855, (that is to say) the Parishes of Clapham, Tooting Graveney, Streatham, St. Mary, Battersea, (excluding Penge), Wandsworth, and Putney, (including) Roehampton. There are 63 Board Schools in the whole of the Lambeth Division for the present year (1879), and 45,000 children on the rolls.

[49] All Elementary Schools in the receipt of Government Grants are annually examined by H.M. Inspector of Schools, and a report of their condition forwarded to the Ed-

parent of every child between the ages of 5 and 13 must cause such child to attend an efficient School during the whole time for which the School is open. The following cases are excepted:—(a) where a child is receiving efficient instruction in some other manner. (b) where a child is not less than 10 years of age has received a certificate that he has passed the 5th Standard of the Code of 1871: in which case he is wholly exempt from attendance at School. (c) where a child of not less than 10 years of age has obtained a certificate that he is beneficially and necessarily at work: in which case he is exempt from the obligation to attend School more than 10 hours a week. (d) where the child cannot attend School through sickness or other unavoidable cause. If a parent commits a breach of the Bye-Laws he may be summoned before a magistrate, and fined 5s.; and the child may be ordered to attend School. B.—By the Act of 1876, if either—(1) the parent of a child above the age of five years who is prohibited from being taken into full-time employment, habitually and without reasonable excuse, neglects to provide efficient elementary instruction for his child; or, (2) a child is found habitually wandering, or not under proper control, or in the company of rogues, vagabonds, disorderly persons, or reputed criminals; the parent may be summoned before a magistrate, and the child may be ordered to attend School. If the attendance order be not complied with, the parent, if in fault, may be fined 5s.; and in cases of continued non-compliance, the fine may be repeated at intervals not less than a fortnight. The child may also, under certain circumstances, be sent to a certified day industrial School, there to be detained during certain hours each day for a stated period; or to an ordinary certified industrial School, there to be wholly detained for a stated period, which, however, must not extend beyond the time when the child will reach the age of 16 years. In either case, the parent may be made to contribute to the maintenance, of the child. II.—REGULATIONS AFFECTING EMPLOYER AND CHILD. The term "employer" includes a "parent" who employs his child by way of trade or for the purposes of gain. A.—No person may employ, in the year 1877, any child who is under the age of nine years; or in subsequent years, any child who is under the age of 10 years. B.—No person may employ a child within certain limits of age, unless the child shall have obtained either a certificate of proficiency that he has reached the fourth Standard of the Code of 1876; or a certificate that he has previously made 250 attendances at least, in not more than two Schools, during each year for a certain number of years, whether consecutive or not, as follows:—

		Unless they shall have obtained a Certificate.	
Age of Children, who may not be employed.	Either of Proficiency, according to the undermentioned Standard.	Or; of previous due Attendance for the undermentioned number of years.

In 1877	Children between 9 and 12, with the exception of those who were 11 before the 1st January, 1877	Fourth Standard of 1876	Two
1878	Children between 10 and 13, with the exception of those who were 11 before the 1st January, 1877	Ditto.	Two
1879	Children between 10 and 14, with the exception of those who were 11 before the 1st January, 1877	Ditto.	Three
1880	Children between 10 and 14	Ditto.	Four
1881 and subsequent years	Children between 10 and 14	Ditto.	Five

The penalty incurred by an employer who acts in contravention of the above provisions is a sum not exceeding 40s. But no penalty will be incurred by the employer (*a*) if the child was lawfully employed on the 15th August, 1876. (*b*) If the child obtains efficient instruction by attendance at School for full time or in some other equally efficient manner. (*c*) If the employment be during a specified time allowed by the School Board for purposes of husbandry, &c. and if the child be over eight years of age and be so employed. (*d*) If the child be employed and be attending School in accordance with the provisions of the Factory Acts, or of the Bye-Laws of the School Board. (*e*) If the employer be *bona fide* deceived as to the age of the child or as to his having obtained a certificate; or if some agent, without the knowledge of the employer, shall have employed the child—in which latter case the agent will be liable to the penalty. Although the employer be exempt from penalty, when the child is lawfully employed under the above regulations, the parent will still be liable for any breach of the Bye-Laws, where the latter are more stringent. III.—REGULATIONS AS TO THE PAYMENT OR REMISSION OF FEES. If a parent is unable, from poverty, to pay the School fee of his child, he may apply either to the Guardians of the Poor for the Parish where he lives, or to the School Board. The Guardians, if satisfied of the poverty of the parent, must pay the school fee, not exceeding 3d. a week, of the child, in any Public Elementary School which the parent may select. If the parent select a Board School, the School Board, on his application, may, if they think fit, remit the school fee. The payment or remission of the school fee will not subject the parent to any disability. IV.—FREE INSTRUCTION. Subject to conditions to be made by an order of the Education Department, a child under 11 years of age who obtains a certificate that he has attended a Public

Elementary School 350 times a year, for two, three, four or five years according to circumstances, and, also, that he has attained a Standard (to be fixed by the Department) in Reading, Writing, and Arithmetic, will be entitled to have his school fees paid for him by the Education Department at a public Elementary School for three years more.

BY ORDER OF THE BOARD.
15th November, 1876.

In 1879 there were 63 Board Schools in the whole of the Lambeth Division and 45,000 children on the rolls.

In Battersea there are 68 taverns for the sale of spirits, etc., and 84 beer-houses, making a total of 152 public-houses. There are also 29 coffee-shops.

A Coffee Palace.—Latchmere Grove.—Plague Spots.—The Shaftesbury Park Estate.

A COFFEE PALACE IN OLD BATTERSEA.—On Saturday afternoon, Dec. 13, 1879, a coffee palace, belonging to the Coffee Taverns Company, Limited, was opened at Lombard Market, York-road, Battersea. This is the 22nd tavern of the kind opened by the Company, and carried on, in regard to the business, on the same principle as others. A well furnished room is provided for public meetings and other gatherings.

LATCHMERE GROVE, which is almost encircled with Railway embankments, was noted for its piggeries. The lane once known as "Pig Hill," leading from Battersea Fields to Lavender Hill, is now a wide open road and forms the west boundary of the Shaftesbury Park Estate.

Somewhere near the foot of "Pig Hill" were two places called in olden time *"Plague Spots"* where many bodies of persons who had died of the Plague were buried.

THE SHAFTESBURY PARK ESTATE[50] formerly the site of Poupart's Market Ground, covers an area of 42 acres, contains about 1100 houses and 8000 inhabitants. The houses are built on the most improved sanitary principles, they are prettily and artistically constructed, having small gardens back and front; on either side of the streets are rows of lime and plane trees which in the course of a few years will give the "Work peoples' Town," a beautiful and pleasant aspect. The Houses are built in four classes, containing 5, 6, 7, and 8 rooms respectively, (the latter including a bath room), and the weekly rental (at first was) 6/6, 7/6, and

[50] The Artizans Labourers and General Dwellings Company (Limited). Capital £1,000,000 in 100,000 shares of £10 each (paid up capital, £583,000). Chief Office: 34, Great George Street, Westminster, S.W. Office hours:—10 till 5 Saturdays 10 till 1. Estate Offices 221 Eversleigh Road, Shaftesbury Park, S.W. 35, A Street, Queen's Park. W.

DIRECTORS.—The Hon. Evelyn Ashley, M.P., Chairman, H. R. Droop, Esq., R. E. Farrant, Esq., John Kempster, Esq., Rev. H. V. Le Bas, F. D. Mocatta, Esq., Samuel Morley, Esq. M.P., Ernest Noel, Esq. M.P., John Peace, Esq., W. H. Stone, Esq. Bankers.—The London and Westminster Bank, Lothbury, E.C. Solicitors.—Messrs. Ashurst, Morris, Crisp and Co., 6, Old Jewry, E.C., Manager J. V. Sigvald Muller, Esq. Secretary.—Samuel E. Platt.

8/-, and the best class £26 and £30 per year, which sums, except the best class includes rates and taxes, but if the tenant is buying the house under the repayment table, the rates, taxes, and ground rent have to be paid by him in addition to the purchase money.[51] The purchasing prices of the houses are £170, £210, £260, £310, and £360; and they are leased for a term of 99 years subject to annual ground rent of £3 10s., £4 4s., and £4 10s. according to the class of house. Each dwelling is thoroughly ventilated by means of improved ventilating valves, which are fixed to every room and connected with air shafts in all the external walls and the same are applied beneath the floors, the houses have concrete foundations and are considered dry and healthy.[52]It is intended to convert the premises used as the Estate Agency Office into a Club house, equal in accommodation to any at the West End, with Library, reading, smoking, and billiard rooms; a small hall to hold about 350 is being built which among other things is intended to be let to benefit clubs and such like societies. It is suggested that the present temporary hall be converted into Swimming and Washing Baths. Brassey Square a space about one and a quarter acres, the Estate Company are going to make into a garden like that on the Thames Embankment, in which seats are to be placed and it is intended to have a

---

The Company was established for the erection of improved dwellings near to the great centres of industry to carry out the objects of the Company in London, large estates have been secured near Clapham Junction and the Harrow Road, that near Clapham Junction called Shaftesbury Park.

[51] The present weekly rental, which includes rates and taxes, except in the case of the first-class Houses is as follows: — An ordinary fourth class House 7/6 third class 8/6 second class 10/- first class 10/- and 11/-. The shops, lower houses, those with larger gardens than ordinary, and some other exceptional houses are subject to special arrangements both as to Rental and purchase.

[52] The scheme thus proposed has been abandoned. The temporary Hall has been taken down and seven houses with shops erected on the site, also a Temperance Hall. The Shaftesbury Club and Institute, Eversleigh House, Lavender Hill, was opened on Saturday, Feb. 2nd, 1878, at 3 o'clock p.m. Previously a movement had been in progress to establish a Club and Institute for the benefit of those large classes of working men who live upon the Shaftesbury Park Estate, and in the crowded neighbourhoods in the immediate vicinity. Nothing of the kind was in existence, and, as a consequence, there was no efficient corrective to the growing evils of intemperance and wasted time among these classes of the people. The movement met with a great and increasing support from the working men themselves, and the Provisional Committee appointed has been busily engaged in the work of organising the Club. The objects of the Club and Institute are thus stated in the Draft Rules: —

"To afford to its members the means of social intercourse, mutual helpfulness, mental and moral improvement, industrial welfare, and rational recreation. The Club shall not identify itself with any political, social, or theological party. As funds permit, there shall be provided: — Library and Reading Rooms, supplied with Books, Periodicals, and Newspapers; Educational Classes; Conversation, Refreshment, and Smoking Rooms, in which various games may be played; Billiard and Bagatelle Rooms; Popular Lectures and Entertainments; Rooms for the Meetings of Benefit and Friendly Societies." Subscription 1s. a month 2s. 6d. a quarter, 10s. a year. Arthur George Thorne, Hon. Secretary. Mr. W. Swindlehurst was the Secretary to the Estate Company. The purchase of the Freehold Land (it is said) cost the Estate Company £28,000. Recently the house rents on the Estate have been raised.

and to play there in summer months. Beside Co-operative Stores, there is a Social Review connected with the Estate, and a Newspaper has been started called "The South Western Advertiser."[53] The London Board School on the estate is situated in Holden Street. Between houses Nos. 21-23 in the Grayshott Road a stone may be seen bearing the following inscription "Healthy homes the first condition of Social Progress." This stone was laid by the Right Honourable the Earl of Shaftesbury, K.G., for the Artizans, Labourers and General Dwellings Company, Limited, on the 3rd of August, 1872. R. Austin, Architect.

No Beer-shop, Inn or Tavern is erected on the Estate but it must not be inferred from this, that all the inhabitants are Total Abstainers. However the ostensible and important objects of the Estate Company are to help the Working Classes to become owners of the House they occupy; to raise their position in the social scale; and to spread a moral influence over their class, tending to foster habits of industry, Sobriety and Frugality. Obedience to moral and physical laws, the right and proper use of material appliances for sanitary purposes, have a tendency to prolong human life and to make life more enjoyable, and the Supreme Governor of the Universe hath so ordained that it should be so. According to the metropolitan average, the deaths should have been 194, but they only numbered 100. In 1877 the births on the Shaftesbury Park Estate were 284. Connected with the Estate is a Volunteer Rifle Corps known as the "26th Surrey." Mr. Samuel E. Platt, Secretary to the Estate Company; Mr. J. V. Muller, Manager. Office, 221, Eversleigh Road. The Missionary who visits in this district is Mr. Vost, who holds meetings in the Temperance Hall, Elsley Road.

Eastward of the Shaftesbury Park Estate is situated Beaufoy's Chemical Works. Entrance, Lavender Hill. Mr. Matthew Cannon, Manager.

This site was formerly a brickfield. When Mr. Henry Beaufoy purchased the land comprising some 17 acres he named it "Pays Bas," signifying in French a *low country*. Recently 7 acres have been let on Lease of 99 years for building purposes, it is proposed to erect thereon 230 houses. In this locality and that of Latchmere it is said the bricks were made for the construction of Chelsea Hospital.

The Metropolitan Artizans' and Labourers' Dwellings Association.

THE METROPOLITAN ARTIZANS AND LABOURERS DWELLINGS ASSOCIATION have just erected three blocks of houses in the Battersea Park Road, designed by Charles Barry, Esq., President of the British Institute of Architects. Accommodation in A Block for 98 families with 3 and 4 rooms each. There are two B Blocks, 45 families in a block, having accommodation for 90 families with one or two rooms each for labourers. The whole of the front window-frames facing the main road are glazed with Plate Glass. Between the pathway and the Blocks is erected an iron palisade and some evergreens have been planted within the

The entrance to Shaftesbury Hall is in Ashbury Road.

[53] The following Newspapers, which are published weekly, contain (Battersea) Local Intelligence and District Board News. "The South London Press," 2d. "Battersea and Wandsworth District Times," 1d. "Mid-Surrey Gazette," 1d. "The Clapham Observer," 1d. "The South Western Star," 1d.

enclosure. There are underground Laundries at the north end of the Blocks with all necessary appliances. The B Blocks have three tiers of balconies supported by iron columns communicating with the dwellings on the upper storeys. The roofs are tiled by the Broomhall Tile Company. The Builders, are Messrs. Downs & Co. Southwark. Major-General Scott, Secretary, office, 9, Victoria Road, Westminster Abbey. It is intended to erect more Blocks on the land adjoining. Chairman, John Walter, Esq.

The buildings are intended as models of the dwellings for Artizans and Labourers, to replace the habitations condemned in various parts of the Metropolis under the Act of 1875. They are built in flats as nearly fire-proof as may be. Each tenement in the Artizans dwellings and each block of four rooms for those of the labourers are entirely separated from others by an open space, each tenement has a constant supply of fresh water, the use of a wash-house and a coal bunker, a dust shoot, and generally great care has been taken to insure to the tenants all the advantages of the best known sanitary appliances. Within the outer door which opens on to a general staircase, are all the conveniences except the wash-houses which are detached from the building. These tenements contain in most cases three rooms, viz.: kitchen, bed-room, and sitting-room. The labourers blocks are so divided that they can be let singly, or in twos, threes, or fours. The dwellings were formally opened on Saturday Afternoon, June 23rd, 1877, by the Earl of Beaconsfield. The ceremony was graced by a select company, among whom were in addition to the Prime Minister, the Earl and Countess of Rosslyn, the Countess of Scarborough, the Earl and Countess Stanhope, the Lord Chancellor and Lady Cairns, Lady E. Drummond, the Marquis of Bristol, the Earl of Ilchester, the Earl of Verulam, the Bishop of Winchester, the Right Hon. R. A. Cross, M.P., Mrs. and Miss Walter, Mr. W. H. Smith, M.P., Mr. Roebuck, M.P., Mr. Montague Corrie, Mr. Algernon Turner, Major-General H. Y. D. Scott, Manager of the Association, and numerous Members of Parliament. Her Majesty who takes a deep interest in this movement for the improvement of the dwellings of her people, commanded Earl Beaconsfield to express Her wish that Her name may be associated with this institution and that in future these buildings will be called the Victoria Dwellings for Artizans.

On the North side of Battersea Park Road is the site for Messrs. Spiers and Pond's New Steam Laundry, contiguous to which (Propert's) Blacking Manufactory is now built. Mr George Ashby Lean, Architect; Mr. Waters, Builder, The Common, Ealing.

Up the centre of the meadow a new road is to be made 50 feet wide. About forty years ago this ground yielded as fine a crop of wheat as any in England. At that time certain Notice Boards were erected with the words *"Any person found plucking an ear of Corn will be fined one shilling."* An old parishioner, who is still living, told the writer that he had been fined three shillings because he had picked up three ears of corn which another man had thrown away.

Latchmere Allotments.—Dove Dale Place.—An Old Boiler.—Lammas Hall.—The Union Workhouse.

BATTERSEA (LATCHMERE, formerly called Lechmore) ALLOTMENTS cover an area of 16¼ acres, and are let to the industrial poor of the parish to encourage habits of industry, the land was applied to the present purpose in the year 1835. Originally there were 74 allotments now there are 156. The Allotments let at 3/- a plot, each allotment being divided into 10 plots. Application must be made to the Churchwardens, William Evill and Joseph William Hiscox, Esqrs.

Pleasantly situated between the Albert and Bridge Roads, Battersea Park Road, is Dove Dale Place, founded by the late Mrs. Lightfoot of Balham, (Widow of the late Dr. Lightfoot) for persons in reduced circumstances professing godliness, whether in connection with the Church of England or members of other Christian Churches having small yearly private incomes of their own. There are twelve accommodations of two small rooms each, there are two four-room cottages one at each end with gardens. In the middle of the centre block is a Chapel and over the window is the representation of a Dove bearing an Olive Branch. There are some pecuniary advantages connected with the foundation. It is in the hands of Trustees.

On a plot of ground by the main road opposite Dove Dale Place stands an *old boiler* that belonged to one Andrew Mann—it has stood (we are told) where it is for the last twenty five years. Before its removal to Battersea, it stood on a piece of land in Vauxhall Bridge Road.

LAMMAS HALL situated in Bridge Road West, is Licensed Pursuant to Act of Parliament of the 25th of King George 2nd, was erected in 1858. The Hall will seat about 400 persons and may be hired for lectures, concerts, and other public purposes. The front part of the building is used as a Vestry Hall and for the transaction of other parochial business. A more commodious Hall is urgently needed in a central part of the parish, so also are required Baths, Lavatory, and a Public Library. Lammas Hall owes its origin from a fund which was paid by the Battersea Park Commissioners for the extinguishment of the Lammas Rights to the Churchwardens, by resolution of the Vestry after several schemes had been brought forward they proposed to build a Hall and Vice Chancellor Stuart appointed the Trustees hence its name "Lammas Hall." Mr Thomas Harrap, *Vestry Clerk.*

THE UNION WORKHOUSE, erected in 1836 is situated within the boundary of Battersea parish at the junction of East Hill and St. John's Hill, it is an extensive brick building with accommodation for 833 inmates. The Infirmary adjoining was added in 1870 at a cost of £40,000. The Casual Ward in addition is constructed for 117 casual paupers. The Union comprises Battersea, Clapham, Putney, Streatham, Tooting, and Wandsworth with a population in 1871 of 125,000 and an area of 11,488 acres. John Sanders, *Solicitor and Clerk*; Edward H. Taylor, *Assistant Clerk*; Rev. William Armstrong, *Chaplain*; T. H. Cresswell, *Medical Officer*; John Hodge, *Master*; Mrs Martha Hodge, *Matron*; Mr. Pettman, *Missionary*.[54]

---

[54] The poor of England till the time of Henry VIII. subsisted as the poor of Ireland until 1838 entirely upon private benevolence. Judge Blackstone observes that till the Statute 26, Henry VIII. cap. 26, he finds no compulsory method for providing for the poor, but upon the total dissolution of the Monasteries, abundance of Statutes were made in the reign of King Henry VIII., Edward VI. and Elizabeth which at last established the Poor's Rate, a legal

Old Battersea Workhouse.—The "Cage."—The "Stocks."

Old Battersea Workhouse, which has long since been pulled down, was situated in the neighbourhood of Battersea Square. In the same neighbourhood is the "Priory," now the residence of Mr. Oakman. Not far from the Raven Tavern was the "Cage," in Surrey Lane, for the confinement of petty criminals. Near the Prince's Head Tavern was the Pound in which cattle were enclosed for trespass until replevied or redeemed. Also a wooden machine called the "Stocks" to put the legs of offenders in, for securing disorderly persons, and by way of punishment in divers cases, ordained by statute, &c., was erected without the gates of Battersea Churchyard, near the waterside.

In the last quarter of the eighteenth century, writes Robert Chambers in his "Book of Days," there flourished at the corner of the lane leading from the Wandsworth Road to Battersea Bridge a tavern yclept "The Falcon," kept by one Robert Death—a man whose figure is said to have ill comported with his name, seeing that it displayed the highest appearance of jollity and good condition. A merry-hearted artist, named John Nixon, passing the house one day, found an Undertaker's company regaling themselves at 'Death's door,' having just discharged their duty to a rich Nabob in a neighbouring churchyard, they had ... found an opportunity for refreshing exhausted nature; and well did they ply the joyful work before them. The artist, tickled at a festivity among such characters in such a place, sketched

---

assessment for the support of the poor. Before the Reformation immense sums of money were appropriated for charitable purposes, and notwithstanding many abuses the religious order of those days never so far lost sight of this original institution as ever to neglect the poor. The famous Statute of the 43rd of Elizabeth, 1601, by which Overseers were appointed for Parishes is the basis of all the poor laws in England. By Statute 23, Edward III., 1342, it was enacted that none should give alms to a beggar able to work. An Act was passed 1531, empowering Justices to grant licenses to poor and impotent persons to beg within certain limits of territory. By the Common Law, the poor were to be sustained by "parsons, rectors of the church and parishioners so that none should die for default of sustenance," and by 15 Richard II. impropriators were obliged to distribute a yearly sum to the poor. An act of 1601 directed that every parish shall provide for its own poor by an assessment to be levied by the Justices in General Sessions and embodied regulations as to how assessment should be made and applied. In 1782 Workhouse Unions were introduced by an Act called Gilbert's Act. The Act of 1834 among other changes established the system of Poor Law Unions. In Scotland the poor were really maintained by the private Alms of individuals and by certain funds under the management of the *Kirk Session*, which when regularly constituted consisted of the Minister, Elders, Session Clerk and Kirk Treasurer. The Presbytery was by law appointed Auditor of the Poor's Accounts of the several parishes. In the event of any difficult case arising in the discharge of this duty the Presbytery could lay it before the Synod for advice. "Scotland and Ireland have been legislated for separately, their poor laws are similar to the English in principle and practice; both are administered by a Central Board, which supervises the local bodies charged with relief, and in both the rate is levied on the annual value of real property. The present system in Scotland was instituted by the 8th and 9th Vic. c. 83 (1845). Scotland is divided into 883 parishes, some of them combined for Workhouse accommodation. The relief is administered by a parochial board, appointed by ratepayers, the Burgh Magistrate and the Kirk Session. They appoint Inspectors of the poor who act as relieving officers. The Scotch law differs from the English and Irish in allowing no relief to able bodied adults."

them on the spot. This sketch was soon after published, accompanied by a cantata from another hand of no great merit, in which the foreman of the company, Mr. Sable, is represented as singing as follows, to the tune of 'I've kissed and I've prattled with fifty fair maids': —

"Dukes, Lords, have I buried, and squires of fame,
And people of every degree;
But of all the fine jobs that ere came in my way,
A funeral like this for me.
This, this is the job
That fills the fob;
Oh! the burying of a Nabob for me!
Unfeather the hearse, put the pall in the bag,
Give the horses some oats and some hay;
Drink our next merry meeting and quackeries increase
With three times three and hurra!"

The Falcon Tavern.—A Cantata.

A portion of the Falcon Tavern erected about 275 years ago at the end of Falcon Lane still remains with the old witch elm tree in front, its hollow trunk, to which a door is attached, answers the purpose of a bin or cupboard where hay is put with which to feed horses, and the old wooden-cased pump, fastened with rusty hold-fasts to the tree, may still be seen. On the 15th of January, 1811, a printed engraving was published representing "Undertakers regaling" by this road-side inn, a copy of which may now be seen within. At that time R. Death was the landlord, he had written outside the tavern in large characters, Robert Death, Dealer in Genuine Rum, Gin, Wine; an Ordinary on Sundays; Tea, Coffee and Hot Rolls; Syllabubs and Cheese-cakes in the highest perfection. The subjoined doggerel lines as a skit or burlesque on the publican's name is published with the engraving:—

"O stop not here ye sottish wights,
For purl nor ale nor gin,
For if you stop whoe'er alights
By Death is taken in.
When having eat and drank your fill
Should ye, O hapless case,
Neglect to pay your landlord's bill
Death stares you in the face.
With grief sincere I pity those
Who've drawn themselves this scrape in,
Since from this dreadful gripe, heaven knows,
Alas! there's no escaping.
This one advice my friend pursue
Whilst you have life and breath,
Ne'er pledge your host for if you do
You'll surely drink to Death."

The Falcon Tavern is now kept by Mr. J. G. Brown.

Origin of Bottled Ale in England.—"Ye Plough Inn."—"The Old House."—Stump of an Old Oak Tree.

Mr. Edward Walford in his work entitled "Old and New London," published by Cassell, Petter and Galpin, London; in Part 66 at Page 479, writes, "Battersea has other claims to immortality: in spite of the claims of Burton and Edinburgh, there can be little doubt, if Fuller is a trustworthy historian, that one of the ozier beds of the river side here was the cradle of bottled ale. The story is thus circumstantially told in 'The Book of Anecdote':—Alexander Nowell, Dean of St Paul's and Master of Westminster School in the reign of Queen Mary, was a supporter of 'the new opinions' and also an excellent angler. But, writes Fuller, while Nowell was catching of fishes Bishop Bonner was after catching of Nowell, and would certainly have sent him to the Tower if he could have caught him, as doubtless he would have done had not a good merchant of London conveyed him away safely upon the seas. It so happened that Nowell had been fishing upon the banks of the Thames when he received the first intimation of his danger, which was so pressing that he dared not even go back to his house to make any preparation for his flight. Like an honest angler, he had taken with him on this expedition provisions for the day, in the shape of some bread and cheese and some beer in a bottle; and on his return from London and to his own haunts he remembered that he had left these stores in a safe place upon the bank, and there he resolved to look for them. The bread and cheese of course were gone; but the bottle was still there—'yet no bottle, but rather a gun: such was the sound at the opening thereof.' And this trifling circumstance, quaintly observes Fuller, 'is believed to have been the origin of bottled ale in England, for casualty (*i.e.* accident) is mother of more inventions than is industry.'"

On the road to Wandsworth and facing Plough Lane was "Ye Plough Inn," erected A.D. 1701. In front of this Inn grew an oak to which an iron ring was fastened, and it is supposed that here Dick Turpin the notorious highwayman occasionally reined up his bonny black mare. When the Inn was re-built in 1875-6 the trunk was removed to the front of the "Old House" in Plough Lane, which formerly belonged to Mr. Carter, who owned extensive market gardens about here. The following lines were written in commemoration of the famous Old Plough Tree, and the present landlord has had the lines enframed for his customers to read:—

> "This stump the remains of the Old Oak Tree,
> That flourish'd when knights of the road roamed free,
> When bands of lawless yet chivalrous knights
> Struck fear to the hearts of purse-proud wights!
> This gay old king of the forest's wilds,
> His proud head bow'd to the sun's bright smiles,
> In glorious prime when his branches were strong
> As shoulders of Atlas in time long gone!
> His leaves in the murmuring breeze did fling
> Their sweet green shade o'er the Old Plough Inn!
> When the knights of the road of their deeds did sing,
> 'Twas there to his side was first fixed the ring

To which Dick Turpin the gallant and bold
When going to the Plough to spend his bright gold
Did tether his mare, swift Bonny Black Bess.
When rider and horse stopp'd here to get rest.
Removed from his place when the Old Plough's head
By time's fell decree in ruin was laid!
This stump that remains of the Old Plough tree
In front of 'The Old House,' in Plough Lane you may see.
Here placed in memory of the Old Plough Inn
An aged memento of things that have been!
Here in his last stage, sapped branchless and grey,
Here in cool September, the trunk's first day,
In the year eighteen hundred and seventy-six,
Was planted by Messrs. J. Goodman and Wilkes."

William Holloway.

Situated in Plough Lane, and nearly opposite the residence of the late Rev. M. Soule, were Alms Houses for eight poor widows, founded by Mrs. Henry 'ritton. The whole of this estate is now built upon and is called May Soule Road.

"Lawn House," Lombard Road.—The Prizes for the Kean's Sovereigns and the Funny Boat Race.—The Old Swan Tavern.—Royal Victoria Patriotic Schools.

At Lawn House, now occupied by Mr. Miller the Barge Builder in Lombard Road, of the Firm of Nash and Miller, lived Mr. Hammett, of the firm of Eisdale nd Hammett, Bankers. He was a great patron of the rowing fraternity and kept an pen house two days in the year. He awarded the prizes for the Kean's Sovereigns nd the Funny Boat Club races on the lawn in front of his house.

The Old Swan Tavern (now kept by Mr. R. Turner) nearly opposite the Star nd Garter, was a kind of half-way house between Lambeth and Putney for the ton and Westminster scholars who used to put in here when training for the great rowing match so strongly contested between them, but who in the zenith of heir fame never obtained such popularity as the annual boat race has done of late etween the Cantabs and Oxonians.

An old-fashioned print represents the former Parish Church of Battersea with quare tower crowned with lantern and pinnacles, not far off is the Swan Tavern vith stairs leading down to the river where persons arriving by boat might land. An excellent wood-cut engraving in "Lysons's Environs" represents not only the New Parish Church but the sign of the Old Swan with two necks. Charles Dibdin n a ballad opera entitled "The Waterman; or the first of August," first performed at he Theatre Royal, Haymarket, August 8th, 1774, Scene III.—Battersea—represents room at the Swan, with a large open window looking on the Thames in which Master Bundle the honest gardener and hen-pecked husband, and Mrs. Bundle the ermagant wife, the Star of Battersea, figure conspicuously. Reference is also made n Scene I. to the "Black Raven," now kept by W. Ambrose. It is said that in olden time this was a Posting Establishment for Royalty.

Situated on Wandsworth Common and overlooking the London Brighton and South-Coast and South-Western Railways are the Royal Victoria Patriotic Schools for Boys and Girls, children of deceased soldiers, sailors and marines. Founded by Her Most Gracious Majesty, 1854-56. The Patriotic Asylum was endowed by the Commissioners of the Royal Patriotic Fund which was instituted in 1854 for the purpose of giving "assistance to the widows and orphans of those who fell during the Crimean and more recent wars, and to provide schools for their children." Within the boundary of Battersea Parish is situated the Asylum for Boys but the Asylum for Girls which is some three hundred yards distant is in the parish of Wandsworth. 200 boys are in the Asylum. *Superintendent*, W. Ridpath; *Office*, 5, St Martin's Place, Trafalgar Square; *Secretary*, W. H. Mugford, Esq.

St. James' Industrial Schools.—Royal Masonic Institution for Girls.

Near the southern boundary of the parish and not far from Wandsworth Common Railway Station, are situated St. James' Industrial Schools.[55]This Institution stands on a portion of 22 acres of land purchased of the Right Honourable Frederick Earl Spencer, K.G., and conveyed to the Governors and Directors of the Poor of the Parish of St. James, Westminster, by Deed bearing dates, the thirtieth day of December, one thousand eight hundred and fifty. The first stone laid 24th September, 1851. The School opened 22nd June, 1852. F. Parkis, Superintendent. There are now 141 boys in the schools. On leaving a premium of £10 is given to each boy to learn a trade. Mrs. Anne Newton, late of upper Harley Street in the Parish of Mary-le-bone, widow, deceased, by her Will left, dated the 12th of March, 1806, £1,000. £429 19s. 3d. has been received through the Court of Chancery. The interest is given to the best boy selected by his fellow scholars, on condition that the Superintendent agrees with their decision.

The Royal Masonic Institution for Girls supported entirely by *Voluntary Contributions*, was instituted on the 25th March, 1788, at the suggestion of the late Chevalier Bartholomew Ruspini, Surgeon-Dentist to his late Majesty, George the Fourth, for the purpose of educating, clothing, and maintaining a limited number of girls, whether orphans or otherwise, the children of Brethren whose reduced means prevented them from affording their female offspring a suitable education. His late Majesty, the Prince of Wales, with other members of the Royal Family, the nobility, clergy and gentry, and many of the most influential members of the craft, gave the project their warmest support, and by their united efforts established this Institution, which has preserved numbers of children from the dangers and misfortunes to which females are peculiarly exposed, trained them up in the knowledge and love of virtue and habits of industry, and cultivated the practice of such social, moral and religious duties as might best conduce to their welfare and eternal happiness. A school-house was erected in 1793, near the Obelisk, St. George's Fields,

---

[55] Mr. Beal sold on Wednesday, March 13th, 1878, at the Mart, 14½ acres of land for £14,500, being part of 20 acres bought in 1850 for the sum of £600. The land is in Battersea Parish, bordering on Wandsworth Common, and was part of the site of the Westminster Union (St. James') Industrial Schools. It was bought by the British Land Company.

on leasehold ground belonging to the Corporation of the City of London. At the expiration of the lease in 1851, it was determined by the Committee to remove to a more healthy locality. Accordingly about three acres of freehold land were purchased on the high ground of Battersea Rise. Upon this land the present building, which is an ornament to the neighbourhood, was erected in 1852. It is constructed of red brick of Gothic architecture from the designs of Mr. Phillip Hardwicke, and is noticeable for its great central clock tower. Since the first erection of the building a wing has been added and the wings of the buildings have been extended in front in order to afford extra school-room, dining room and dormitory accommodation. Detached from the main building an Infirmary has been erected in the grounds, including *convalescent room, laundry, and every appliance necessary thereto.* The establishment consists of a Matron; a Governess; three Assistant Governesses; an Assistant to the Matron, and six Junior Teachers; a Gardener and his Wife; and eight female Servants. Since its establishment, one thousand and ninety-one girls have been educated, clothed, and maintained within its walls. There are now *one hundred and sixty-two* girls in the Institution. The school is open for inspection every day from eleven to four (Sundays excepted) and can be reached by any train stopping at Clapham Junction which is closely adjacent.

Clapham Junction.—Battersea Provident Dispensary.

CLAPHAM JUNCTION is in the direction of St. John's Hill, at the north-eastern extremity of Wandsworth Common. "The station itself which was at first one of the most inconvenient, was re-built a few years ago, and now with its various sidings and goods-sheds cover several acres of ground." It is one of the most important railway junctions south of the Thames, offering facilities to persons desirous of travelling not only to any part of the Metropolis but to all parts of England. Easy access can be had to the eight different platforms for "upline" and "downline," etc., on entering the tunnel. Booking office for Kensington, Metropolitan line, etc., on the ground floor at the north end of the tunnel and facing No. 2 platform; Booking office South-Western line No. 5 platform; Booking office Brighton and South-Coast No. 8 platform; also Telegraph office ditto ditto.

At the Junction there are thirteen waiting rooms, two refreshment bars, two cab ranks, two carriage roads to the Junction from St. John's Hill. Nearly 1,000 trains pass through the Junction daily. The staff of railway employés are respectful and obliging to passengers; there is none of that bull-dog growl in reply to questions which characterize some men with surly dispositions who fill public positions.

> "Evil is wrought from want of thought
> As well as want of heart."

London, Brighton and South-Coast Railway: Station Master, Mr. John B. Carne; South-Western Railway: Station Master, Mr. Thomas Green. West London Extension Railway: Battersea Station, High Street.

BATTERSEA PROVIDENT DISPENSARY, 175, High Street, founded 1844, re-organized 1876; President, The Rev. Canon Erskine Clarke, Vicar of Battersea;

Hon. Secretary and Treasurer, Mr. B. W. Bayley; Committee for 1881, Dr. J. Brown, Mr. J. H. T. Connor, Mr. Heale, Mr. Merry, Mr. Pilditch, Rev. S. G. Scott, Rev. H. G. Sprigg, Rev. J. Toone, Mr. Trehearne, Mr. Tyrer, Mr. H. Urwicke; Elected Representatives of Benefit Members, Mr. King, Mr. Whensley; Medical Officers, Mr. Oakman, The Priory, Battersea Square; Mr. G. F. Burroughs, Queen's Road, and Grayshott Road; Dr. R. Frazer, Sisters Terrace, Lavender Hill; Mr. Biggs, 93, Northcote Road; Mr. Sewell (Kempster & Sewell), 247, Battersea Park Road; Resident Dispenser, Mr. Whitehead; Collector, Mr. Chatting.

The Funds of the Institution are derived from two sources. (1) From the weekly payments of Subscribers who are termed members. (2) From annual contributions of the more affluent, who on subscribing to the Institution become honorary members. Medical attendance and medicine are supplied to persons earning not more than 30/- a week on payment of one penny per week for those over 14, and one half-penny per week for those under 14; but no greater sum than fourpence shall be required from any family residing together as such. To persons earning more than 30/- and not more than 50/- per week, double the terms named above. Members select their own medical attendant from the medical officers of the Institution. The medical officers attend at the Dispensary at appointed hours, but give advice at their own residences, and visit the sick at their own houses when necessary. The Dispensary is open for the supply of medicines daily, except Sunday, at 10, 3 and 7; but medicines are supplied at all hours in urgent cases.

Wandsworth Common Provident Dispensary.—Charity Organization Society.—The Penny Bank.—No. 54 Metropolitan Fire Brigade Station.—Origin of Fire Brigades.

WANDSWORTH COMMON PROVIDENT DISPENSARY, Bolingbroke House.—President, The Rev. Canon J. Erskine Clarke; Honorary Secretaries and Treasurers, Rev. J. H. Hodgson, Church House, Bolingbroke Grove; J. S. Wood, Esq., Woodville, Upper Tooting; Honorary Dentist, A. J. East, Esq., St. John's Hill, New Wandsworth; Resident Medical Officer, Dr. John H. Gray.

CHARITY ORGANIZATION SOCIETY, 1, Clifton Terrace.—Office hours, 9 till 10 a.m. and 5 to 6 p.m. Joint Secretaries: J. H. Ward, Esq., and Frank Knight, Esq., Agent, Mr. J. T. Thornton. Sub-office: St. George's Mission Room, New Road.

THE PENNY BANK, 1, Clifton Terrace, Battersea Park Road, is open on Mondays and Saturdays, from 7 to 8 p.m.

Conspicuously situated at the corner of Simpson Street, Battersea Park Road, is No. 54 Metropolitan Fire Brigade Station, erected 1873-4, is substantially built of red brick, with turret. In case of fire two engines and one fire-escape are kept on the premises. Staff: one officer and four men.

"We are indebted to Germany for the invention of the first fire engine."

Respecting the origin of fire brigades: "In 1774 an Act was passed requiring every Parish to provide itself with one large and one small engine, &c., and everything necessary in case of fire. The first London fire brigade was an Institution

ntirely independent of the parishes, as indeed also of the Government and of the
Corporation of London. It was created and exclusively supported by the Insurance
Companies of the Metropolis. At first every Insurance Company had its own fire
ngine and men to work it, but in 1825 some of them joined, and when the advan-
age of union was seen most of the others desired to take part in the combination
lready formed, the result of which was that in 1833 a more extensive organization
vas made, to which the name of the London Fire Brigade was given. Such was
he state of matters until by Act 28 and 29 Vict. cap. xc., July 5th, 1865, the duty of
xtinguishing fires and protecting life and property in case of fire was declared
o be entrusted to the Metropolitan Board of Works within their jurisdiction, and
provision was made for the establishment of the Metropolitan Fire Brigade. The
Act provides for its support from three sources, viz.: 1st, £10,000 Grant from Trea-
ury; 2nd, ½d. in the £ Rate; 3rd, £35 for every £1,000,000 insured in the Metropolis
rom Insurance Companies, which in the year ending December 31, 1872, realized
£16,267. All the Stations are in direct communication by telegraph with the Central
Station, so that any required number of engines or men may be summoned to any
given spot without delay. In 1872 the cost of maintenance was: Brigade, £67,520;
Stations, £8,793; Total, £76,313. All the Dock Companies have engines, and some
large private firms." — *Popular Cyclopedia*, Blackie & Son.

By 1833 all the important Companies combined and the London Fire Brigade
vas formed, organised and raised to an efficient standard under the management
of the late and much lamented Mr. James Braidwood, who met with his death in
he act of discharging his duties at the great conflagration which broke out in the
afternoon of Saturday, June 22nd 1861, in one of the warehouses on the banks of
he river, close to the Surrey side of London Bridge, which in spite of increasing
efforts to extinguish it, continued to burn until it destroyed property worth nearly
£2,000,000. The destruction of property thus caused by the fiery element is without
a parallel in the Metropolis since the great fire of 1666. "Three acres of ground were
gradually covered with a mass of fire, glowing and crackling at a white heat like a
ake of molten iron. The saltpetre, the tallow, the tar and other combustibles stored
in the warehouses ran blazing into the Thames until the very river appeared to be
covered with the flames. Ships were burned as well as houses, and the danger to
life was almost as great on the river as in the street. The glare of the conflagration
was not only visible but strikingly conspicuous 30 miles off."

The Metropolitan Police.—Police Stations, Battersea.—St. John's College of the National Society.

THE METROPOLITAN POLICE.—The organization of the present effective
Police force is due to Sir Robert Peel's bill of 1829. The force is divided into the
City Police, confined to the City proper, whose office is in the Old Jury, and the
Metropolitan Police, which consists of about 8,200 men, and whose Chief Station
is in Scotland Yard.

Metropolitan Police Station, Battersea, V. Sub-Division, Bridge Road. *Superintendent*, Mr. Digby; *Inspectors*, Mr. McCrory, Mr. Steggles. Number of men about
70. W. Division New Police Station, Battersea Park Road.

The full force of the Metropolitan Police in 1876 was 10,238.[56]

Board of Works for the Wandsworth District, Battersea Rise, S.W. Arthur Alex Corsellis, *Clerk of the Board.*

ST. JOHN'S COLLEGE of the National Society is situated in Lombard Road fo the training of young men who are intended to become schoolmasters in school: connected with the Church of England. There are at this time about 80 students The Rev. Evan Daniel, M.A., Principal; Rev. Edwin Hammonds, Vice-Principal Mr. George White, Secretary and Tutor; Mr. Arthur Macken, Tutor; M. Alphonse Estoclet, French Master; Mr. E. C. May, Teacher of Music; Mr. W. Taylor, Norma Master; Mr. E. Mills, Organist; Dr. Connor, Medical Attendant.

The College owes its origin to Dr. J. P. Kay-Shuttleworth and Mr. E. C. Tufnell Assistant Poor-Law Commissioner, who with the view of establishing a Norma School in this country for imparting to young men that due amount of knowledge and training them to those habits of simplicity and earnestness which might ren der them useful instructors to the poor, travelled to Holland, Prussia, Switzerland Paris and other places that they might witness the operations of such educationa schemes as had been projected by Pestalozzi, De Fellenberg and others interestec in promoting the education of the poor. The plan suggested by Dr. Kay-Shuttle worth and Mr. Tufnell met with the hearty and most cordial approval of the Vicar the Hon. and Rev. R. Eden, who offered them the use of his village schools to carry out their benevolent intentions. In 1840 they selected a commodious manor house near the river Thames, at Battersea. Boys as students were first obtained from the School of Industry at Norwood, who were to be kept in training for three years Subsequently some young men joined the Institution whose period of training was necessarily limited to one year. In 1843, the Directors, Dr. Kay-Shuttleworth and Mr. Tufnell, who had supported the Institution by their own private means, had it transferred into the hands of the National Society. The Continental modes of instruction which had been adopted, such as Mulhauser's method of writing, Wilhelm's method of singing, Dupuis' method of drawing, etc., were so satisfactory that a grant of £2,200 for the enlargement and improvement of the premises was made to them by the Committee of Council on Education which was transferred to the National Society and without delay disbursed in completing the alterations required. In the early part of 1846 a new class-room was erected. "The Institution is supported by the National Society's special fund for providing schoolmasters for the manufacturing and mining districts. Only young men are received as students, whose term of training is generally two years."

The Vicarage House School.—Various Wharves and Factories.

THE VICARAGE HOUSE SCHOOL is also situated here. Principal: Miss

[56] The Report of the Commissioners of Police for the year 1879 shows that in December the Metropolitan police numbered 10,711, which was an increase of 234 over the previous year. The number of felonies committed during the year was 21,891, for which 11,431 persons were arrested. The loss by thefts was £101,798, of which £22,460 was recovered. The Director of Criminal Investigations reports that photography and engraving have been extensively used in the tracing of criminals, with very satisfactory results.

Crofts. Fees from half a guinea to a guinea per quarter, according to age and attainments. The only extra subjects are Music and French.

On the border of the river between Albert Bridge and Watney's Distillery are several wharfs and factories. Ribbon Factory of Cornell, Lyell and Webster; the Glove Factory of Fownes & Co.; Garton, Hill & Co.'s Sugar Refinery now in course of erection; Orlando Jones & Co.'s Rice Starch Manufactory; Denny's (Creek) Flour Mills;[57] Price's Patent Candle Company's Factory; B. Freeman & Co.'s Varnish and Color Works; T. Whiffin's Chemical Manufactory; Nash and Miller, Barge Builders; A. B. Cox, Barge and Boat Builder; Watney's Malt Houses.

Mr. George Chadwin.—T. Gaines.—Tow's Private Mad House.—The Patent Plumbago Crucible Company's Works.

On the site where now stands Fownes & Co.'s Glove Factory, formerly used as a silk factory, was Bonwell and Waymouth's Distillery. This firm furnished a Corps of (Battersea) Volunteers, of which the late Mr. George Chadwin was an ensign. Mr. Jonathan Browne, who used to preach at the Old Baptist Meeting House, York Road, was the grandfather of Mr. George Jonathan Chadwin, of Lombard Road, who was Vestry Clerk for 29 years in conjunction with his father.

T. Gaines, a celebrated Horticulturist and Florist, resided in an ancient mansion that stood in Surrey Lane, thought by some to have been a private residence of Queen Elizabeth. The house has been pulled down.

J. Tow kept a Private Mad House in High Street, It is now occupied by Austin & Co., Dyers.

It is supposed by some that there was in olden time a Foundry in Battersea for casting shot, etc., for the Tower of London.

THE PATENT PLUMBAGO CRUCIBLE COMPANY'S WORKS, which are the largest crucible works in the world, cover a large space of ground and have a river frontage. The principal elevation in Church Road is a conspicuous feature in the neighbourhood. It is Italian in character freely treated and somewhat Continental in design. The clock tower rises about 100 feet high, in which is an illuminated clock that may be seen at a considerable distance. A portion of the basement of this elegant structure is appropriated to the private office of the manager and clerks' offices where every quality of plumbago is represented by specimens from all the most celebrated mines, particularly those of Ceylon, Germany, Spain, Siberia, Canada, Finland and Borrowdale. The other departments are the stores, grinding room, mixing room, potters' room, drying room, the clay department, store room, etc. Crucibles for melting and refining metals have been used ever since man threw aside his hatchet and bone-chisel for bronze. For scientific research the crucible has occupied an important place. It was constantly used by the first alchemists and has truly been styled the cradle of experimental chemistry. The word crucible from the Latin crux-crucis recalls the alchemical practice of marking the vessel with the protective sign of the cross. Crucibles of different shapes and sizes are extensively employed by the refiner of gold and silver, the brass founder, melters of copper,

[57] A pair of 4-ft. stones will grind four bushels per hour.

zinc and malleable iron, the manufacture of cast steel, the assayer and the practical chemist. For ordinary metallurgical operations clay crucibles are extensively employed. At the International Exhibition of 1862 the only prize medal for crucible was awarded to the Company and another prize medal for blackleads. The Company's crucibles are now used exclusively by the English, Australian and Indian Mints; the Royal Arsenals of Woolwich, Brest, and Toulon, etc., etc., and have been adopted by most of the large engineers, brass founders and refiners in this country and abroad. Their great superiority consists in their capability of melting on an average forty pourings of the most difficult metals, and a still greater number of those of an ordinary character, some of them having actually reached the extraordinary number of 96 meltings. These crucibles never crack, become heated much more rapidly than any other description, and require only one annealing, may be used any number of times without further trouble, change of temperature (they may be plunged while cold into a furnace nearly white hot without cracking having no effect on them. The Patent Plumbago Crucible Company are the greatest consumers of the Ceylon Graphite brought to the United Kingdom. The total quantity of Graphite exports from Ceylon in 1862 was 40,195 cwt., of which 34,730 cwt. was shipped to Great Britain.

This Company are at present carrying out very extensive improvements on the river side along the front of their premises in the construction of a river wall built of Portland Cement Concrete, the foundations of which are carried down four feet below Trinity Low Water Mark, which have been done without the aid of a coffer-dam. These works when completed will reclaim a very valuable frontage of the river. The total length of wall and camp-shedding together with the adjoining property of Messrs. May and Baker's Chemical Works will be about 500 feet.

These improvements if extended westward towards the Parish Church will be the means of doing away with the unsightly mud banks which now exist, there is no doubt then a clean foreshore will be accomplished similar to the south side lower down the river where more extensive embankment works have been constructed. Behind a portion of the wall which the Plumbago Company are constructing will be some extensive cellars, which will be covered over with a concrete floor carried on wrought iron girders and supported by cast iron columns, and on the top of this floor will be a tram seven feet wide for the use of a heavy steam crane, and when completed will be able to unload goods out of barges alongside and deliver the same into the second floor of the present warehouse.

These works have been constructed from the designs and under the superintendence of Mr. W. H. Thomas, C.E., of 15 Parliament Street, Westminster, Engineer to the Patent Plumbago Crucible Company, and now being carried out by Messrs. B. Cook & Co., of Phœnix Wharf, Church Road Battersea, Mr. Maples acting as Clerk of the Works.

The same firm are also constructing large river-side works at Nine Elms for the London Gas-Light Company for a Ship's Berth, from the design and under the superintendence of Robert Morton, Esq., the Company's Engineer.

A very striking feature is connected with the latter works, as it is proposed to bring vessels up the river capable of carrying 1,000 tons of coals which will be discharged by the use of hydraulic cranes and delivered by tram direct into the Gas Works.

Silicated Carbon Filter Company's Works.

Adjacent are the Silicated Carbon Filter Company's Works. Whenever man has arrived at any considerable degree of civilization the subject of water supply had a share in his solicitude, and it is questionable if our modern works for supplying water surpass those of ancient Judea, Greece, Rome, Mexico and other places. The effect of impure water on the health and life of the community was alas, too painfully evinced by the outbreak of cholera in 1854-1866, and by the reports of medical officers as to the cause of typhoid fever.

The Silicated Carbon Filters are so constructed that the solid matter deposited on the filtering medium can be easily cleansed away. They entirely remove from water all organic matter and every trace of lead, and for all domestic purposes they may be said to render water absolutely pure. Testimonials from eminent authorities describe the extraordinary power possessed by these filters of entirely freeing water from every noxious quality.

Condy's Manufactory.—Citizen Steamboat Company's Works.

Contiguous are the premises belonging to Mr. H. Bollman Condy, the Inventor, Patentee, and Manufacturer of Antiseptic Aromatic Vinegar, "Condy's Fluid," and "Condy's Ozonised Sea Salt."

Adjoining are the Citizen Steamboat Company's Works and Dock, whose steamboats leave Battersea to London Bridge and intervening piers every ten minutes from 8 a.m. till dark. Entrance: Bridge Road. Manager: Mr. M. Williams.

Situated in Wellington Road is A. Ransome & Co.'s Battersea Foundry.

S. Williams' Barge Works, Albert Road.

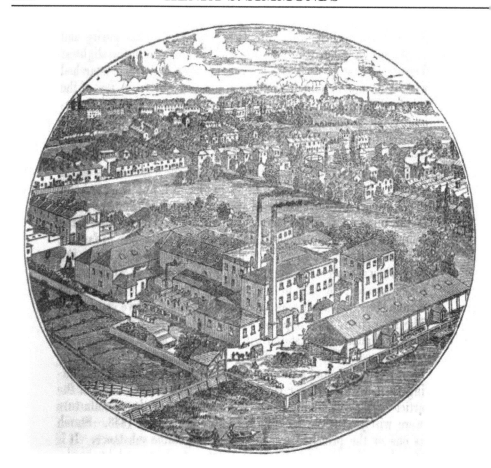

Orlando Jones & Co.'s Starch Works.

ORLANDO JONES & CO.'S STARCH WORKS.—Oryza is the name by which rice was known to the Greeks and Romans and which has been adopted by botanists as the generic name of the plant yielding that valuable grain. The name *Paddy* is applied to the rice in the natural state, or before being separated from the husk. The genua Oryza has two glumes to a single flower; paleae two, nearly equal, adhering to the seed; stamens six, and styles two. The common rice *Oryza Sativa* unlike many cultivated grams is still found in a wild state in and about the borders of lakes in the Rajahmundy Circare though the grain in its wild state is white, palatable and considered wholesome the produce when compared with the varieties of cultivation is very small. The rice plant is described as a native of India from which country it has spread over a great part of the world especially in Asia where it forms the principal portion of the food of the inhabitants. A failure of the rice crop is most disastrous as has been experienced too painfully by the natives of India during the late famine in that region. "A rice field produces a much greater quantity of food than the most fertile corn fields. Two crops in the year, from thirty to sixty bushels each, are said to be the ordinary produce of an acre." Rice is now extensively cultivated in North and South Carolina, and in Georgia, also in Italy and the South of Spain and likewise a little in Germany. There are forty or fifty varieties of rice. Dr. Roxburgh divides them into two kinds. One called in Telinga, Poonas Sans; the second division of cultivated rice is called Pedder Worloo by the Telingas.

Rice Starch is principally used for laundry purposes it will be found distinguished from all others by its singular purity and brightness of color. It will not stick to the iron in the slightest degree. It may be used with hot or cold water, and articles starched with it do not lose their stiffness in damp weather. A few of the principal sources of the various known starches are sago, arrowroot, yams, the manioc-root and horse chesnuts in addition to those resorted to by manufacturers, viz.: wheat, potato, maize and rice, the latter being a great novelty and illustrating more than any other the progress of chemical science. Wheat starch is the oldest known. It is alluded to by Pliny in the 'Natural History,' and the discovery of the method of its extraction is attributed by him to the inhabitants of the Island of Chios. The starches used three centuries ago, when such enormous ruffles and frills were in fashion were made from wheat; in fact down to modern times it was the only known source of starch. Owing to a scarcity of wheat at the commencement of the present century the use of wheat for the manufacture of starch was prohibited by a legislative enactment. The restrictions thus imposed were considered most oppressive, no one could manufacture starch without a licence and a tenement rent was exacted. The details of manufacture were subject to Government regulations and a duty of 3¼d. per pound was levied, amounting to more than 75 per cent. of the present market value of the article. These hindrances to the extension of the manufacture were wisely removed by our Legislature in the year 1833. Starch is one of the principal constituents of vegetable substance. It is stored up in the seeds, roots and piths of plants and by its decomposition furnishes the materials for keeping up respiration and supplying the animal heat. It has an organised structure and when examined by the microscope presents the form of rounded grains or granules composed of concentric layers which differ in size and shape in the starch of different plants the granules varying in diameter from 1000th to 300th of an inch. However the composition is the same, consisting of seventy-two parts of carbon and eighty-one of water. "In its pure state starch is a fine white powder without taste or smell. It is not soluble in water or alcohol, or ether, but mixed with boiling water it swells, bursts, and forms a kind of mucilage, which cools into a semi-transparent paste or jelly." The process of manufacturing starch from rice was discovered and patented about the year 1840 by Mr. Orlando Jones, founder of the house of the same name. His invention consists in the treatment of rice by a caustic alkaline solution during the steeping, grinding and macerating of the grains. The alkali used is either caustic potash or soda, of such a strength as to dissolve the gluten without destroying the starch; it must consequently vary with the character of the grain and hence the utmost nicety is required. The Battersea Works of Orlando Jones & Co. were built in 1848, the firm having previously carried on their manufacture in Whitechapel, they are situated on the banks of the Thames near the works of Price's Patent Candle Company, and occupy ground extending from the river to York Road; thus the firm possesses facilities of conveyance both by land and water—this latter is particularly valuable to them to enable them to save all dock, landing and warehousing charges. A large new store has been recently built on their wharf to which rice is barged direct from the ship. From the wharf also the manufactured article itself is conveyed to the docks for shipment to the Continent and our Colonies, with which a large trade is carried on. As an illustration of the extent of Orlando Jones & Co.'s operations it may be added that the box making department is a little factory in itself, and the machinery employed for the various purposes of sawing, dusting, cleaning, lighting, pumping, stirring, and grinding is driven by steam engines. It will be obvious that the manufacture of rice starch on a large scale requires no little capital and skill, and takes high rank among those industrial enterprises which are so peculiarly the characteristic and the glory of our age and country. Messrs. Orlando Jones & Co's manufacture has been awarded nine prize medals at International Exhibitions, and the grand distinction of the gold medal of the Académie Nationale of Paris. These medals have been awarded 'for introduction of the process,' 'for excellence of manufacture' and 'for large production.'

It is worthy of note that Messrs. Orlando Jones & Co. are the manufacturers of Chapman's Patent Prepared Entire Wheat flour especially distinguished by its richness in earthly phosphates which are essential to the development of bones and teeth. This farinaceous food for infants, children and invalids is much recommended by the medical faculty.

Battersea Laundries.—Spiers and Pond's.—Propert's Factory.—The London and Provincial Steam Laundry.

Battersea is becoming quite noted for Laundries. There is Strutt's (Lawn) Laundry, Orkney Street; Royal Albert Laundry, Battersea Park Road; Laundry, Sheepcote House; Latchmere Laundry; Alder's South Western Laundry, Surrey Lane; Lombard Road Laundry; Palmer's Laundry, Chatham Road, Wandsworth Common; and many others.

But one of the largest and most gigantic of Laundries is the Colossal Steam Laundry, belonging to Messrs. Spiers & Pond, erected 1879. The Laundry is situated on the North side of Battersea Park Road, it is constructed of yellow brick, with stone window-sills, and Beart's white-moulded brick for string courses, window jambs, arches, and cornices. The Building and Works are from designs by Mr. Kemp, Architectural Engineer. Mr. Priddle of Hounslow was the Contractor; and Mr. Warburton, Clerk of the Works, under whose superintendence the work was carried out.

The Building and Grounds extend over an area of one acre, the principal frontage which is 170 ft. in length, faces the East in a road leading to the South gate of Battersea Park, now called Alexandra Avenue. The central portion has an elevation of 45 ft. in height consisting of three floors containing, Manager's Residence, Clerk's Offices, etc., also a mess-room for the Employés, with bath-room and domestic lavatories. A spacious archway leads into the court-yard. This entrance is

10 ft. in width and 15 ft. in height. The wings of each side of the central portion have an elevation of two floors. Other blocks each containing one lofty floor are built on the North, South and West sides, to nearly one half the extent of the site. The remaining open space which is set apart as a drying ground is furnished with necessary appliances. Securely fixed in the ground by means of struts are 96 poles, to which is firmly attached a galvanic wire-rope for bleaching purposes. A separate block at the South West corner is for stables, adjoining which is the engine and boiler house with a chimney-shaft 70 ft. high, 7 ft. wide at the base and 4 ft. at top. This part of the Building is fitted up with a horizontal Engine and 2 Boilers by Manlove, Alliott and Co. of Nottingham of sufficient power to drive the Machinery requisite for the various processes of the Laundry; the Patent Machines used are made by Mr. Bradford of London and Manchester. The boundary wall enclosing the building and grounds is 7 ft. high. On the South side of the laundry is a sorting-room 63 ft. in length by 18 feet in width for the reception of articles as they arrive in the vans. The washing-room is 50 ft. square with large open *louvres* in the ceiling for the purpose of ventilation and to allow the steam to escape. The drying-room is 70 ft. by 30 ft. A flue-pipe 70 ft. in length is placed horizontally immediately along the floor in this department and about 1,200 ft. of corded piping are utilized for the heating chamber. In the West block are the folding and the mangling rooms, their dimensions being respectively 40 ft. by 30 ft., and 52 ft. by 30 ft. In the North block is the ironing room which is 55 ft. by 25 ft., next to which is the packing room 40 ft. by 25.

Estimated cost of building and machinery about £12,000.

Matron, Mrs. Tobin. Number of employés 60.

Propert's (Blacking Factory) built 1878-9. Hunting Mark a fox's head. Hunting preparations, established 1835, South Audley St.

B. Beddow and Son, Sole Proprietors.

A site past Propert's factory has been selected by the London and Provincial Steam Laundry Co. Limited. Ernest Turner, Architect, 246, Regent St. W. Mr. Austin, Secretary.

The London and Provincial Steam Laundry (Company Limited) is elaborately fitted up with Machinery of the very best description—the building is said to be the largest in the world and it occupies an acre and a half of ground. Its working-staff is composed mostly of females numbering 150 including 32 who reside upon the premises, and there are 20 males. The Laundry is capable of turning out from 80,000 to 90,000 pieces weekly. The Architect was Mr. Ernest Turner of Regent Street. Messrs. Bradford and Co. of Manchester and London, supplied the machinery which was specially designed for this Laundry. The works are entered at the west by double gates which lead into a second court-yard where the vans can discharge and receive their freight in all weathers. The main body of the building is cut off from the resident portion by a second pair of gates. The general Laundry is divided longitudinally into three sections. The wash-house is fitted up with machinery adapted for speed and economizing labour.

The washing machines which are of various sizes are known as Bradford's

"Vowel A." Then there is a range of boiling troughs, and again the hydros in which the articles when washed and rinsed are put and whirled round at the rate of 400 revolutions per minute "till every drop of extractable moisture is driven off through the side holes." The Ironing-room is in the central hall and occupies an area of 80 by 70 ft. being 20 ft. high. For curtains, lace, etc., there is a separate room. The boiler-house is provided with two 15-horse power horizontal engines, driven by two 20-horse Cornish boilers. There is a disinfecting chamber, and the severest penalties are demanded, not only against any person sending infected articles, but against any of the employés neglecting to give immediate notice of any case of infectious disease, with which he or she shall be brought into contact. Mr. J. T Helby, Manager.

It is interesting to know how enormously property has increased in value in Battersea, within the last one hundred years. The Battersea Bridge Estate which contains about 4 acres, was sold by auction at the Mart by Norton, Trist, Watney and Co., 62, Old Broad Street, on Thursday, May 20, 1880, realizing £35,000. At Mid-summer 1791, this property was let on three leases for 90 years, at ground rents amounting together to £90 per annum.

The Workman's Institute erected two years ago has full complement of 150 members. It has a kitchen, library, newspapers, games, etc. One of the workmen has been thirty-eight years and a few others thirty years in the service of the firm.

> The man how wise, who, sick of gaudy scenes,
> Is led by choice to take his fav'rite walk,
> Beneath death's gloomy, silent, cypress shades,
> Unpierc'd by vanity's fantastic ray!
> To read his monuments, to weigh his dust;
> Visit his vaults, and dwell among his tombs!
>
> *Young's Night Thoughts.*

St. Mary's (Battersea) Cemetery.—Numerous Epitaphs and Inscriptions. Scale of Fees, etc.

Situated on Battersea Rise at the commencement of Bolingbroke Grove, Wandsworth Common, is St. Mary's Cemetery used as a place of interment for the parishioners. It covers an area of 8 acres, and cost £8,000, including the erection of mortuary, chapels, etc. The ground thus purchased formed part of an estate that belonged to Mr. Henry Willis. It was opened Nov. 1860. It is fringed on the north and west sides with stately elms, and partially on the east boundary with poplar trees.

Grassy hillocks, planted with flowers and evergreens, monumental inscriptions and tombstones, together with the number of each grave denote the spot where many a tributary tear of fond affection has been died by the surviving relatives and friends of loved ones who have departed this life, but whose mouldering dust lies sleeping here. The congregation of the silent dead seems to make the place sacred, and gives it a solemn air. Here lie the mortal remains of the late Venerable John S. Jenkinson, M.A., for 24 years Vicar of Battersea, he died 17th

October, 1871, aged 74, much beloved and greatly lamented. An appropriate text of Holy Scripture, I Thess. 4, 14, is engraved round the beautiful block of granite that covers his grave. On the occasion of his decease the following lines were composed by a parishioner, dated October 17th, 1871:—

> Our Vicar has been called away,
> From earthly ties has risen,
> To take the place prepared for him;
> Our Vicar rests in Heaven.
> His journey ended, trials o'er;
> Now all his sufferings cease,
> He's gone to be with Him who said,
> "In Me ye shall have peace."
> He ever faithful to his charge,
> The Saviour's love set forth
> To sinners that they might be saved;
> Was faithful unto death.
> Full twenty years and more he trod,
> God's house His flock to lead;
> In sickness words of comfort gave,
> In want assist their need.
> May we his flock example take,
> Before our sun go down;
> That when our Saviour comes, we too
> May win a heavenly crown.

A mourning or memento card headed "Falling Leaves" bears the following lines written on the Funeral of the Rev. J. S. Jenkinson:—

> 'Twas Autumn—and a mournful train
> Proceeds beneath the trees,
> Our Vicar in the tomb was laid,
> Amid the falling leaves.
> Fit emblem of the hoary head,
> And many such were there;
> Methought they spoke in silent words
> For this event prepare.
> The mighty shepherd of his sheep,
> In seasons such as these,
> Speaks gently, that each one may take
> A lesson from the leaves.

> A PARISHIONER.
> *October 21st, 1871.*

Here is a superb monument of red polished granite in memory of John Humphrey Esq., Alderman of London and late M.P. for the borough of Southwark who died 28th September, 1863. Ætat. 69.

Here is a tombstone with epitaph in memory of Mary Davies, who departed this life January 24th, 1872, aged 88 years. "For more than sixty-two years she was connected with Battersea Chapel Sunday School, where by her consistent Christian character and entire devotedness to her work, she won the esteem of all. Being dead she yet lives in the hearts of many teachers, scholars and friends, who erect this stone in remembrance of a course of quiet usefulness which they deem worthy of all honour.

"Not myself, but the truth that in life I have spoken,
Not myself, but the seed that in life I have sown
Shall pass on to ages—all about me forgotten
Save the truth I have spoken, the things I have done."

Here is a marble obelisk.—In memory of the Rev. James Milling, A.B., Curate of St. Mary's Battersea, who entered into rest the 11th of January 1865 aged 27 years. His last words were "Not by works of righteousness which we have done, but according to his mercy he saved us by the washing of regeneration and renewing of the Holy Ghost which he shed on us abundantly through Jesus Christ our Saviour." *Titus iii* 5 *and* 6. This monument was erected by the parishioners and children of the Parochial Schools.

On another tombstone is an inscription to the memory of Mr. John Nichols, a devoted husband and estimable father, Baptist minister and Editor of Zion's Trumpet, a magazine devoted to the interest of the Aged Pilgrims' Friend Society and its Asylum; who fell asleep in Jesus Feb. 1st, 1867, aged 67 years.

"His presence guide my journey through and crown my journey's end."

In the faith of Christ here also rests the Rev. Philip Pennington M.A. of Christ's College, Cambridge, sometime civil chaplain of the Island of Mauritius. And God shall wipe away all tears from their eyes, and there shall be no more death neither sorrow, nor crying, neither shall there be any more pain for the former things are passed away.

Many are the pledges of conjugal endearment which help to tenant these graves.

"Ah! those little ice-cold fingers,
How they point our memories back
To the hasty words and actions,
Strewn along our backward track!
How those little hands remind us,
As in snowy grace they lie,
Not to scatter thorns—but roses,
For our reaping by and by."

We perceive here that ruthless death with his scythe pays no regard to infantile age, and that others in the vigour of their youthful prime as well as the matured adult and hoary-headed have been suddenly cut down by an awful surprise.

Here is a grave planted with flowers, the stone at the head of the grave states that William Gobell was accidentally killed on the London and Brighton Railway, March 4th, 1873, aged 65 years. Here is another stone in affectionate remembrance f William James, late Engine driver on the L.B. and S.C.R., who was killed while n the execution of his duty on the 29th of July 1876, aged 38 years. This stone has een erected by his fellow mates, as a token of respect to his memory.

Another stone is erected in memory of Henry Blunden, who was killed on the . and S. W. Ry., on the 17th October, 1871, aged 22 years.

> "All you that come my grave to see,
> Oh think of death and remember me,
> Just in my prime and folly skilled;
> When on the Railway I was killed,
> Take warning, hear, and do not weep,
> But early learn thy grave to seek."

Sacred to the memory of Thomas Hutchinson Higerty, who departed this life)ctober 13th, 1869, aged 5 years and 2 months.

> How very soon is age upon us,
> Ere we know our way to earth,
> But in heaven there's no sorrow,
> There's nothing but joy and mirth.
> How soon hath time closed around us,
> First a child and then a man,
> How soon he's turned to mouldering dust
> Which from a few years back he sprang.

The head-stone states that the above lines were written by his brother, aged welve years.

> I like that ancient Saxon phrase which calls
> The burial ground God's acre! It is just:
> It consecrates each grave within its walls,
> And breathes a benison o'er the sleeping dust.
> God's acre! yes, that blessed name imparts
> Comfort to those who in the grave have sown
> The seed that they had gathered in their hearts,
> Their bread of life—alas! no more their own.
> Into its furrows shall we all be cast,
> In the sure faith that we shall rise again
> At the great harvest, when the archangel's blast
> Shall winnow, like a fan, the chaff and grain.
> Then shall the good stand in immortal bloom,
> In the fair gardens of that sacred birth;
> And each bright blossom mingle its perfume
> With that of flowers which never bloomed on earth.

Longfellow.[58]

---

[58] The word *Sepulchre* comes from the Latin *Sepelio* to bury. It is the place where the dead body of a human being is consigned, whether it be in the ground or an excavation in the rocks.

Abraham buried Sarah, his wife in the cave of the field of Ephron, at Machpelah, whic he purchased in the presence of the children of Heth, for 400 Shekels of silver, 1860 B.C Genesis 23.

The word Cemetery *Koimeterion* comes from the Greek *Koimao (Koimaein)* to sleep. I is the sleeping place, and "Christianity has turned the Sepulchre into a Cemetery assuring us, as it does, that those who die in Jesus, *Sleep in Him*, awaiting a future awakening, i augmented vigour, and with renovated powers. To the Christian, the grave should be as sociated with the idea of calm and undisturbed repose, after a life of honourable toil, with the hope of a glorious and blessed resurrection." The Greeks had their burial places at distance from the towns. Lycurgus allowed his Lacedemonians to bury their dead within the city and around their temples that the youth being inured to such spectacles might be the less terrified with the apprehension of death. Two reasons are alleged why the ancient did not allow burials within their cities. 1st. they considered that the sight, touch or neigh bourhood of a corpse defiled a man, especially a priest. 2nd. to prevent the air from being corrupted by putrifying bodies, and the buildings from being endangered by the frequenc of (Cremation) funeral fires. The custom of burning bodies prevailed amongst most Easter nations, and was continued by their descendants, after they had peopled the different part of Europe. Hence we find it prevailing in Greece, Italy, Gaul, Britain, Germany, Sweden Norway and Denmark, till Christianity abolished it.

The Romans had their places of interment in the suburbs and fields especially the high ways; hence the necessity of inscriptions. We have a few exceptional instances of person buried in the city a favour allowed to only a few of singular merit in the Commonwealth Burying within the walls was expressly prohibited by a law of the xii Tables. Plutarch say those who had triumphed were indulged in it. Val. Publicola and C. Fabricius, are said to have had tombs in the Forum, and Cicero adds Tuberius to the number. Places of buria were consecrated under Pope Calixtus I. in A.D. 210. (*Eusebius.*) Among the primitive Chris tians, cemeteries were held in great veneration. It appears from Eusebius and Tertullian tha in the early ages they assembled for divine worship in the cemeteries. Burying in churche for many ages was severely prohibited by Christian Emperors. The first step towards it was the erection of churches over the graves of martyrs in the cemeteries, and translating the relics of others into churches in the city. Subsequently Kings and Emperors were buried in the Atrium or church porch. The first Christian burial place it is said, was instituted in 596 buried in cities, 742; in consecrated places, 750; in church yards, 758. It is said however in the 6th century the people began to be admitted into the churchyards; and some Princes, Founders and Bishops into the churches. The practice adopted at the consecration of ceme teries, was something after this fashion—the Bishop walked round it in procession with the crosier or pastoral staff in his hand, the holy water pot being carried before, out of which the aspersions were made. Many of the early Christians are buried in the catacombs at Rome. Vaults erected in churches first at Canterbury, 1075. Woollen shrouds only permitted to be used in England 1666. Linen scarfs introduced at funerals in Ireland 1729, and Woollen shrouds used 1733. Burials taxed 1695. A tax conducted on burials in England—for the bur ial of a Duke £50, and that of a common person 4s., under William III 1695, and George III 1783. Acts relating to Metropolitan burials, passed 1850-67. In 1850 the Board of Health was made a Burial Board for the Metropolis, and power was given to the Privy Council to close the City grave-yards. Parochial Registers instituted in England by Cromwell, Lord Essex, about 1538.—*Stow.*

Earth to earth system of burial advocated by Mr. Seymour Haden. Wicker Coffins ex hibited at Stafford House, 17th June 1875. With the view of rendering the death of persons of quality more remarkable, it was customary among the Greeks and Romans to institute funeral games, which included horse-racing, dramatic representations, processions and

Another stone bears the following inscription:—

In loving remembrance of William Hayward; born April 4th, 1850, died December 8th, 1874.

> "Time, how short—Eternity, how long."
> Reader, this silent grave contains
> A much-loved son's remains;
> Death like a frost has nipt his bloom,
> And sent him early to the tomb;
> In love he lived, in peace he died,
> His life was craved, but God denied.

This stone is erected by his mother as a small token of love for him.

Also of Thomas Hayward, brother to the above; born October 26th, 1855, died June 8, 1876.

> Had He asked us, well we know
> We should cry, Oh! spare this blow;
> Yea, with streaming tears should pray,
> Lord we love him, let him stay.

A grave stone records the death of Henry Stening, who met with sudden death on the 25th November, 1875, aged 59 years. "In the midst of life we are in death."

Here is a white marble head stone with gilded monogram (I.H.S.) and stone border to grave prettily decorated with flowers, sacred to the memory of Alfred Thomas Martin, who died September 29th, 1876, aged 31.

Also of Nelly, died July 19, 1875, aged 7; Alfred William, died March 17, 1876,

---

mortal combats of gladiators; these games were abolished by the Emperor Claudius, A.D. 7.

The custom of delivering a funeral oration in praise of a person at his funeral is very ancient, it was practised by the Egyptians, Hebrews, Greeks and Romans. The old heathens honoured those alone with this part of the funeral solemnity who were men of probity and justice, renowned for their wisdom and knowledge, or famous for warlike exploits. This custom was very early obtained by the Christians. Some of their funeral sermons are now extant as that of Eusebius on Constantine, and those of Nazianzen on Basil and Cæsarius; and of Ambrose on Valentinian, Theodosius, and others.

One of the oldest established and most celebrated of the European cemeteries is that of Pere la Chaise near Paris. In the Scottish cemeteries no such distinctions exist as in England where the cemeteries are divided into two portions—one consecrated for the burials of members of the Established Church over whose remains the funeral service is read and one unconsecrated for the burials of dissenters.

The Burials Law Amendment Act 1880, has given to Parishioners in England the right of burials in Church-yards without the rites of the Church of England. Though the Incumbent of a parish has no longer the exclusive right of officiating at interments in consecrated ground yet none of his rights are actually abrogated. He is still custos of the grave yard and must be consulted about the hour and place of interment as well as the inscriptions on grave stones. While in the case of lay funerals contemplated under the Act, it is not necessary to have any service at all, the service if performed must be Christian and orderly.

aged 6; Charles Percy, died February 23, 1877, aged 18 months, children of th above. "The Lord giveth and the Lord taketh away."

Within the precincts of this cemetery is entombed the body of Henrietta, Lady Pollock, widow of Field Marshal Sir George Pollock, Baronet, G.C.B., G.C.S.I., died February 14, 1873, aged 65 years. "Jesus said, I am the Resurrection and the Life." *John xi.* 25-26.

Here is a vault in memory of William Henry Wilson, of Chapel House, Battersea Park, and 6, Victoria Street, Westminster, born 4th of September, 1803, died 8th March, 1871; also of Margaret Isabel (Daisy,) third child of John Wilson; and Margaret Isabel Theobald, died 3rd March, 1876, aged 3 years and 1 month.

Not far from the gravel walk is a grave-stone at the head of which is a dove with a scroll on which is engraved "Thy will be done." Sacred to the memory of Mary Jane Webb, the beloved and only child of Charles and Mary Webb, who departed this life Nov. 30th, 1869, aged 8 years and 8 months, deeply lamented by her sorrowing parents and regretted by all who knew her.

> She is not dead, the child of our affection,
> But gone into the School,
> Where she no longer needs our poor protection,
> And Christ Himself doth rule.

Here is a grave-stone; an opening in the stone which is glazed, represents a female in a recumbent position reading a book. In affectionate remembrance of George Barrett, who departed this life January 9th, 1871, aged 2 years and 3 months; also Louisa Barrett, who departed this life September 24th, 1872, aged 16 years and 6 months.

> Dear to their parents! to their God more dear,
> Brother and Sister sweetly slumber here;
> Blest in their state from fear and danger free;
> To us they died; they live O Lord with Thee.

Also Daniel Barrett, father of the above, who departed this life August 23rd, 1873, aged 46 years.

> Even as he died a smile was on his face,
> And in that smile affection loved to trace,
> A cheerful trust in Jesus' power to save,
> An aged Pilgrim's triumph o'er the grave.

Here is a grave planted with Laurels, having a Rhododendron in the centre, the stone at the head bears the inscription—In affectionate remembrance of Philadelphia Emma, the beloved wife of Ephraim Wilson, of Bridge Road, Battersea, who departed this life, June 24th, 1875, aged 27 years.

> The losing thee, our comfort is, to know
> That those relying on a Saviour's love,
> Have left this troubled world of sin and woe
> To be at rest with Christ in heaven above.

Here is a grave covered with a white marble slab and cross, bearing this simple inscription; Phillis, wife of Wyndham Payne, taken to her rest, 26 July, 1870.

Here is a grave-stone; in affectionate remembrance of Clara Cahill, who died 20th of December, 1871, aged 2 years and 3 months.

Dear lovely child, to all our hearts most dear,
Long shall we bathe thy memory with a tear;
Farewell, to promising on earth to dwell;
Sweetest of children, farewell! farewell!

Also Albert, Brother of the above, who died August 7th, 1874, aged 14 months, interred in St. Patrick's cemetery, West Ham.

Oh! why so soon! just as the bloom appears,
Strayed the brief flower from this vale of tears;
Death viewed the treasure to the desert given,
Claimed the fair flower, and planted it in heaven.

Also Caroline, sister of the above, who died March 1st, 1876, aged 1 year and 7 months.

Yes, dearest Carrie, thou art gone,
Thy brief career is run,
Thy little pilgrimage is past
All sorrowing here is done,
Just like an early summer's rose,
Thou did'st come here to bloom,
But long ere thou beganst to blow,
Death snatched thee to the tomb.

A head-stone marks the grave of Mary Childs, who died Nov. 24th, 1865, aged 68; for 33 years a faithful servant in the family of George Scrivens, of Clapham Common.

A beautiful granite Grecian cross is erected in memory of the dear loved wife of Arthur Steains, Jun., born 8th January, 1844, taken to her eternal rest 22nd June, 1875. "Blessed are the pure in heart, for they shall see God."

Here is a stone—sacred to the memory of Wm. Chas. Brewer, who died June 11th, 1875, aged 21 years. Remember the days of thy youth. This stone was erected by some of his fellow employés, as a token of affection. Our time will not allow us to comment upon the different inscriptions, but it is gratifying to observe how many grave-stones have been erected as a tribute of generous affection by working men themselves, in memory of their deceased fellow workmen. A noble feature this in the British Mechanic, a quality possessed and not unfrequently displayed by English hearts and hands.

At the head of a grave is a marble stone, erected to the memory of Anne Grover, late of Wendover, Bucks, who died April 30th, 1877, aged 54 years. "The Lord is a stronghold in the day of trouble, and He knoweth them that trusteth in Him." —*Nah. i. 7.*

A small stone is erected in loving memory of Catherine Weedon, who departed this life, December 24th, 1876, aged 38; underneath are the following well known lines.

> We cannot tell who next may fall,
> Beneath Thy chastening rod;
> One must be first—but let us all
> Prepare to meet our God.

At the head of a grave is a stone erected by the friends and companions, in memory of Alfred Fell, and Arthur Ronald, who were accidentally drowned while bathing in the River Thames, July 6th, 1873, both aged 19 years. The subjoined lines read—

> Mark the brief story of a summer's day,
> At noon, in youth and health they launched away,
> Ere eve, death wrecked the bark and quenched their light;
> The parent's home was desolate at night,
> Each passed alone that gulf as eye can see,
> They meet next moment in eternity.
> Friend, kinsman, stranger, dost thou ask me where?
> Seek God's Right Hand and hope to find them there.

A few yards from the spot is a stone in memory of Alfred Halsted who died May 1st, 1873, aged 2 years and 5 months.

Also of Emma Halstead who died January 3, 1875, aged 12 years.

Also of Emma Halstead sister of the above who died June 28th 1879 aged 18 months.

> "Speak gently to the little child,
> Its love be sure to gain;
> Teach it in accents soft and mild,
> It may not long remain."

Here is a private grave with a stone in affectionate remembrance of Agnes Eliza Waller, who fell asleep in Jesus, April the 6th, 1871, in her 15th year; also Elizabeth Waller, mother of the above who died in the Lord, February 27th, 1873, in the 37th year of her age. Looking unto Jesus the Beginner and Finisher of our faith.—*Hebrews xii.* 2.

Here also lie buried the mortal remains of James Waller, who died July 7th, 1880, he was an earnest and successful city-missionary.

Here is a monumental stone, in form of an Iona cross, encircled with a ring emblematical of the Unity and Catholicity of the Christian Church. The epitaph states, that Laura Susan Cazenove, "fell asleep," August 24th, 1861, in her 22nd year. "There shall be one fold and one Shepherd."

Here is a sepulchre stone, in memory of Frances Elizabeth Scrivens, widow of George Scrivens, Esq., of Clapham Common, who died March 11th, 1867, aged 81 years.

In this cemetery are interred the mortal remains of Arthur Miller Rose, who died 12th July, 1864, aged 67; also Susannah, his wife, who died 30th December, 1870, aged 75. "The memory of the just is blessed." —*Proverbs x. 7.*

Near this spot we observed an iron label, with the number of somebody's grave; there was no hillock, the surface was completely flattened; over the label was placed by fond hands a faded wreath.

Covering a brick vault is erected a superb monument, bearing the following inscriptions—in affectionate remembrance of Marianne, the beloved wife of Robert Jones, of Clapham Common, born May 9th, 1808, died November 17th, 1868; also in memory of Anne, second daughter of Robert and Marianne Jones, born July 2, 1841, died October 22, 1872. "He hath prepared for them a city." —*Hebrews xi.* 6.

"O Paradise! O Paradise!
Who doth not crave for rest?
Who would not seek the happy land
Where they that love are blest?
Where loyal hearts and true,
Stand ever in the light;
All rapture through and through,
In God's most Holy sight."

Also Falkland Robert, the third son of Robert and Marianne Jones, who died 29th November, 1875, aged 23 years.

Adjacent to that of his parents, is erected a monument of Scotch granite, mounted with a white marble urn, partially covered with a cloth or veil. Sacred to the memory of Joseph May Soule, second son of the late Rev. I. M. Soule, who departed this life, 15th March, 1875, aged 33. "I am the Resurrection and the life." —*John xi.* 25. On the south side of the beautiful obelisk erected over his Parents' grave is an epitaph to the memory of Hannah Turnbull, for 13 years a devoted nurse in the family of the Rev. I. M. Soule, who died June 9th, 1866, aged 44 years. Fallen asleep in Jesus.

By the side of one of the gravel walks a modest head-stone is erected in memory of Elizabeth Ursula, wife of James Pillans Wilson, Esq., born October, 1836, fell asleep in Jesus, 11th May, 1869, in her 33rd year. She was a regular attendant at the public worship of God, from her childhood, and sought sincerely to please Him, but did not become a worshipper of Him, 'in spirit and in truth,' by believing in the Lord Jesus Christ, and being saved until her twentieth year, from which time she knew Him indeed as her Father, and walked with Him in this world as His child. Subjoined is the following address to the reader—

Dear reader, how is it with you? Are you still only an outward worshipper, or perhaps not even that? O! believe in the Lord Jesus Christ, as having died on the cross for your sins, and ask Him to make Himself known to you in your heart as your own Saviour, and then you also will walk this earth as a happy child of God, loving and serving Him by the power of His Spirit in you, till He shall take you home to Himself to the fulness of joy in His presence, and the pleasures at His right hand for evermore.

And as it is appointed unto men once to die, but after this, the judgment; so Christ was once offered to bear the sins of many, and unto them that look for Him shall He appear the second time without sin, unto Salvation.—*Hebrew ix.* 27-28 *Isaiah liii.* 6. *Acts xvi.* 30-31.

Here is a grave with stone border and marble head-stone—in memory of the Rev. Edwin Thompson, D.D., Vicar of St. John's Parish, and honorary Chaplain of the Royal Masonic Institution for Girls, Battersea Rise, who died February 2nd 1876, aged 51 years. "Knowing that he, which raised up the Lord Jesus shall raise up us also, by Jesus, and shall present us with you."—*II. Cor. iv.* 14.

Also of Hannah Thompson, mother of the above, who died July 1st, 1876, aged 80 years. "This is the victory that overcometh the world—even our faith."—*I. John v.* 4.

We must tread softly among these grassy mounds, for yonder at the end of the gravel walk is situated our Darling Teddie's grave, (No. 7217). Edward George Curme Simmonds, who was drowned off Battersea Park embankment, October 16 1875, aged 10 years. In another part of the cemetery is interred all that is mortal of our beloved daughter Hannah, who died June 12, 1873, aged 18. "My faith looks up to Thee, Thou lamb of calvary, Saviour divine!"

But we have tarried almost too long, and as time is precious we must leave for the present our meditations among the tombs, only observing that as we examined the records of mortality, and thought of the promiscuous multitude rested together without any regard to rank or seniority within those thousands of graves, we were reminded of the words of the Rev. James Hervey, when gazing upon a similar scene in a church yard. "None were ambitious of the uppermost rooms, or chief seats in this house of mourning; none entertained fond and eager expectations of being honourably greeted, in their darksome cells. The man of years and experience reputed as an oracle in his generation, was contented to lie down at the feet of a babe. In this house appointed for all living, the servant was equally accommodated and lodged in the same story with his master. The poor indigent lay as softly, and slept as soundly as the most opulent possessor. All the distinction that subsisted was a grassy hillock, hound with osiers, or a sepulchral stone, ornamented with imagery." In Thy fair book of life divine; My God inscribe my name.

> My flesh shall slumber in the ground,
> Till the last trumpet's joyful sound;
> Then burst the chains with sweet surprise,
> And in my Saviour's image rise.
> How many graves around us lie!
> How many homes are in the sky!
> Yes for each saint doth Christ prepare, a place with care,
> Thy home is waiting, brother there!

On the south side of the centre gravel walk east of the mortuary Chapels is a neat marble head-stone. Sacred to the memory of Elizabeth Farmer, born January 13th, 1810, died February 1st, 1873. Also of William Farmer, born May 14th, 1802, died May 26th, 1877, he was for 36 years a faithful servant in the employ of Messrs. Thorne, Brewers, Nine Elms. "The memory of the Just is blessed. They rest from their labours." — *Rev. xiv.* 14. This stone as a tribute of filial affection is erected in loving remembrance by their sons.

On the west-side of the cemetery is erected a small red granite cross in loving remembrance of John Hext Ward, Churchwarden of Battersea, 1874. Died 9th December, 1877, aged 40. A few of his friends thus record their admiration for his sterling worth, for his manly godliness, and for his self-denying efforts to help the poor to help themselves. "Thy Kingdom come."

Here is a grave adorned with pretty flowers and rose trees a glass shade covers a wreath, in the centre of which is an image representing the Redeemer. At the head of the grave a memento card is framed and glazed, In loving remembrance of Kate Ellen Wilson, who departed this life July 2nd, 1878, in her 21st year.

> The stem broke and the flower faded.
> When my final farewell to the world I have said,
> And gladly lie down to my rest;
> When softly the watchers shall say "she is dead,"
> And fold my pale hands on my breast;
> And when with my glorified vision at last,
> The walls of that city I see;
> Angels will then at the beautiful gate,
> Be waiting and watching for me.

Conspicuously by the side of the carriage road may be seen a stone obelisk tapering like a spire, with hand and forefinger pointing to the sky. On front of the obelisk is a dove with marble scroll with the words "for of such is the kingdom of heaven." In memory of Jessie Felicia, the beloved wife of Frederick Reed, of Wandsworth, late of Battersea; who died 22nd October, 1874, aged 31 years. Also Emily Kate, the beloved daughter of the late C. Q. Baker, of Margate, Kent; who died 6th January 1877, Aged 2½ years.

A grave stone with dove and scroll with the words "Jesus wept" is erected in affectionate remembrance of Rozinia Sarah eldest daughter of Henry and Rozinia Osborn, and grand-daughter of Mrs. M. E. McBain; who departed this life October 14th 1868, aged 8 years and 7 months. "The sting of death is sharp—But the love of Christ surpasseth all."

Another stone sacred to the memory of Mrs. Mary E. McBain who died July 8, 1866, aged 68 years.

Also of James Fairbain McBain, husband of the above who fell asleep in Jesus, May 18th, 1879. For many years he had been a temperance advocate and successful evangelist.

Here is a stone in affectionate remembrance of Little Marke, the dearly beloved child of Philipp and Rose Konig, who fell asleep February the 3rd, 1876, aged 22 months.

> Our loss is his great gain,

We trust in Christ to meet again.

Another stone in memory of Elizabeth the beloved wife of John Tyler Larking who after a painful mental and bodily disease fell asleep in the dear Lord Jesus August 27th, 1878, in her 76 year. "For I reckon that the sufferings of this present time are not worthy to be compared with the glory which shall be revealed in us."

On the right hand side of the principal road from the main entrance to the cemetery is a grave-stone erected in loving undying remembrance of Kate Ellen Wilson, whom it pleased God to take from this world of care on the 2nd of July 1878, aged 21 years.

> "Gone for ever in the blossom of life and love,
> After scarcely a moment's warning.
> Eloquence is lost in attempting to describe her noble qualities
> Loving, faithful, generous and pure,
> Thou wert the bright star that guidest me on,
> Toiling for thee and rank among strangers.
> Thy smile my reward when the battle was won,
> In sickness or sorrow, in sadness or sleeping
> Thy smile ever near to guide me along,
> Whispering hopes of a bright tomorrow
> My sad spirits cheering with dreams of relief,
> But e'er one summer passed away
> That gentle voice was hushed for aye
> I watched my Love's last smile and knew,
> How well the angels loved her too,
> Then silent. —
> Then silent but with blinding tears
> I gathered all my love of years,
> And laid it with my dream of old,
> When all and loved slept white and cold."

On the border stone are the words "the property of Walter Scott." No. of grave 8747.

We observe another stone in memory of Mahalah the beloved and affectionate wife of Henry Noble Williams, who died November 12th, 1873, aged 38 years. In her prostrated affliction she "endured as seeing Him who is invisible" and longed to behold "the King in His beauty."

> How calm and easy was her parting breath,
> No conscious sorrow shook her bed of death
> No infants fall when wearied sleep oppressed
> So did her soul sink to eternal rest
> "Until the morning breaketh."

"She looked well to the ways of her household, and ate not the bread of idleness." *Prov. xxxi.* 27.

Also the above named, Henry Noble Williams, who died October 28th, 1879, aged 44 years.

"This mortal shall put on immortality." *I. Cor. xv.* 53.

Here is a grave the head-stone is erected in affectionate remembrance of John Allison Peel, who died March 23, 1871, aged 40 years.

> Then let our sorrows cease to flow,
> God has recalled His own;
> But let our hearts in every woe,
> Still say Thy will be done.

Also of John William Peel son of the above, who was accidentally killed by the falling of a boat swing June 18,1872. Aged 11 years.

Here is another stone erected by loving hands. In memory of Sarah Appleton who died June 5, 1860, aged one month. Also of Minnie Appleton who died March 10, 1864, aged 13 months. And of Rose Appleton who died Dec. 17, 1865, aged 4½ years, children of George Appleton of Battersea Park. Also of Mary Appleton, who died March 16, 1866, aged 79 years; grandmother of the above children.

Added to this epitaph are the lines with which most persons are familiar:—

> Forgive blest shade the tributary tear
> That mourns thy exit from a world like this
> Forgive the wish that would have kept thee here
> And stayed thy progress to the realms of bliss.

A plain head-stone marks the resting place of all that was mortal of that good man William Henry Hatcher, born at Salisbury 21st January, 1821. Died at Sherwood House, Battersea, 2nd August, 1879. This stone was erected by his colleagues and Fellow Workers.

THE UNCERTAINTY OF LIFE.

> Beneath our feet and o'er our head
> Is equal warning given;
> Beneath us lie the countless dead,
> Above us is the heaven.

> Death rides on every passing breeze,
> He lurks in every flower;
> Each season has its own disease,
> Its peril every hour.

> Our eyes have seen the rosy light
> Of youth's soft cheek decay,
> And fate descend in sudden night
> On manhood's middle day.

> Our eyes have seen the steps of age
> Halt feebly towards the tomb;
> And yet shall earth our hearts engage,
> And dream of days to come?

Turn, mortal, Turn! thy danger know, —
Where'er thy feet can tread
The earth rings hollow from below,
And warns thee of her dead.

Turn, Christian, turn! thy soul apply
To truths divinely given;
The bones that underneath thee lie
Shall live for *hell or heaven!*

The Burial Ground of St. Mary, Battersea, was purchased 1860, and secured
for the use of the Parishioners, by Act of Parliament, xv. and xvi. Victoria Cap. 85

This was the Scale of Fees of the Burial Board of St Mary, Battersea.

	First Ground, A.		Second Ground, B.		Third Ground, C.	
	ADULT.	INFANT.	ADULT.	INFANT.	ADULT.	INFANT.
	£. s. d.	£. s. d.	£. s. d.	£. s. d.	£. s. d.	£. s. d.
INTERMENT FEE for PARISHIONERS without purchase, viz.:—						
Fee for Interment, including Turfing and Digging Grave	0 18 6	0 13 0	0 16 6	0 10 6	0 10 6	0 6 0
Tolling Bell (if required)	0 5 0	0 5 0	0 2 6	0 2 6	0 1 0	0 1 0
Total	1 3 6	0 18 0	0 19 0	0 13 0	0 11 6	0 7 0
INTERMENT FEE at Expense of Union—						
Fee for Interment					0 10 6	0 6 0
Tolling Bell					0 1 0	0 1 0
Total					0 11 6	0 7 0
Purchase of Grave—Brick	3 3 0	3 3 0	2 2 0	2 2 0	2 2 0	2 2 0
Purchase of Grave—Earth	2 2 0	2 2 0	1 10 0	1 10 0	1 10 0	1 10 0
Conveyance, if required, 5s.						
Fee for Interment in Vault or Brick Grave	1 1 0	1 1 0	0 10 6	0 10 6	0 10 6	0 10 6

Fee for Interment out of regulated hours (Extra)	0 7 6	0 7 6	0 5 0	0 5 0	0 2 6	0 2 6
Fee for Interment of Still Born and Infants less than One month old.		0 2 6		0 2 6		0 2 6
Register Fee for entry in Register of Vaults or Grave in perpetuity.	0 1 0	0 1 0	0 1 0	0 1 0	0 1 0	0 1 0
Certificate.	0 2 7	0 2 7	0 2 7	0 2 7	0 2 7	0 2 7
Searching Register of Burials, for one year.	0 1 0	0 1 0	0 1 0	0 1 0	0 1 0	0 1 0
Searching Register of Burials for each additional year.	0 0 6	0 0 6	0 0 6	0 0 6	0 0 6	0 0 6
Certificate of Entry	0 2 7	0 2 7	0 2 7	0 2 7	0 2 7	0 2 7
Fee for Erecting Headstone, ... } Fee for Erecting Footstone . . . . . . }	0 14 0	0 14 0	0 10 0	0 10 0	0 10 0	0 10 0
Fee for Erecting Mural Monument	10 10 0					
Fee for Erecting or placing Tomb or Flat Stone, &c.	1 1 0					

OTHER FEES.

Keeping Monuments and Graves in perpetuity, according to Agreement.

Planting with Flowers and keeping in order a private Grave, per annum, 10s.
d.

Turfing with Flowers and keeping in order a private Grave, per annum, 3s.

For Removing and replacing Head and Foot-Stone, 10s.

For Removing Ledger Stone, 14s.

Digging Grave Extra Depth, per foot—1-ft. 2s. 2-ft. 3s. 3-ft. 4s. 6d. 4-ft. 6s. 5-ft.
s. 6d. 6-ft. 10s. 7-ft. 14s. 8-ft. 17s. 9-ft. £1.

Fee for Additional Inscription, 5s.

Fee for Change of Stone or Monument, 15s.

NON-PARISHIONERS DOUBLE FEES.

By Order,
THOMAS HARRAP, Clerk.

Approved by the
SECRETARY OF STATE,
For the Home Department,
December 21*st*, 1876.

The Battersea Charities.

THE BATTERSEA CHARITIES. Most of which are by will of the founders administered by the Vicar and Churchwardens.

1. ANN COOPER, in 1720, gave £300 to purchase an estate, the profits thereof to
e disposed of to poor people not receiving alms or to bind out poor children with
he approbation of Henry Lord Viscount St. John. This estate is land consisting of
bout 15 acres, situated in South Cerney in Gloucestershire, and produces a rental
f £18 15s. per annum.

2. THOMAS ASHNESS, in 1827, bequeathed £100 in trust for the use of the poor of
his parish, to be distributed amongst them as the Vicar and Wardens shall think
it, and the dividend from this is £3 8s.

3. ANTHONY FRANCIS HALDIMAND, by will of 1815, bequeathed £200 for the
ame purpose, the dividend of this sum is £3 12s. 8d.

4. REBECCA WOOD, in 1596, bequeathed £200, the interest of which is to be dis-
ributed annually among 24 decayed families of the parish, the dividend from this
s £6 4s. 9d.

5. HENRY SMITH, in 1626, bequeathed several pieces of land, situated in the
parishes of Sevenoaks, Seal and Kensing, in the County of Kent, the profits thereof
o be applied to the relief of the impotent and aged poor who have resided 5 years
n one of the twelve parishes named in his will, to be distributed in apparel of one
colour. The dividend received as the portion due to this parish is £17 1s.

6. JOHN CONRAD RAPP, in 1830, left £200, the interest to be divided at Christmas between four poor men and four poor women as the Vicar and Wardens in the discretion should think most necessitous and deserving of such relief. The amount from this benefaction is £6 9s. 4d.

7. JOHN PARVIN, in 1818, left £1,000, the interest to be laid out in coal, candle, broad and flannel and distributed among 40 poor widows actually residing in Nine Elms and Battersea Fields. Also a further sum of £1,000 upon trust to pay one-fourth part of the interest annually to the trustees of schools formed by the late Lord St. John in this parish. One-fourth part to be expended in purchasing of bread to be distributed on the Sunday in every fourth week of the month. Two fourths for the use of poor aged men and women equally in the Workhouse, and to be in the habit of attending Divine Service in Battersea Church. The last distribution of one-fourth to parties in the Workhouse was up to December 26th, 1836. One-fourth of the second £1,000, was paid away in 1853 for meeting law charges in the information of B. Starling and C. Bowes renew Scheme of Sir Walter St. John's Schools, and the two fourths transferred to the trustees of Sir Walter St. John's Schools in 1863 by order of the Charity Commissioners. The sum now available from this source for Christmas distribution is £33 5s. 8d.

8. JOHN CONSTABLE left £50 bequest in 1856 for the poor of this parish. The dividend from this now is £1 19s. 4d.

9. JOHN BANKS, in 1716 left by will to five poor men and five poor women 50s. each per annum, inhabitants of this parish. Candidates' names for recipients of this charity are forwarded by recommendation to the Haberdashers' Company of London who distribute this fund.

10. HENRY JUER, in 1874, bequeathed the sum of £500, the dividend thereof to be distributed on the 6th February in each year to 12 needy parishioners of the age of 60 years and upwards.

11. JOHN EDMUNDS, who in 1708 left £10 per annum for putting out boy-apprentices. The property bequeathed consisting of a small tenement in the City has increased in value, and so few applications of boys or masters are received at the Lammas Hall that the sum of £730 1s. 10d. is now on deposit to the credit of this charity.

Parish Officers.—Vestrymen.

The Parish Officers issue a form to be filled in by all applicants and to be endorsed by a householder.

"He that hath pity upon the poor lendeth unto the Lord; and that which he hath given will he pay him again."—*Prov. xix.* 17.

"Inasmuch as ye have done it unto one of the least of these my brethren, ye have done it unto me."—*Matthew xxv.* 40.

The "Imperial Gazetteer," Vol. p. 130, states that Battersea has a free school with £160 and other charities with £121.

Churchwardens. — Joseph William Hiscox, Altenburg Terrace, Lavender Hill; Edward Wood, 6, Shelgate Road, Battersea Rise.

Overseers. — Andrew Cameron, 65, Salcott Road; William Daws, 49, High Street; Robert Steel, Sleaford Street; B. T. L. Thomson, 6, Crown Terrace, Lavender Hill.

Vestry Clerk. — Thomas Harrap, Crown Terrace, Lavender Hill.

The following is the List of Vestrymen and Auditors Elected under the provisions of the Metropolis Local Management Act, 1881.

Vestrymen Ex-officio. — Rev. John Erskine Clarke, Vicar, 6, Altenburg Gardens; Joseph William Hiscox, 2, Altenburg Terrace, Lavender Hill; Edward Wood, 6, Shelgate Road, Battersea Rise.

WARD No. 1. (Vestrymen who retire in 1882).—William Duce, 21, Ponton Road, Nine Elms; James Dulley, 85, Battersea Park Road; Rev. Thomas Lander, St. George's Vicarage, 33, Battersea Park Road; Samuel Lathey, 1, St. George's Road, New Road; Nathaniel Purdy, 1, Ponton Terrace, Nine Elms; Thomas D. Tulley 22, Queen's Square, Battersea Park. (Vestrymen who retire in 1883).—John Gwynne, 64, Stewart's Road; Edwin Lathey, 1, St. George's Road, New Road; Thomas Read, 41, Battersea Park Road; Frederick Rummins, 49, Lockington Road; George T. Smith, Wandle Road, Upper Tooting; Robert Steele, Sleaford Street. (Vestrymen who retire in 1884).—Thomas Anderson, 37, Battersea Park Road; Charles Clench, 161, Battersea Park Road; John Samuel Oldham, 18, Battersea Park Road; Patrick James O'Neil, 145, Battersea Park Road; John Whiting, 38, Patmore Street; Eleazer Williams, 180, New Road. *Auditor.* — John Douthwaite, St. George's Schools, New Road.

WARD No. 2. (Vestrymen who retire in 1882).—George F. Burroughs, 1, Queen's Crescent, Queen's Road; John Merritt, 1, Prospect Cottages, Falcon Grove; John Merry, 237, Battersea Park Road; Thomas Poupart, 399, Battersea Park Road; Rev. S. G. Scott, St. Saviour's Parsonage, Battersea Park; George N. Street, 491, Battersea Park Road; Henry Walkley, 351, Battersea Park Road. (Vestrymen who retire in 1883).—Horace E. Bayfield, 1, Somers Villas, Lavender Hill; Wm. Jno. Folkard, 12, Rushill Terrace, Lavender Hill; Charles E. Gay, 41, Orkney Street, Battersea Park Road; Henry John Hansom, Grove End House, Falcon Lane; Charles Heine, 219, Battersea Park Road; B. T. L. Thomson, 6, Crown Terrace, Lavender Hill; George Ugle, 21, Acanthus Road, Lavender Hill. (Vestrymen who retire in 1884).—Charles Donaldson, 177, Battersea Park Road; John Elmslie, 241, Battersea Park Road; William Sangwin, 533, Battersea Park Road; Samuel Hancock, 339, Battersea Park Road; Samuel Bowker, 6, Crown Terrace, Lavender Hill; Frederick Aubin, 393, Battersea Park Road; Charles Spencer, 4, Wycliffe Terrace, Lavender Hill. *Auditor.* — George Fowler, 20, Queen's Square.

WARD No. 3. (Vestrymen who retire in 1882).—James Chorley, 69, High Street; William Daws, 49, High Street; George Durrant, 22, Bridge Road West; William Gerrard, Lombard Road; William Hammond, 72, York Road; Henry May Soule, Mayfield, St. John's Hill; Horsley Woods, 38, Bridge Road West. (Vestrymen who retire in 1883).—Bernard Cotter, 228, York Road; George Thos. Dunning, 45, Winstanley Road; William Gosden, 3, Spencer Road; John Thos. Gurling, High Street;

Joseph Oakman, The Priory, High Street; Rev. John Toone, St. Peter's Parsonage, Plough Lane; John Trott, 75, High Street. (Vestrymen who retire in 1884).—George Brocking, 27, High Street; William J. Bromley, 12, Olney Terrace, Plough Lane; John W. Denny 108, York Road; Thomas Gregory, Station Road; William Griffin 44, High Street; Joseph James Kilsby, 189, York Road; William Wingate, Sen., 1, High Street. *Auditor.*—Charles Earl Holmes, 80, Bridge Road.

WARD No. 4. (Vestrymen who retire in 1882).—James Clarke, 2, Rushill Terrace, Lavender Hill; John Davis Hatch, Bolingbroke Grove, Wandsworth Common; Alfred Heaver, Homeland, Benerley Road; Joseph William Hiscox, 2, Altenburg Terrace, Lavender Hill. (Vestrymen who retire in 1883).—Andrew W. Cameron, 65, Salcott Road; John Cleave, Eaton Villa, Vardens Road; Horace Turnor, 63, Northcote Road; Edward Wood, 6, Shelgate Road. (Vestrymen who retire in 1884).—Francis Cowdry, 25, Belleville Road; William Haynes, Rotherstone House, Salcott Road; R. W. Oram, 13, Clapham Common Gardens; William Wilkins, St. John's Road, Battersea Rise. *Auditor.*—John Tomkins, Heather Villa, Nottingham Road, Wandsworth Common.

Parish Clerk.—James Spice, Bridge Road West.

Beadle.—William Edwards.

Registrar of Births, Deaths and Marriages.—William Griffin, High Street.

District Surveyor of North Battersea.—H. J. Hansom, Grove-end House, Falcon Lane.

A Parochial Assembly for conducting the affairs of a Parish, so called because its meetings were formerly held in the Vestry—a room appended to a Church in which the sacerdotal vestments and sacred utensils are kept. Vestrymen are a select number of persons in each parish elected for the management of its temporal concerns.

The Vestry is the organ through which the Parish speaks, and in numerous matters relating to church rates, highways, baths and wash-houses and other sanitary matters, it has important functions to discharge and is a conspicuous feature of Parochial management. The Vicar is entitled to be chairman. It is the duty of the Churchwardens and Overseers to keep a book in which to enter the minutes of the Vestry. The Vestry appoints annually Churchwardens, nominates Overseers, etc. A Church rate can only be made by a Vestry, and if the majority choose, to make none. The Vestry Clerk is chosen by the Vestry; his duty is to give notice of Vestry meetings; to summon the Churchwardens and Overseers; to keep the minutes, accounts and Vestry books; recover the arrears of rates; make out the list of persons qualified to act as Jurymen, and to give notices for to vote for Members of Parliament.

Churchwardens in England are Ecclesiastical officers appointed by the first Canon of the Synod of London in 1127. Overseers in every parish were also appointed by the same body, and they continue now as then established.—*Johnson's Canons.*

Churchwardens, by the Canons of 1603, are to be chosen annually. The Common Law requires that there should be two Churchwardens, one of whom is appointed by the Incumbent and the other is chosen by the Parishioners in Vestry assembled. Their primary duty is to see that the fabric of the Church is kept in good repair, superintending the celebration of public worship, and to form and regulate other Parochial regulations. The appointment and election take place in Easter Week of each year.

Overseers are officers who occupy an important position in all the parishes in England and Wales, they too are appointed annually. Their primary duty is to rate the inhabitants to the Poor rate, collect the same, and apply it towards relief of the poor, besides other miscellaneous duties, such as making out the list of voters for Members of Parliament. The list of persons in the Parish qualified to serve as Jurors, the list of persons qualified to serve as Parish Constables. They are bound to appoint persons to enforce the Vaccination Acts, etc., etc.

When the birth of a child is registered, the registrar is to give notice of vaccination; and the child must be vaccinated within three months. Penalty for not bringing the child to be vaccinated 20s. If any registrar shall give information to a justice that he has reason to believe any child has not been successfully vaccinated, and that he has given notice thereof, which notice has been disregarded, the justice may order the child to appear before him, and he may make an order directing such child to be vaccinated within a certain time, and if at the expiration of such time the child shall not have been vaccinated, the parent or person upon whom the order has been served is liable to a penalty not exceeding 20s.

Guardians of the poor, in the English parochial law are important functionaries elected by a parish or union of parishes; they have the management of the workhouse and the maintenance, clothing and relief of the poor, and in the regulations must comply with the orders of the Poor Law Board, a central authority, whose head is a member of Parliament, their duties are entirely regulated by these orders, and by statutes.

Relieving Officers.—Mr. Murphy, Wye Street, York Road; Mr. Tugwell, 479, Battersea Park Road.

Medical Officers.—Dr. Kempster, 247, Battersea Park Road; Dr. Oakman, The Priory, Battersea Square.

Surveyor and Inspector of Nuisances.—Mr. Pilditch, Stone Yard, Battersea, to whom complaints should be made.

Dust Contractor.—Applications to be addressed Board of Works, Battersea Rise.

Turn-cock.—R. Gray, 24, Dickens Street; *Assistant ditto.* W. Moore, 24, Parkside Street.

Collectors of Parochial Rates.—Mr. E. Stocker, 37, St. John's Hill Grove; Mr. G. Nichols, Pembroke Villa, Falcon Lane; Mr. G. J. Chadwin, Lombard Road; Mr. O. Shepherd, 15, Middleton Road, Battersea Rise.

Collectors of Queen's Taxes.—Mr. A. G. Iago, Gatcombe Villa, Harbutt Road, Plough Lane, New Wandsworth; Mr. Lewis, Bridge Road.

Battersea Tradesmen's Club.—Temporary Home for Lost and Starving Dogs.

The Battersea Tradesmen's Club commenced October 1875, may be regarded as a local Institution. Its founder was Mr. Elmslie, the register contains the names of 200 elected members, having for their object the general interest, improvement and prosperity of the parish. The club has sustained a heavy loss by the sudden death of its respected Treasurer, Mr. Henry Kesterton, he was a guardian of the poor, a member of the vestry, and also of the board of works. His straightforwardness and generosity inspired much respect. Deep sympathy with his wife and family was manifested at his funeral, which was attended by a great number of the leading members of the club, and other parishioners. His mortal remains were interred at Norwood Cemetery.

The following gentlemen form the Committee.—

Mr. J. Pochin, 291, Battersea Park Road; J. Evans, 367, Battersea Park Road; Mr. W. Sangwin, 533, Battersea Park Road; Mr. T. Bowley, 535, Battersea Park Road; Mr. E. Evans, 287, Battersea Park Road; Mr. J. Douglas, W. L. Com. Bank; Mr. G. N. Street, 353, Battersea Park Road; Mr. H. Walkley, 351, Battersea Park Road; Mr. F. Sturges, Orkney Street; Mr. C. E. Gay, 21, Orkney Street; Mr. B. Hickman, 100, Gwynne Road; H. Winter, 52, Park Grove; W. Marsh, Battersea Park Road.

Secretary.—Mr. Robert Gooch, 21, Queen's Square, Queen's Road.

Any person wishing to have his name enrolled as a member of the Club, must subscribe 10s. yearly.

The temporary Home for lost and starving Dogs, Battersea Park Road, (removed from Holloway.) Established October 2nd, 1860. The late Mrs. Tealby was the foundress and unwearied benefactress of this Institution. In 1875 more than 3,200 dogs were either restored to their former owners, or sent to new homes, being an increase of 1094, over the previous year. The home has been visited by many of the nobility and gentry, and by great kennel owners, and all have expressed themselves very much pleased with the cleanliness, and general good order, which they have observed. It is gratifying to know that of the many thousands of dogs which have been brought into the home there has been *no case of hydrophobia*. Every precaution is taken by the committee not to allow any dog to be sold for the horrid purpose of vivisection. There are in stock at the home more than 300 dogs. Keeper at the home—Mr. J. Pavitt; open daily from 8 a.m. to 6 p.m.; (the home is entirely closed on Sunday.)

"I cannot understand that morality which excludes animals from human sympathy, or release man from the debt and obligation he owes to them."—*Sir John Bowring.*

> "He prayeth best, who loveth best;
> All creatures great and small;
> For the great God who loveth us,
> He made and loves them all"

—Coleridge.

"With eye upraised, his master's look to scan,
The joy, the solace, and the aid of man;
The rich man's guardian and the poor man's friend.
The only creature faithful to the end."

London, Chatham and Dover Railway—Battersea Park Station— York Road Station (Brighton Line).—West London Commercial Bank. London and South Western Bank.—Temperance and Band of Hope Meetings.—South London Tramways in Battersea—Fares.

London, Chatham and Dover Railway—Battersea Park Station, Battersea Park Road, booking office to Victoria, Crystal Palace, main line and City trains, Blackheath Hill, for Greenwich. Station master, Mr. H. Lankman.

York Road Station, Battersea Park—London, Brighton and South London Line. Station master, Mr. Henry Mead.

West London Commercial Bank, Limited, Established 1866. Incorporated, under the Joint-Stock Companies' Act 1872. Head Office—34, Sloane Square, London, S.W. Battersea Park Branch, 1, Victoria Road. Manager, Mr. George Patrick McCourt.

London and South Western Bank, Head office, 7, Fenchurch Street. Battersea Branch, Battersea Park Road, opposite Christ Church. Manager, Mr. J. Barr.

Temperance and Band of Hope Meetings are held at St. George's Mission Room, New Road; Arthur Street, Mission Hall, Battersea Park Road; Grove School Room, York Road, Conductor Mr. G. Mansell; Temperance Hall, Tyneham Road, Shaftesbury Park Estate; The Institute, Mill Pond Bridge, Nine Elms Lane, every Tuesday, commencing at 8 p.m. President, George Howlett, Esq.; Vice-President, Mr. T. O. Shutter; Treasurer Mr. D. Greaves; Financial Secretary, Mr. H. Gitsham; Registrars, Mr. F. Clarke, Mr. W. R. Josslyn; Corresponding Secretary, Mr. R. Curson, 6, Horace Street, Wandsworth Road, S.W.

SOUTH LONDON TRAMWAYS. In 1879 a Tram-way was constructed in Battersea Park Road. (Turner, Contractor, Chelsea). Tram cars first commenced running for the conveyance of passengers between Falcon Lane and the Rifleman January 6, 1881. The second portion of the South London Tramways Company's line from Nine Elms to Clapham Junction was opened for traffic on Saturday March 12th, 1881.

The Queen's Road and Victoria Road Lines being now completed, in addition to those previously worked in Falcon Lane and Battersea Park Road and Nine Elms Lane, Cars are running as under:—

EVERY TEN MINUTES THROUGHOUT THE DAY, FROM

THE FALCON TAVERN, CLAPHAM JUNCTION,	} to	NINE ELMS LANE.
First Car leaves 7.45 a.m. Last Car do. 10.10 p.m. Do. Sat'days do. 11.55 p.m.		First Car leaves 8.15 a.m. Last Car do. 10.10 p.m. Do. Sat'days do. 11.55 p.m.
PRINCE'S HEAD, HIGH STREET, BATTERSEA,	} to {	CHELSEA BRIDGE STEAMBOAT PIER, viâ VICTORIA ROAD.
First Car leaves 7.55 a.m. Last Car do. 9.45 p.m. Do. Sat'days do. 11.33 p.m.		First Car leaves 8.20 a.m. Last Car do. 10.20 p.m. Do. Sat'days do. 11.10 p.m.
LAVENDER HILL END OF QUEEN'S ROAD,	} to {	BRIGHTON RAILWAY STATION, BATTERSEA PARK ROAD.
First Car leaves 8.10 a.m. Last Car do. 10.0 p.m. Do. Sat'days do. 11.10 p.m.		First Car leaves 8.25 a.m. Last Car do. 10.15 p.m. Do. Sat'days do. 10.50 p.m.

In Battersea Park Road the Cars run every 5 minutes between "Prince's Head" and Victoria Road (South End).

Workmen's Cars will run as heretofore.

On Sundays the Cars commence running about 10 a.m. and finish as on Week-days.

FARES.

"The Falcon" to "Clock House"	1d.
"Prince's Head" to Victoria Road (South End)	1d.
"Clock House" to "Rifleman"	1d.
Victoria Road (South End) to Nine Elms	1d.
Lavender Hill to Chelsea Bridge	1d.
Beyond the above distances	2d.

N.B.—The Tickets are only available for a Single Journey upon the Car where issued.

Lector House believes that a society develops through a two-fold approach of continuous learning and adaptation, which is derived from the study of classic literary works spread across the historic timeline of literature records. Therefore, we aim at reviving, repairing and redeveloping all those inaccessible or damaged but historically as well as culturally important literature across subjects so that the future generations may have an opportunity to study and learn from past works to embark upon a journey of creating a better future.

This book is a result of an effort made by Lector House towards making a contribution to the preservation and repair of original ancient works which might hold historical significance to the approach of continuous learning across subjects.

HAPPY READING & LEARNING!

LECTOR HOUSE LLP
E-MAIL: lectorpublishing@gmail.com

9 789389 539615